PROVENCE

ART · ARCHITECTURE · LANDSCAPE

PROVENCE

ART · ARCHITECTURE · LANDSCAPE

Edited by Rolf Toman

Text by Christian Freigang

Photographs by Achim Bednorz

KÖNEMANN

Key to maps

Church/monastery/convent

Ruined church/monastery/convent

Castle/château

Ruined castle/château

Museum

Secular and important buildings

Roman remains

Beauty spots

Lookout points

©1999 Könemann Verlagsgesellschaft mbH
Bonner Str. 126, D-50968 Cologne, Germany

Editing and Production: Rolf Toman, Espéraza,
Nikolaus Hoffmann, Bergisch Gladbach, Thomas Paffen, Münster
Picture Research: Monika Bergmann, Cologne
Graphics: Ehrenfried Kluckert, Bremgarten
Maps: Detlef Maiwald, Norderstedt
Production: Mark Voges, Cologne
Reproductions: litho niemann + m. steggemann gmbh, Oldenburg

Original title: Provence. Kunst, Landschaft, Architektur

© 2000 for this English edition:
Könemann Verlagsgesellschaft mbH

English Translation: Paul Fletcher, Debra Nicol, Brian Malley, Susan Kunze,
Clare Charters, Christine Bainbridge in association with Chanterelle
Translations, London
Typesetting: David Tsai, Chanterelle Translations, London
Project Management: Josephine Bacon
Project Coordination: Nadja Bremse and Russel Cennydd
Production: Ursula Schümer
Printing and Binding: Neue Stalling, Oldenburg

Printed in Germany
ISBN 3-8290-2714–1

10 9 8 7 6 5 4 3 2 1

Contents

The History of Provence

The name "Provence" derives from the Latin *provincia*, meaning "the province," and indicates that even in Antiquity, southeast France was remote from the center of the Empire. Life in this distant spot was better, the soil more productive, and the climate more temperate than in Rome. That, at least, was the opinion of the Roman author, Pliny the Elder, who described the province which lay between the Alps and the Mediterranean as "another Italy" producing oil and wheat in abundance. The earlier Greek colonists probably felt the same way. Even today, the French themselves see Provence as a byword for leisure and relaxation, and as such the diametrical opposite of Paris, the bustling capital. Juxtapositions such as center and periphery, business and leisure, frenzied activity and relaxation, have always ascribed the more agreeable of these qualities to Provence, well before the region became a winter retreat for the English aristocracy in the eighteenth century.

These are clichés, of course. It should not be forgotten that Provence was politically independent for a long time and that even today, tourism is far from its only source of income. The rich historical legacy and the diversity of climate and landscape between the Mediterranean and the Alps make Provence one of the most varied and interesting parts of Europe.

Prehistory and early history

The first traces of Stone Age settlers, found in a cave at Vallonnet (Roquebrunne), date back around 950,000 years and are the earliest evidence of cave dwellers in Europe. The mild climate and the countless caves and caverns in the limestone of the Alps offered prehistoric Man suitable living conditions. Traces have been found of Stone Age hunter-gatherers from as early as the sixth millennium; these people made increasing use of stone to construct their dwellings. The remains of the oldest settlement found in the region so far were discovered near Courthézon in the Département of Vaucluse and date from around 4,650 BC. Bories, primitive drystone dwellings (see illustration on the right and on pp. 164-165, Gordes), were probably also developed at around that time in order to shelter their inhabitants from the weather and protect them from enemies. Metal came into use only around 2,500 BC, but was used mainly for decorative purposes, such as jewelry and small copper artefacts. Weapons at that time continued to be made of stone. Only after bronze had been discovered in around 1800 BC did metal replace flint as the most important material for tools.

The Iron Age constituted a period of increased social differentiation. From the sixth century BC onward, the indigenous settlers, called Ligurians

Drystone hut (borie) in the
Village des Bories near Gordes

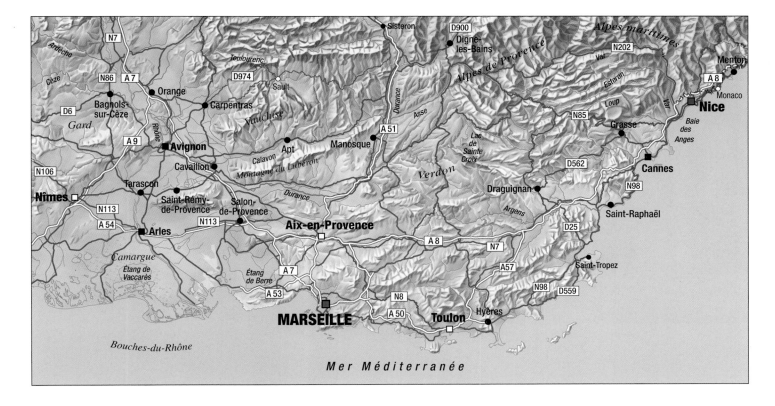

Aix-en-Provence
Oppidum d'Entremont
Excavations of the ancient
settlement

St-Rémy-de-Provence
Julian monument in the
Roman cemetery at Glanum

by the Greek colonists, began to mix with the Celts who were moving into the region from the north, and different tribes began to emerge. The area around Marseille was ruled by the Saluvians; the Vokontians ruled the northern part, between the rivers Durance and Isère. These tribes lived in town-like settlements called *oppida* (from the Latin word for "town"), similar to those which can be seen today at Entrement near Aix (above) or Roquepertuse in the Département of Bouches-du-Rhône. Their art was a sophisticated one, as can be seen from the large group sculptures of seated male figures and horses' heads exhibited in the museum at Marseilles.

Antiquity

Around 600 BC, the first Greek traders arrived from Phocea in Asia Minor and founded a trading post which they called Massalia. It was in an ideal location, a bay sheltered by high cliffs. This was the original Marseille. When Phocea was destroyed by the Persians between 545 and 540 BC, Massalia became the refuge for many of its citizens and the capital of the Greek colony. It went on to become the center of Greek colonization in the area, from which a network of trading posts was developed. These included Nicea (Nice), Antipolis (Antibes) and Olbia (Hyères). The Greeks also crossed the river Rhône to expand their activities northward. However, they did more than merely pursue their commercial interests, and were responsible for building the first real towns in Provence, as can be seen from the excavations at St-Blaise on the Etang de Berre, in Marseille and in Glanum near St-Rémy (see illustration on p. 112). In the second century BC, the Greeks emerged as faithful allies of the Romans, whom they supported against Carthage in the second Punic War. The Romans, for their part, aided the Greeks in their numerous battles with the indigenous Celtic and Ligurian tribes.

The Roman armies were first invited into Provence by Marseille in 125 BC in order to help the Greeks defend themselves against the allied indigenous tribes. Once they had defeated the Celts and Ligurians, the Romans remained in southern France to ensure that the land bridge between the Roman colonies in Spain and the Italian mother - country remained secure. They created a new administrative province which they first called Gallia Cisalpina, but renamed Gallia Narbonensis with the foundation of the new capital of Narbonne in 118 BC. The Roman presence was permanently secured in 49 BC, when Julius Cesar subjugated Marseille. The Greek colony had made the mistake of allying itself with his rival, Pompey. This was the beginning of a comprehensive Romanization of the region, marked by the foundation of numerous Roman colonies to house former legionnaires. Apt, Arles, Avignon, Fréjus, Riez and Vaison are some of the towns that were founded in this manner. Even today temples, theaters, amphitheaters, bridges, aqueducts, and Roman baths bear witness to the cultural and technical revolution that occurred within the space of little more than two generations. Progress mainly affected the larger towns and traffic routes, as well as the large farm settlements (*villae*). The mountainous, inaccessible hinterland remained largely unaffected by the new developments. The period spanning the end of the third and the beginning of the fourth centuries was a time when Gallia Narbonensis underwent administrative reorganization. The new provinces of Gallia Viennensis and Alpae Maritimae were created to the east of the

OPPOSITE:
Pont du Gard (above)

Nîmes
The Temple of Diana (below)

Arles
Roman baths, the
northern apse

Rhône, which included the towns of Digne, Embrun and Senez. In 375, Gallia Viennensis was divided in two and a new province, Narbonensia Secunda, was created, with Aix as its capital.

The highly developed administrative structure of the Roman provinces, in which the *civitates* constituted the regional centers, also fostered the spread of Christianity and predetermined the borders of the bishoprics and archbishoprics. Evidence has been found of Christianity being practiced in the third century. One of the most important synods of early Christianity, attended by bishops from most Roman *civitates*, was held in Arles as early as 314.

The upper classes in the towns embraced many of the forms of Christian burial culture, as can be seen from the many surviving sarcophagi of late Antiquity (the fourth and fifth centuries) decorated with Christian motifs. Most of these can be found in Arles (see pp. 86-89). A further indication of the comprehensive spread of Christianity is the early religious buildings, especially the baptismal churches, which were usually erected on the sites of old forums, the central public square. Examples of these early churches can be seen in Fréjus, Aix, Riez and Cimiez.

The Middle Ages
The fifth century witnessed a decline in urban culture. The administrative infrastructure ceased to operate effectively, forcing many people to move to the country for their very survival. Local fiefdoms now developed around the farming settlements and formed the basis of the feudal power structures of the Middle Ages. Subsequent decades were characterized by the brutal conquests of the Visigoths, Burgundians and Ostrogoths.

The Franks annexed the region in 535, although in practical terms Provence remained politically independent. This situation changed dramatically in the third decade of the eighth century, however. When several towns joined forces to attack the Franks at a time when the Franks themselves were attempting to repel the invading Saracen forces at Tours and Poitiers, the Franks, under their leader Charles Martell, violently subjugated the rebellious province and annexed it. Around 800, Provence was part of the Frankish empire under Charlemagne. Under

his successors, the Merovingian kings, Provence was particularly affected by the partitioning of the Holy Roman Empire. At the Peace of Verdun, the province was allocated to the Emperor Lothar, who had inherited the middle lands of the old Empire, then, after Lothaire's death in 855, it became part of a new kingdom of Provence under his son Charles. That kingdom included a large section of Gallia Viennensis as well as the area around Lyon. In 947, all this was incorporated into the kingdom of Burgundy, which covered a huge area, extending to present-day Switzerland.

The High and Late Middle Ages, when rule over Provence was divided between various counts, are not only significant in historical terms, but also for the development of the distinctive Provençal identity used as a basis for the resurgent nationalism of the early 19th century.

In 1032, the kingdom of Provence-Burgundy fell to the German empire, whose rule, however, remained sybmolic despite numerous visits by various emperors. Frederick II Barbarossa was crowned King of Burgundy in Arles in 1178, but the real power lay with the counts and viscounts who were pursuing their own interests. In the tenth century, rivalries between these petty rulers led to the emergence of a Margravate Provence, the so-called Arelate, which covered the territories of the three archbishoprics—Arles, Aix and Embrun. Similarly, in 1125 a system of alliances led to the division of Provence between the Counts of Barcelona and those of Tolouse. The lands west of the Rhône and to the north of the Durance went to the Counts of Tolouse and formed a new Margravate Provence. The region between the Rhône, the Durance, the Alps and the Mediterranean went to the Spanish counts (Comté Provence). The region around Avignon, later called the Comtat Venaissin, remained undivided. In addition, the county of Forcalquier emerged at the foot of the Alps. Despite the ongoing fighting between the counts, Provence experienced marked economic growth during this time, mainly due to trade across the Mediterranean and along the Rhône. To organize the flow of goods, administrative bodies were set up in many towns, such as Arles, Aix and Orange, which developed into a sort of local militia. At the same time, the arts flourished. Romanesque church building and sculpture sought to instil new life into ancient traditions in art.

The Albigensian Wars interrupted this economic boom. Between 1218 and 1229 the French Kings Louis XIII and Louis IX organized a crusade against the heretic movement which had sprung up mainly in Languedoc. This resulted in Raymond VII, the last Count of Tolouse, who had supported the Albigensians or Cathars, being driven from power. Most of his territories fell to the crown, while the previously insignificant town of Beaucaire became part of the royal seat of administration. The policies of the Counts of Barcelona had similar results.

In 1246, Beatrix, daughter of Count Raymond Berenger V, married Charles of Anjou, a brother of the French King Louis IX . In 1266, Charles received the Kingdom of Naples in fee from the Pope. The whole of Provence was now part of the hereditary lands of the Capetian dynasty, whose importance in the fourteenth and fifteenth centuries was to be of major significance far beyond this region of the western Mediterranean. The house of Anjou immediately suppressed the liberties of the towns, encountering strong resistance along the way, and attempted to make Aix one of their towns of residence. Soon, however, they were forced to turn their attention to their Italian territories, where their rule was being contested by the House of Aragon. Under Charles II of Anjou (1285-1309) the towns regained their self-governing status.

Another important force also determined the historical development of Provence in the fourteenth century, when Avignon became the Papal residence. As a result of the Albigensian Wars, in 1274, the Comtat Venaissin fell under Papal rule. Following the advice of the French king, Pope Clement V left Rome because of its political turmoil and established a provisional Papal residence in Avignon, thereby gaining control over its significant hinterland and acquiring the protection of the French. The conflict between his successor John XXII (1316-1334) and Emperor Ludwig the Bavarian resulted in the provisional residence becoming a permanent one. Supported by rigorous fiscal policy, Avignon developed into one of the cultural centers of the late medieval world. When the Papacy returned to Rome in 1376, Avignon became the seat of the antipope pretenders until the fifteenth century.

The Black Death visited Provence in 1348 and decimated the population, only to be followed some years later by a new threat. Marauding mercenaries returning from the Hundred Years War between the English and the French laid waste to the land, plundering, raping, and murdering. The most infamous of these bands was led by Arnaud de Cervole between 1357 and 1358, but there were others, such as that of Du Guesclin in 1365 and Raymond de Turenne's band at the turn of the century.

Political infighting weakened the influence of the old Anjou line, and this, in turn, affected Provence. In 1360, a new dynasty was appointed by Jean II the Good and ruled Provence until 1481. Although the eastern part of the region, including Nice, fell to Savoy in 1419, the fifteenth century as a whole brought renewed prosperity after the devastation of the previous decades. Many towns in Lower Provence, the lowlands along the river Rhône, erected city walls and became more urban in character. The little villages at the foot of the Alps and along the coast were also fortified, as can still be seen today in places like Vence, St-Paul-de-Vence, and Èze. King René I, who ruled from 1434 to 1480, was the personification of the new prosperity. While this

OPPOSITE:
Gorges de la Nesque
Looking south from Mont
Ventoux (top)

Arles
Les Alyscamps with
St-Honorat (center)

Cavaillon
Cathedral cloister (below)

Pernes-les-Fontaines
Tour Ferrande
Detail of frescoes

monarch lost the Italian territories to Aragon, thereby making his claim to the crowns of Sicily and Jerusalem a claim in name only, he was able to devote all the more attention to his hereditary lands, Anjou and Provence. Court life was extravagant, and, as in Burgundy, the arts prospered (see p. 100), influenced as they were by the Early Italian Renaissance. Certain Italian artists, such as Francesco Laurana, even worked in Provence.

After the death of King René, his son Charles du Maine inherited the province, but survived his father by only a year. In his will, he bequeathed Provence to the King of France. Systematically, old established rights and privileges were modified and adapted to developments in the ambitious up-and-coming French monarchy. The installment of the *parlement* in Aix as the highest judicial body and the introduction of French as the language of law and administration were important measures within the context of annexation by the French kings, culminating in the centralist policies of Louis XIV in the seventeenth century. The life of the Jews, too, was influenced by the annexation by France. They had originally enjoyed a certain degree of religious freedom and tolerance, but now they were subjected to anti-Semitic pogroms, leading many Jews to seek refuge in the ghettos of the Comtat Venaissin and Nice, or to convert to Christianity.

The Early Modern Era up to 1789

The conflict between King François I of France and the Emperor Charles V over northern Italy also affected the neighboring Provence. On a number of occasions between 1524 and 1536, imperial troops stood before Aix and Marseille, but

failed each time to capture these cities. For the remainder of the sixteenth century, the history of Provence consisted of a series of episodes of religious strife. The religious sect known as the Waldensians, followers of the Lyonnaise physician Pierre Valdès, had survived the war against the Albigensians in the thirteenth century. Its members, who rejected any kind of religious authority, had mainly retreated to the remote villages of the Luberon. When the sect enthusiastically adopted the teachings of Calvin in 1532, King François organized a campaign to exterminate them, and in 1544 this ended with the sect's almost total annihilation.

The bloody conflicts between Catholics and Protestants which kept France in turmoil for the second half of the sixteenth century moved southward as the war spread. In Provence, where French royal influence was traditionally viewed with suspicion, many towns began to adopt Protestantism from around 1560. Orange, which had been in the possession of the governor of the Netherlands since 1544, was even known as "Little Geneva." As Protestantism viewed the adoration of Christian icons and statues as idolatry, innumerable medieval figures were destroyed during this time. Only a small fraction of the Romanesque sculpture to be found in Provence before the iconoclasm of the Reformation survived those terrible times. From 1584 onward, the Catholic League began to win the upper hand in the civil war. In 1588, it conquered Aix, and Marseille in 1596. In Avignon and Arles, Jesuit convents were founded to secure the Catholic faith in the region.

In addition to the armed conflicts, Provence suffered from recurring plague epidemics, the

Nîmes
Jardin de la Fontaine

Field of lavender

OPPOSITE:
Villefranche-sur-Mer

RIGHT:
Vallignières
Clock tower with
wrought iron decoration

Nîmes
Musée des Beaux-Arts
Detail of portal area
of the façade

most severe being in the years 1580 and 1629. In 1720, another terrible epidemic broke out which lasted for two years, claiming about 100,000 victims, 38,000 of them in Marseille alone.

Under these adverse conditions, a process of economic differentiation set in, whose repercussions can even be felt today. While cultural and economic activity was concentrated on a few large towns like Marseille, Aix and Arles, most of the medium-size towns like Tarascon, Sisteron, Beaucaire, Orange, or Carpentras stagnated. The economy continued to depend on agriculture and small industry, while the sea trade, which from the eighteenth century onwards became increasingly concentrated in Marseille and Toulon, was still the single most important economic sector.

The triumph of Catholicism and the political influence of the monarchy had important consequences for the outward appearance of the towns. Church and political institutions introduced new representative architectural forms, based on both the French and Italian baroque. Town halls, the townhouses of the nobility, and the building and rebuilding of churches were the most important architectural projects, introducing an extensive and elaborate repertoire of architectural forms.

From the French Revolution to the present

The French Revolution began in Marseille as early as the spring of 1789, when the populace revolted against nobility and magistrates. It was from Marseille that republicanism found its way into other towns of Provence and here that the French national anthem, the Marseillaise, originated. But counter-revolutionary forces organized quickly in this generally conservative region, and up to the 1830s, Royalism remained the dominant political force, especially in Lower Provence, while more liberal tendencies could be discerned in the hinterland. A change became evident only with the Revolution of 1848, when the political left had a large majority which it continued to maintain until the beginning of the twentieth century. Numerous members of parliament and statesmen of the Third Republic, such as Georges Clemenceau, came from the "Red South."

One of the most influential developments of the French Revolution was administrative reform. In 1790, the administrative districts of Bouches-du-Rhône, Var and Basses-Alpes were formed. The papal possessions of the Comtat Venaissin were annexed in 1791 and formed the nucleus of the district of Vaucluse. In 1793, revolutionary troops captured Nice and created the Alpes-Maritimes département. When Nice again became French in 1860, on the basis of a referendum, this administrative district, was also re-established.

Provence's economy remained mainly agricultural and rural until well into the nineteenth century. The exceptions are Toulon and, of course, Marseille, whose meteoric rise to the status of an international port resulted in a population structure of merchants, traders and dockers which was very different to that of the rest of the region. Radical sociological changes only set in toward the end of the nineteenth century. The introduction of compulsory school attendance raised the level of education, and French began to replace Provençal as the dominant language.

The Industrial Revolution was ushered in when, in 1849, a railway line opened to connect Avignon with Marseille. Up until the end of the nineteenth century, the railway system expanded, making Provence easily accessible from Paris as well as from Italy. The previously remote areas at the foot of the Alps were now increasingly part of the trade routes. The fertile areas between the Rhône and Luberon, especially, were now better able to market their produce. But the concentration of population in the coastal towns lead to an exodus from the mountain regions, a trend which continued into the second half of the twentieth century. This caused the suburbs of Avignon and Marseille to become overcrowded slums.

The development of the traffic routes rapidly advanced tourism in the area. This was the birth of Belle Epoque culture, when the Côte d'Azur became a fashionable meeting place for high society, and artists and writers from all over the world congregated in such fashionable spots as Cannes, Nice, and Monte Carlo. Elaborate residences were built and soon the unforeseen demand for building sites started a wave of property speculation. After the World War II, tourism turned into mass tourism. The new motorways and the airports of Marseille and Nice began bringing so many tourists to the Côte d'Azur each year that the region were bursting at the seams, particularly in the summer.

There has also been a reaction to the rapid modernization and fundamental structural changes that Provence has undergone since the beginning of the nineteenth century, in the form of the rediscovery of a regional identity. One of its leading advocates, Frédéric Mistral, gained world renown having spent his life collecting and promoting the folklore of the Provence. With his *Trésor dóu Felibrige* he created a complete dictionary of the Provençal language, a language which also became the vehicle for his poetry.

After Mistral, regionalism created a rather lopsided view of Provence as an "exotic" region, which is a positive view, but also open to misinterpretation. Alphonse Daudet's *Letters from my Mill*, and the novels and plays of Marcel Pagnol give a burlesque picture of a boastful and sensuous but not always very intelligent people, which has greatly influenced the way they are perceived. The traditional outsider's view of the Provençal character is perpetuated in the novels of Peter Mayle and especially his *A Year in Provence*. The image of Provence which is generally promoted as being carefree and

traditional reflect what tourists want to see rather than the historical reality.

Provence suffered greatly in World War II. In August 1944, Allied troops landed on the coast between Toulon and Cannes and recaptured the coastline which German troops had held since 1942, all of which caused severe damage. Moreover, the retreating Germans destroyed parts of Marseille and Tarascon.

After the war, a crisis in industry hit the larger cities, caused mainly by the rapid decline of colonial trade and the international crisis in the shipbuilding sector. The war in Algeria and the gaining of independence by most of France's former colonies, especially those facing Provence across the Mediterranean, lead to a wave of immigration mainly of North African origin, into southern France. This has caused social tensions and problems, especially in the densely populated areas around Marseille and the Etang de Berre, which have played into the hands of the xenophobic political parties of the extreme right. As elsewhere in Europe, the decline of heavy industry has been accompanied in recent decades by increased development of the tertiary sector. Technological research centers, the so-called *technopoles*, especially in Marseille and in the

new towns of Fos-sur-Mer and Sophia-Antipolis now play a leading econmic role in the region.

Another development of increasing economic importance is ecological tourism. The protection of water and the environment has been enshrined in legislation, and the unrestricted growth of the cities has been checked in recent years. The number of music, theater, and folklore festivals is immense, especially in the summer. Furthermore, there is not a town in Provence that does not have at least one museum worth visiting, as well as an inviting botanical garden or an *ecomusée*.

In the countryside, there are great opportunities to go hiking and rambling or pursue other recreational activities which offer alternatives to life at the beach, including such water sports as whitewater rafting, canoeing and kayaking, and canyoning.

However, what attracts visitors most of all is the natural beauty of the surroundings and the centuries-old cultural artefacts, which include not just the Roman amphitheaters and Romanesque churches, but magnificent buildings, public and private, of every age, right down to nineteenth century industrial architecture, magnificent hotels from the Belle Epoque, and the flora and fauna on water and land.

About this book

The Provence presented in the following chapters covers the largest historical area known by that name as it extended both eastward and westwards. Certain places are also included which lie outside these historical boundaries, such as Nîmes, Uzès, or the Pont du Gard, since they are so closely associated with Provence that many assume them to be part of it. Along the north-south axis, a few restrictions had to be made. Areas too far to the north could not be included in this volume as to do so would have reduced the space available for describing the "classic" travel destinations.

The route through Provence which this book follows begins with the lower Rhône valley, the heights of the Gorges d'Ardèche, the Tricastin and Orange. From there we travel southward and explore first the areas in the southwest and then those in the southeast. We continue on towards the great regional capitals of Aix and Marseille, and then continue eastward along the coast. Throughout the book, there are side-trips into the hinterland, until we reach journey's end, via the magnificent landscape of the Alpes-Maritimes and the miniature Grand Canyon of the Gorges du Verdon.

On the Threshold of Provence

Gorges d'Ardèche, the countryside around Tricastin, and Orange

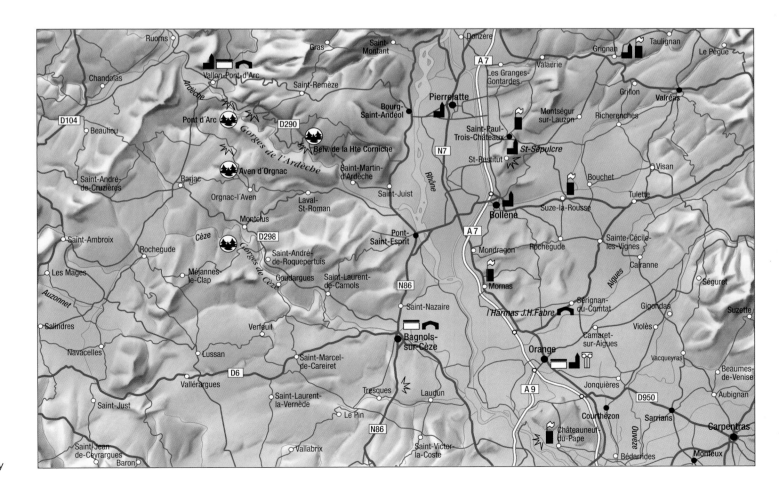

The Gorges of the Ardèche

The River Ardèche rises at an altitude of 4,890 ft (1,467 m) in the Mazan Massif. After flowing for over 75 miles (119 km), it enters the Rhône Valley. In its upper reaches it negotiates steep gradients, but lower down, the riverbed cuts deep into the limestone strata. It also flows underground in places, carving out countless caves and potholes. Local weather conditions can have a dramatic impact on the water level. Water flow can range from 8.3 to 23,333 cu. ft (2.5 to 7,000 cu. m.) per second! In the fall, the river in spate reaches spectacular levels. Sometimes walls of water rush through the valley at speeds of up to 12½ m.p.h (20 km/h). The strength of these floodwaters is such that near

Pont-St-Esprit at the confluence with the Rhône, the course of the latter is pushed eastward. In 1890, the waters of the Ardèche swept across the eastern banks of the Rhône, completely submerging the Lauzon breakwater.

The Ardèche Gorge (see illustration on page 16) is one of the natural wonders of France, but the adjoining plateaux, from the north the Plateau des Gras to the south the Plateau d'Orgnac, are also of interest. They are uninhabited regions where nature runs wild. The scenic D 290 road follows the left-hand crest of the gorge, while footpaths run beside it through the valley. Many people enjoy the adventure of a canoe or kayak ride along the sometimes gentle, sometimes rapid, waters of the Ardèche between Vallon-Pont-d'Arc and Aiguèze. The Pont d'Arc (see illustration above) marks the entrance to the steepest and most dramatic section of the valley. This natural bridge was once a rock around which the river flowed, but constant erosion eventually cut a hole through it. In 1994, a cave was found left of the Cirque d'Estre that contains a wealth of cave-paintings estimated to be at least 30,000 years old. Animals and hunting scenes are depicted on the walls in black and red. The astonishing quality and abundance of these paintings are comparable with those in the Lascaux caves. Scientific investigations are continuing, but a temporary exhibition describing the finds can be seen in Vallon-Pont-d'Arc. Visitors to the Gorge may also stumble across the ruins of small châteaux such as the Belvédère du Serre de Tourre or the Belvédère de Gaud.

Gorges d'Ardèche
Pont-d'-Arc, a natural bridge over the Ardèche cut out of the rock. It is 113 ft (34 m) high and about 200 ft (60 m) long.

LEFT AND BELOW:
Orgnac-l'Aven
Aven d'Orgnac
Pothole

La Garde-Adhémar
General view (above)
Mid-12th century Romanesque
parish church (right)

Le Tricastin

On the other, eastern side of the Rhône, well away from the beaten tourist trail, lies Le Tricastin, a hilly region swathed in early summer with yellow sunflowers and purple fields of lavender. La Garde-Adhémar is a small town visible from the Rhône valley motorway (see illustration above). Its origins date back to the 10th century when it is thought that the inhabitants of Val-des-Nymphes sought refuge from the Saracens on this hilltop above the Rhône Valley. The church was built around the middle of the twelfth century. Its simple exterior contrasts with the belltower, richly ornamented with blind arches. One unusual aspect of the church's ground plan is that, like its counterpart in the village of Bourg-St-Andéol on the other side of the Rhône valley, it has a chancel apse both to the east and the west. While many Romanesque churches in northern Europe were designed in this style, there is nothing comparable in France. An ornate system of rectangular piers and struts form the stepped pillars of the small triple-naved basilica. In contrast to other Provençal buildings from the same era, there are no motifs from Antiquity. Simple transom plates are used to support the arches.

A narrow lane leads eastward to the chapel of Val-des-Nymphes, which was probably built in the first half of the twelfth century, but for many years it has been an abandoned and is surrounded by trees and broom scrub (see illustration on page 19, below.) The rich pattern of the round-arched niches on the upper half of the west wall and, inside, the apse, which is split into two zones, are particularly striking.

St-Paul-Trois-Châteaux

The region's main town, whose name is derived from the surrounding area, is St-Paul-Trois-Châteaux. In pre-Roman times, it was the home of the Tricastini, but, during the Roman era, the settlement became the administrative center (*civitas*) for Le Tricastin and was named Augusta Tricastinorum. Its function as a regional capital explains why such a modest town was to become a bishopric in Christian times. A church building was mentioned in records in 852, but work on the present building with chancel and transept (see illustration on page 20) did not start until around 1120. Next came the nave, followed in turn by the vaulting. The complexity of the layout and the quality of the sculptural decoration mark out this triple-naved basilica with its transept and three apses as one

LEFT:

Val-des-Nymphes
Romanesque chapel, western façade with blind arches

of the finest and most important examples of Romanesque architecture in Provence. It is possible to differentiate the plain apses and north transept from the nave and south transept, both of which exhibit features from Roman antiquity (pilasters, pediments, etc). Similar characteristics are visible on the incomplete west portal, which is set into a regular sequence of pilasters, closely resembling ancient triumphal arches. An overarching pediment was probably planned as the concluding section. The west side of the south transept is decorated with relief figures of riders and hunting scenes.

The interior is also unusual. The features that are typical of twelfth-century Provençal architecture—stepped pillars, transverse vaulting, superb masonry—are enriched by a series of unusual motifs. The upper gallery area is integrated into a series of blind, triforium-style arcading, reminiscent of similar designs in

Burgundy (Cluny, Paray-le-Monial, Autun), but it is also a replica of styles from antiquity, in particular the amphitheater in Nîmes. Beneath the arches there is a cornice of relief tendrils and a frieze with a curtain relief. At the edges of the piers, small figures adjust the curtain hanging (see illustration above left) and at the same time bring to life what is only a purely decorative arrangement.

The piers above the arcade transoms consist of partially twisted Corinthian columns. Unlike most other examples in the region, these columns do not conform to the classical rules of proportion. Breaking through the triforium cornice, they have a long, thin appearance in keeping with Gothic style.

The floor mosaic in the main apse depicts the city of Jerusalem. In one or two places, fourteenth and fifteenth-century frescoes have survived (see illustration center left and left).

St-Paul-Trois-Châteaux
Interior view, carved decorations and wall paintings (14th and 15th C.) and ground plan of the Romanesque cathedral.

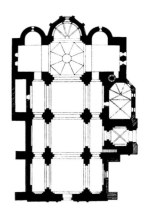

St-Restitut

According to ancient legend, St. Restitutus was the blind man whose sight was restored by Christ. He was originally known as Sidoine, but assumed a new name after the miracle. Sidoine/Restitutus is said to have arrived in France from the Holy Land with the three Marys. Otherwise, very little is known about the picturesque village on the crest of a hill. It was subject to the jurisdiction of St-Paul-Trois-Châteaux and attracted many pilgrims until the Calvinists destroyed the shrines in 1561. The single-naved church, dating from the second half of the twelfth century (see illustration right), has a huge tower on the west side. Its substructure predates the present church. This can clearly be seen from the small ashlar blocks on the north side, which are quite different from the large, square-cut stone blocks of which the present church was built. Beneath the cornice

there is a frieze of panels carved in relief. They date from the Romanesque period and are one of the earliest examples of Provençal sculpture. An enthroned Christ sits in the center, beside whom there are various secular motifs, such as portrayals of the months and animals, hunting scenes, knights and stone masons—a detailed medieval, pictorial encyclopedia. The structure of the church has some similarities with neighboring St-Paul-Trois-Châteaux, not least because of the portal's ornamentation, a faithful reproduction of antique style. Inside, there is a similarly stepped, three-dimensional wall design with small columns at the top.

Grignan

The barony (since 1558 the comté) of Grignan has been in the hands of the aristocratic Provençal Castellane-Adhémar family since the Middle Ages. Their residence (see illustration

ABOVE RIGHT:
St-Restitut
The Romanesque church of St-Restitut. Second half of 12th century.

RIGHT:
St-Sépulcre chapel, near St-Restitut. Although built in 1508, this cemetery chapel still displays elements of the late Romanesque architectural style.

Madame de Sévigné

Marie de Rabutin-Chantal was born in Paris in 1626. Orphaned at an early age, she married Marquis Henri de Sévigné in 1644. The marriage did not last long. Seven years later, after a life of wild excess, her husband died in a duel. From then on, the young widow devoted herself to her children, in particular her daughter, Françoise-Marguerite, whom she idolized. In 1669, she arranged for her daughter to marry the Parisian, François Adhémar de Grignan. However, plans for keeping in close contact with Françoise-Marguerite after the marriage were scuppered when her son-in-law was appointed to the post of Deputy Governor of Provence, and the whole family had to move south. Assisted by a regular stage-coach postal service, there followed a very frequent exchange of letters, mainly between mother and daughter. Letters from Countess Grignan were soon lost, but those of her mother have survived to this day. Her correspondence describes in detail and very sympathetically life at the Paris court of Louis XIV with all its Baroque pomp and splendor, court gossip, ceremonies, intrigues, and suicides. The letters display a spontaneity which sets them apart from the formality of the literary style associated with that era. They can in no way be regarded as frivolous chatter. Madame de Sévigné writes with great style, using cleverly constructed images. Her wit and turns of phrase are far from stilted, but seem effortless and fresh. On three occasions, she spent long periods at Grignan. She wrote enthusiastically in her letters of the magnificent views of the Provençal landscape and of the sumptuous meals. But compared to the eventful daily round of Versailles, the small town seemed isolated and remote. Madame de Sevigné died on her last visit to Provence.

page 22-23) still dominates the small, picturesque town built around the hill. At the beginning of the sixteenth century, Gaucher Adhémar de Monteil modernized the original complex, which comprises several buildings grouped around a courtyard. In 1544, his son Louis, the Lieutenant-General of Provence, began work on converting the courtyard façades in the style of an Italian cortile, similar to the contemporaneous château at Suze-la-Rousse (see illustration on page 24). However, only the eastern and southern wings were given a lavish Renaissance facelift with lateral window surrounds, in addition to delicate, ornamental frieze on the pedestal. In 1547, the owner, who had been involved in a massacre, was flung into jail and the building work came to a halt. Louis Adhémar was pardoned after five years and revived the project, but he was now more interested in a grandiose show (see illustration above), so the old south wing was extended to the east. Grignan now has one of the best classical château façades in Provence.

The façade of the three-story structure has a central portal at its center, with large round pavilions at each corner, rather like some of the châteaux in the Loire valley, such as Chambord. The horizontal structure is rhythmic in style. Wide windows alternate with narrow or framed niches. The wide axes are enclosed by columns, the narrow ones by pilasters. In the seventeenth century, when the daughter of the famous letter writer, Madame de Sévigné, owned the château (see page 22), the old west wing was removed and the prelate wing built. After the Revolution, the whole complex suffered badly. It was the beginning of the twentieth century before work on its reconstruction and restoration began.

Grignan
Façade of the 16th-century château (above)
Château Grignan
General view with the château (left)

Suze-la-Rousse
Château (originally built between the 13th and 15th centuries).

Many old pieces of furniture and tapestries are on display inside the château.

Suze-la-Rousse

Suze-la-Rousse is another fine example of a Tricastin hilltop village. As at Grignan, the village here is dominated by a château that belonged to the local lord (see illustration above). During the Middle Ages, this was the Bishop of Orange. Rostaing de Suze, during his time as Bishop of Orange (1543-1545), had a courtyard built into the original château complex which was built between the thirteenth and fifteenth centuries. Designed—probably by the same architect who worked in Grignan—in Italian Renaissance style, it has three stories clearly separate from one another. The column orders are based on those found in the Roman Coliseum and in the sequence that

became a requirement of the architectural dogma of the sixteenth century, i.e. the Doric, Ionic and Corinthian orders. On the other hand, medieval tradition survives in the windows with their prominent frames and stone window frames. Some rooms inside the château are open to visitors (mainly the banqueting hall and dining room.) The château is also the headquarters of the Université du Vin, which organizes training and exhibitions for vine-growers and wine-lovers.

Orange

Orange is the real gateway to Provence. The famous triumphal arch (see illustration page 25, below) makes this absolutely clear. The appeal of Orange, however, has more to do with the two well-preserved ancient monuments and less to do with any charm unique to so many

OPPOSITE:
Orange
Detail of relief showing mounted combat (above)
Monumental Roman arch
General view (below)

Provençal towns. In the outlying areas surrounding this important hub to the east of a busy motorway intersection, industry and the military set the tone. The St-Eutrope hill to the south of the town was fortified by the Celts. In 105 BC, the Cimbrians and the Teutons destroyed the Roman army here, but in 36 BC the Romans founded a town in honor of Augustus in which veterans of the Second Legion could settle. Every new colonist was given a piece of land of about the same size and the town was laid out to a neat, checkerboard pattern. Arausio, the name adopted by the Romans, can be traced back to a Celtic god of water. But the town which flourished in antiquity later fell victim to the vagaries of history. From the ninth century, Orange was a *comté*, later becoming a *principauté*.

In 1544, William of Orange, later to become governor of the Netherlands, became the Duke of Orange and founded the Nassau-Orange line here. The town became part of the Netherlands, its inhabitants predominantly Protestant. As a result, the town suffered badly during the Wars of Religion. In the seventeenth century, Maurice of Nassau fortified the town by converting existing ancient buildings or re-using the masonry. Orange later passed to Prussia and in 1713 to France. The title of Prince of Orange passed back to the Netherlands, via the new Nassau-Orange.

Ancient monuments

The monumental Roman arch still stands on the main route northward out of the city on an extension of the town's north-south axis, the Cardo Maximus. The arch itself is neither a city gate nor a triumphal arch. It was built outside the city walls and, in any case, triumphal entrances were only allowed to take place in Rome itself. The monumental gates of Orange and other Roman provincial towns were built mainly to mark the founding of a town. They demonstrated clearly that a town or a region was part of the Roman Empire. From the holes for the letters on the north side it has been possible to reconstruct an inscription added after its construction (around 26 or 27 AD), in praise of the Emperor Tiberius as the restorer of the colony. The arch had been built earlier, probably under Augustus.

Now that the many medieval and modern additions and alterations have been removed, today's gate must be one of the best preserved monuments of its kind in France. Flanking the three arches on each side are four Corinthian half-columns supporting the entablature. The central opening is highlighted by a pediment. Above it rises a huge, double attic. Architectural features emphasize the square, angular structure of the gateway, but do not emerge as key elements in its design. Apart from several ornamental motifs, the rich decorations mainly features military matériel, in particular Celtic

weaponry which must be assumed to have been trophies. The arrangement of the objects appears to be haphazard, but in fact it follows a cleverly planned layout. Reliefs showing equestrian battles occupy the wide, central panels of the main façade on its upper and lateral surfaces (see illustration page 25 above). All the relief work is accurate in every detail, but at the same time it is imbued with a strong three-dimensional quality and a deep-set contour line. The composition attempts to create diversity of form and a sense of spatial depth in a Baroque style that contrasts with the classically stark sculptural approach adopted in Rome at the same time. In Orange at least, it seems that the influence of Hellenism, an example of which is the great Altar of Pergamon, was still very much in evidence.

The Roman theater

The great theater of Orange must be one of the best-preserved ancient buildings of its type. The designers used the slope of St-Eutrope Hill to create an orchestra and tiered semi-circle for about 9,000 spectators. On the north side, however, it was necessary to build large supporting constructions from vaulted gangways. The three tiers are separated by aisles. There were 20 rows in the lowest tier, nine in the middle section, and five in the upper section. The front rows, at least, were broken up according to the social ranking of the spectator. Marbled chairs stood on the first three steps of the orchestra for senators, decurions, and other guests of honor. Corbels pierced with holes lined the external upper ledge. These were for masts which would support a network of ropes above the auditorium. Triangular canvases, which could be moved according to the position of the sun, were secured to the ropes.

The stage was slightly raised and decorated with a front wall of columns and capitals. Behind this lay the curtain pit. The 43 ft (13 m) deep stage is set against a monumental three-story stage backdrop wall, known as the *scenae frons*. Hardly any others have survived in such good condition though its marble decorations have been lost, the niches and columns simply have to be imagined. But the surviving core enables visitors to see clearly how the stage wall was broken up dramatically by projections and recesses. It contains three openings through which the dignitaries entered. The Emperor or his representative entered through the central doorway, flanked by four columns, while the local elite took their seats through the side doors. The actors, on the other hand, arrived on stage from the side-entrances. In the niche above the regal doorway stands a statue of the Emperor wearing a cuirass and carrying a baton (see illustration left). It was re-assembled from many broken fragments and probably depicts Augustus. Up above, a kind of awning designed to improve the acoustics, sheltered the stage wall. Putting a date on the structure is not easy,

Orange
The ancient theater
The theater wall is 43 ft (13 m)
long and 126 ft (38 m) high

OPPOSITE:
Statue of Augustus
in the theater wall of the
ancient theater

but it is generally assumed that it was built at the beginning of the first century, the Augustinian era. This means that the moving relief on the stage façade was something of a novelty in Orange, but it was an idea adopted later by many other Roman theaters.

To the west of the theater lie the remains of another semi-circular complex at the center of which once stood a large raised temple. The Capitol, consisting of a group of three parallel temples with their porticos facing toward the town, once stood on St-Eutrope hill. The town's main road ran along the extension of this line as far as the monumental gate outside the town. Anyone living at the time who viewed the town from this vantage point would surely have been impressed by the spectacle of the temple façades on the hillside.

The new Cathédrale Notre-Dame was consecrated in 1208, but it suffered badly during the Wars of Religion. The interior, which was

Roman theater
The years in which the Romans transformed the infrastructure of many towns in southern Gaul coincided with a period of serious domestic crises, which ended with the fall of the Roman Republic and the proclamation of Caesar Augustus as Emperor. Stone theaters were henceforward to be very much part of the southern French scene, but this was an expression of the fact that the theater setting was increasingly a place in which the people were made to feel the power of the Imperial ruler.

The style of the performances was also changing. Tragic and comic plays which had been performed under the Republic were disappearing, giving way to crudely comic mime as well as pantomime, particularly of the old myths, in which dramatic theatrical effects and fables formed the climax. The stages were accordingly brightened up with scenery and lavish backdrops, with thunder and lightning effects, water features and even scent machines. Pantomime placed the emphasis on artistic and physical virtuosity, with rôles and characters being interpreted to richly-orchestrated musical accompaniment.

Gradually, sensual pleasures came to dominate the stage with pantomime actresses symbolizing depravity; the bloodthirsty combat that took place in the amphitheaters was also staged in the theaters.

On the other hand, theaters continued to be venues for political gatherings up until the sixth century. Not only were they the places where rulers received acclaim, they also sometimes provided the opportunity for the people to freely express their opinions.

originally built as a triple-naved chapel with narrow side-aisles or as a single-naved room with
side-chapels, was rebuilt in the form of a single-
nave church with a longitudinal vaulted arch.

Sérignan

Sérignan on the N976 is famous for the nearby
L'Harmas estate, now a botanical garden and
museum but formerly the field study center for
Jean-Henri Fabre, one of the world's greatest
entomologists. It was here from 1878 through
1923 that the scientist studied thousands of
insect species, minerals, and plants. The museum includes his laboratory and a comprehensive
collection of botanical and zoological exhibits,
as well as the home of the polymath, together
with his musical instruments. Hundreds of
watercolors, on which Fabre recorded the fungi
of Provence for posterity, also deserve close
examination.

The Musée-Atelier Werner Lichtner-Aix in
Sérignan is worth a visit. The German painter
settled here in 1969 to capture the light and life
of Provence in his paintings and graphics. He
died in Munich in the year 1987, aged 48, and
bequeathed his studio to the municipality.

Châteauneuf-du-Pape

To the south of Orange lies Châteauneuf-du-
Pape, where one of the finest Provençal wines
is produced. The town was originally built as a
fortress by Pope John XXII. It served as an
outpost and summer residence for the papal
city of Avignon. Largely destroyed during the
sixteenth-century Wars of Religion, the town
lost its surviving keep in 1944 when it was
blown up by German troops. The town offers

Châteauneuf-du-Pape
General view
with vineyards

16th-century wine press

a fine view of Avignon and Villeneuve-lès-Avignon. There is an important Musée des Outils des Vignerons, in Père Anselme's wine-cellar. The museum documents the history of vine cultivation with the aid of antique tools and equipment.

Benefiting from an extraordinarily favorable climate, the Châteauneuf-du-Pape region has been associated with wine production since the fourteenth century and the days of the Popes. The soil in the Rhône alluvial plain consists chiefly of large pebbles which absorb the heat of the day and then release it at night, so the microclimate is ideal for the cultivation of grapes. In 1923, Baron Le Roy de Boiseaumarié took the opportunity to establish an Appellation d'Origine Contrôlée (AOC) covering the vineyards of Châteauneuf and some in the surrounding locations. Curiously, wine producers here are allowed to blend up to 13 different grape varieties in order to achieve the dark, full-bodied wine. In 1939, the district adopted its own distinctive bottle shape. A relief of the papal coat-of-arms is now impressed on the shoulder of the bottle.

Around the Olympus of Provence

Carpentras, Mont Ventoux, and Vaison-la-Romaine

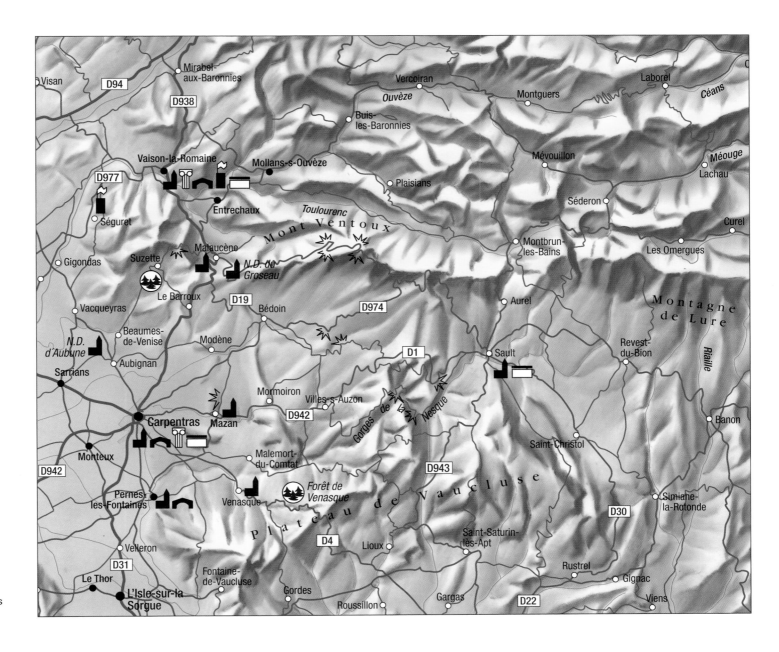

OPPOSITE:
Séguret near Vaison-la-Romaine is one of the most picturesque villages of the Côtes du Rhône and is famous for its full-bodied red wine.

Carpentras
The Hôtel Dieu hospital built in 1750. Detail of the façade

Carpentras

A Celtic tribe of the Caraveli, called the Memini, once lived here on the Molasse Plateau which descends sharply to the northeast, ending at the banks of the small river of Auzon. When the Romans, under Caesar or Augustus, founded the new city here, they named it Colonia Julia Meminorum Carpentoracte. In the Middle Ages, Carpentras was the main residence of the county of Venaissin, ruled by the counts of Toulouse. Their defeat in the Albigensian Wars in 1274 caused Carpentras to be incorporated into the papal state, where it remained until 1791. So as not to compete with the bishop, who ruled the city, Venaissin was ruled from Pernes until 1320. Carpentras flourished in the fourteenth and fifteenth centuries, when popes and cardinals frequently stayed here.

Thanks to the construction of a side-canal from the Durance river in 1768, an irrigation system was developed which turned the area around Carpentras into fertile farmland. The local produce supplies the whole of France, especially since the building of the railroad. Even today, the city has the retained its narrow, crooked streets and central marketplace in which a major theater, dance and folklore festival is held in the second half of July. The town is known for its striped fruit-flavored candies known as Berlingots de Carpentras.

The Cathedral

The largest building in the city is the cathedral which is dedicated to St. Siffrein, the bishop of the city in the third quarter of the sixth century. By the tenth century at the latest, a cathedral created from a group of churches on the site came into being, of which the baptistry survived into the late Middle Ages. In the last third of the twelfth century, a new building, the core of the current structure, was built. The remains of the Romanesque church are still visible on the north side of the choir. The church possessed a single nave with a barrel-vaulted ceiling similar to the cathedrals in Cavaillon and Avignon. Inside, massive blind arches support the side walls. The cupola, whose eight-sided foundation is supported by ascending arches, is still easily visible. The so-called trompe retains lovely relief portrayals of the evangelists. The most remarkable aspect, however, is the ribs of the cupola set upon high bases and topped with Corinthian capitals. Around the beginning of the thirteenth century, the portal on the north side was finally completed; the design is based on older models such as those of St-Paul-Trois-Châteaux and Aix-en-Provence. This can be seen from features such as the twisted columns with their acanthus-leaf capitals or the frieze above the portal adorned with cherubs holding leaves and fruiting vines. The uniform stone masonry technique can be traced back to classical examples.

When the Romanesque structure collapsed in 1399-1400, work on a Gothic replacement began on a site somewhat to the south of the original. The building progressed slowly and the records name many architects who, in most cases, were also active in Avignon. As with the preceding structure and like many Gothic churches in Provence, a wide, single nave was built with a slightly smaller choir. The side-chapels are not quite as high as the outer walls of the nave, which gives the impression of there being three naves. In the 1570s, a Geneva architect named Blaise Lécuyer built a monumental portal on the south side, which became known as the Porte Juive (see p.33). The pointed arch of this entrance is framed by two giant pinnacles on each side whose finials reach to the roof line and are strongly reminiscent of the portal of St-Pierre, built by the same master in Avignon (see p.63).

A conscious intention to build in an antiquated style is noticeable inside the cathedral. The thick pillars are certainly not typical of the clear-cut, late Gothic forms, nor are the plant and animal depictions on the capitals. The six-part vault system that was employed at the east end, where the building was begun, can also be attributed to the rest of the archaisms. Only after Blaise Lecuyer suggested that a four-part solution was more "secure," was the plan changed in the year 1470. From

Carpentras
Passage Boyer,
mid-19th century

Carpentras
Neogothic cathedral spire of St-Siffrein, 1899-1902. The architect, Henri Revoil, had previously built St-Martial in Avignon.

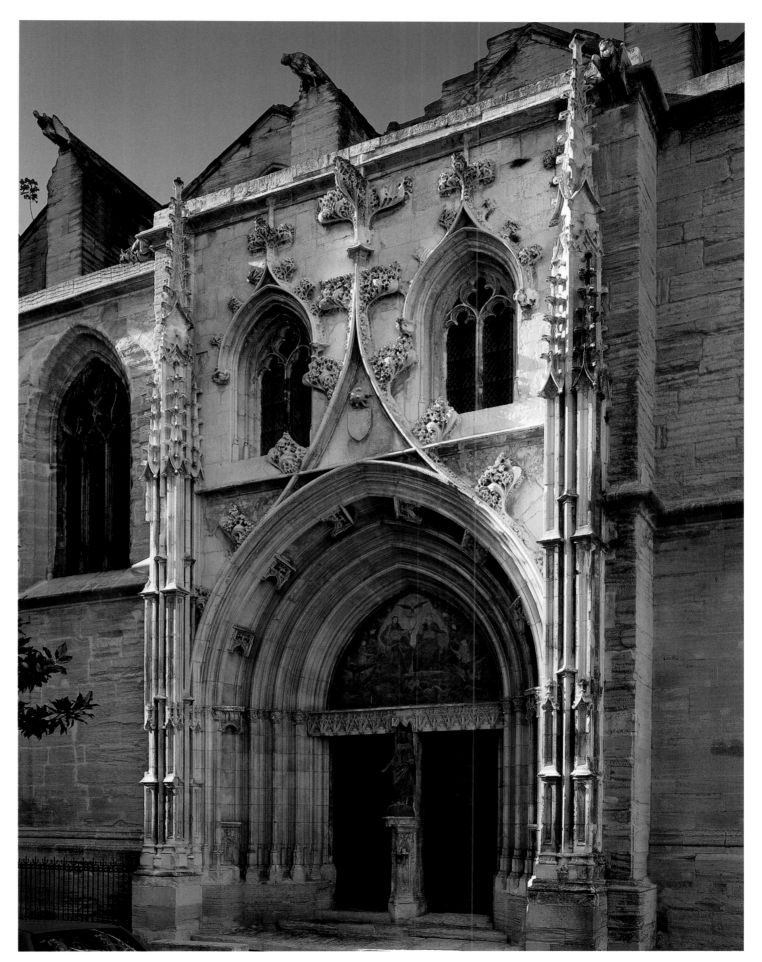

Carpentras
The cathedral of St-Siffrein.
Entrance on the south side,
known as The Jews' Gate
(*Porte Juive*), dating from 1470.

Carpentras
Roman Arch
(north of the cathedral of
St-Siffrein)

pilasters with composite capitals. The corners are accentuated by three-quarter columns. In contrast to the comparable examples in Orange and St. Rémy, the emphasis is on the sides. The entrance is thus made into a self-sufficient, dominating monument whose relatively small size suggests that it was once used as a plinth for a statue or similar object. The reliefs portray two prisoners, chained at the side to a victory sign in the shape of a tree (*Tropaia*). Their specific tribal classification is intentionally ambiguous. The fur-coated warrior is Teutonic, the other, because of his tunic and fur hat, is possibly Asiatic. Clearly, the sculptor combined different motifs to generally symbolize the "imprisoned barbarian." An inset frame isolates the figures from the relief background. The flatness of the relief and the heavy outlines suggest that a local workshop was still creating carvings in the Hellenistic tradition, well after the turning-point in history.

The Bibliothèque Inguimbertine and the Comtadin-Duplessis Museum are located in the same building complex and contain rich treasures of manuscripts, works of art, and paintings by artists such as Rigaud, Lieferinxe, Vernet, mostly from the collection of the art-loving bishop Malachie d'Inguimbert (1735-57).

Pernes-les-Fontaines
Tour Ferrande
General view of the exterior

OPPOSITE PAGE:
Wall paintings in
the Tour Ferrande,
built in 1285.

the lavish design of the structure erected in 1694, Jacques Bernus was probably modeling his "great road of glory" on Bernini's example in St. Peter's in Rome. In the choir, there is a painting of the coronation of the Virgin Mary, accompanied by St. Michael and St. Siffrein, probably from the workshop of Enguerrand Quartons (circa 1460). Other paintings are displayed in the treasury, north of the choir.

The Palais de Justice and the Roman Arch
The former palace of the bishop (now the court-house) was built in 1640 according to the plans of R. Fr. de La Valfrenière who was clearly inspired by the Palazzo Farnese in Rome.

To the north, in the shadow of the cathedral, where it appears to stand rather awkwardly, is the only remaining example of Roman construction in Carpentras (see above.) In the Middle Ages, it served as a portico for the church. The entrance is formed by a rounded arch that is framed by fluted

The Synagogue
The synagogue is of particular interest, since it is the oldest extant in France. It stands in what was once the ghetto and was rebuilt between 1741-43. The first synagogue was constructed in the fourteenth century. However, when the Jewish community grew to about 2,000 (about 20 percent of the total population) Bishop d'Inguimbert finally gave the community permission for a new building, on condition that it be lower in height than the cathedral. Because the ghetto was demolished in the nineteenth century, the synagogue no longer stands amongst a profusion of dwellings, as was earlier the case, but at the edge of a courtyard. The basement contains the ritual baths (*mikva*) used for the purification of the women, and on the first floor there is a bakery for making unleavened bread for Passover (*matzo*). The wood-paneled prayer room (see illustration right) is on the second floor. Here everything has been kept in its original condition. There are side-galleries in which the women sat during the services, the ark containing the scrolls, and the throne of Elijah (used for circumcisions) which is set in a little niche.

Although they were expelled in 1320, the Jews enjoyed special protection in the papal Comtat-Venaissin from 1342. They were forced, however, to wear a yellow star on their clothes and to stay in their own quarter under a system of self-government. With the Edict of Tolerance of 1787, the ghettos of

Carpentras
Synagogue, showing the
ladies' gallery and the Ark
(1741-43).

Cavaillon, Carpentras, Avignon and L'Isle-sur-la-Sorgue began to disperse. For the first time, Jews began to establish themselves elsewhere, especially in Nice, Marseille, and Aix. The significant roll which Judaism plays in Provence can be witnessed by the storm of indignation which swept through all levels of French society when youths vandalized a Jewish graveyard in 1990.

An imposing building standing in front of the gates of the old city was built by Antoine d'Allemand in 1750-51 on behalf of Bishop d'Inguimberts as a hospital (*Hôtel Dieu*). At the top of a wide staircase there is an ancient pharmacy on the first floor which is still equipped with its old cabinets painted with love scenes, imaginary landscapes and cavorting apes.

A few miles away in the direction of Bédoin (D 974), stands an impressive aqueduct that was built between 1720-30 to improve the original water supply system which dated from the Middle Ages.

Pernes-les-Fontaines

Atop a slight elevation just to the south of Carpentras lies the little city of Pernes-les-Fontaines which served as the principle city of the Comtat-Venaissin from 968 through 1320, until the pope transferred this function to Carpentras. As protection against the Grandes Compagnies (see p. 53), strong fortifications were built in the fourteenth century, some of which are still standing. The city's name derives from its 36 springs and fountains, most of which were built in the eighteenth century. They are fed from from a spring near the chapel of St-Roch.

The former priory church of Notre Dame de Nazareth serves today as the parish church. A new nave was built in the apse of the eleventh century church in the third quarter of the twelfth century. More chapels were added in the fourteenth century. The portal, with its entrance hall in the fourth bay, is flanked by columns. The entablature and extensions to the pediment show considerable similarities to the entrances to the churches of St. Gabriel and St. Restitut. The interior contains some exquisite Romanesque sculptures on the impost, cornice, and friezes.

The Tour Ferrande (see p.34, above right), perhaps once a part of the Knights Hospitalier order, retains exceptionally interesting wall paintings in its upper story, which dates from about 1285 (see right). They depict the victory of the Pope and Charles of Anjou over the Hohenstaufen. In the upper panel on the east wall, Clement IV grants Charles the kingdom of Sicily. The south side depicts the French victory over Manfred in the battles of Tagliacozzo and Benevent. At the top of the west wall, there is a portrayal of a scene from a knightly romance: William, Duke of Aquitaine is shown killing the giant Ysoré.

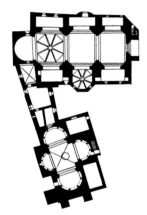

Venasque

From the sixth to the tenth and eleventh centuries this town perched on the ledge of a rocky cliff served as the official seat for the bishops of Carpentras. The church of Notre Dame (see above) is the successor to the original cathedral. The three-bay church shows all the characteristics of the Provençal Romanesque, in the deep, blind arches along the walls, the pointed barrel vaults, and the quadrilateral cupola. The portal on the south side, including the chapel, is a later addition. The oldest part of the church is the eleventh century rectangular main apse.

The so-called baptismal font on the north side of the church (see opposite) is built over a cloverleaf-shaped ground plan. The two wings are of differing length, however. The corner pilasters of the central area were renovated in the thirteenth century. The remaining parts of the building must date from the eleventh century. The most interesting feature are the early blind arcades. The large columns with Corinthian capitals under the apse arches are reused antique stones, next to which there are early Romanesque capitals with stylized ionic scrolls and a woven pattern. Even today, the exact functions of this so-called baptismal font remain a mystery. It was once assumed to be a baptismal church for early Christians, but today it is believed to have once served as a memorial for martyrs. Similar holy grave and holy cross chapels are also found in Montmajour and on the island of St. Honorat.

The Dentelles de Montmirail and the Surrounding Area

North of Carpentras, the Dentelles de Montmirail—buttresses, so to speak, of Mont Ventoux—are reminiscent of the Dolomites with their bizarre, needle-like formations, surrounded by pine forests (see pp.40-41). These forms were caused by sediment deposits shifted into a vertical position and then weathered. The mountains are dotted with picturesque villages.

The heights of Notre Dame d'Aubune were settled in Grecian times. The present church (see p.38) was an ambitious building when it was constructed in the middle of the twelfth century. The church has a transept from which three apses extend, as well as a tall tower that was built somewhat later. Its slenderness is emphasized by the over-extended pilasters that are copies of classical examples, though their elongated proportions reflect a Gothic style.

The village of Beaumes-de-Venise nestles at the base of a cliff and is topped by a ruined château. Le Barroux also has an imposing château with an interior Renaissance courtyard. At Malaucène, there is an interesting parish church that, although built in the beginning of the fourteenth century, still contains some Romanesque features. Some miles to the east stands the ruined twelfth-century chapel of Notre-Dame-du-Groseau, of which only the rectangular choir bay and apse remain.

OPPOSITE:
Notre-Dame-d'Aubune
Romanesque church, second
half of the 12th century.

RIGHT:
**Landscape around
Beaumes-de-Venise**

PICTURE ON PP. 40/41:
Dentelles de Montmirail

PICTURE ON PP.. 42/43:
Mont Ventoux
Arid mountain landscape.

Carpentras, Mont Ventoux, Vaison-la-Romaine

Mont Ventoux

Mont Ventoux dominates the horizon of Carpentras rising to a height of 6363 ft (1909 m). The pyramid-shaped silhouette and whitened top, giving the impression that snow lies on the summit year round, can be seen from far away. This, however, is only the case between December and May; but here the Mistral blows which such a merciless ferocity (up to 143 m.p.h. (230 km/h) that every speck of dust is carried off, leaving only naked-white stone at the top. In fact, the name of mountain is believed to refer to the wind (*vent*). The mountain also has other interesting features. The temperature changes very rapidly during the day and is on average 52°F (11°C) cooler at the peak than at the foot of the mountain. It rains twice as much on the mountain, making it an important water source for the surrounding area. The springs of Groseau near Malaucène as well as the Fontaine de Vaucluse, some 15 miles (24 km) away, are fed by water from Ventoux. The range of climatic conditions that correspond to changes in altitude, have allowed for the cultivation of various biotopes, which were developed in the nineteenth century after the slopes were almost entirely deforested by the shipping industry. Lebanon Cedars are counted among the botanical curiosities and on the peak, even arctic vegetation has taken root. In order to experience the variety of fauna, numerous hiking trails have been provided for visitors. In the winter the area is a beautiful place to ski. For drivers, the D 974 is recommended for the ascent. It was specially designed as a scenic route and offers many new views of the sun-drenched mountain. It is also possible to negotiate the wild Gorges de la Nesque in the south, or drive through the valley of Toulourenc in the north, climbing the mountain (by way of Sault) from the east. At the summit, there is a viewing platform, from which the panorama is amazing. One can see from the Alps (Massiv du Vercors), Luberon, and the Montagne Ste-Victoire as far as Marseille, and when the weather is good, even to the Pyrenees. At night, the stars glitter and sparkle, while the lights from hundreds of Provençal towns and cities as well as the lighthouses of Marseille and Sète shine in the darkness.

Petrarch and the Climbing of Mount Ventoux

"Moved by the unfamiliar fragrance of the air and the free view, I stood benumbed. Looking back, the clouds were at my feet and the mountains of Athos and Olympus seemed less incredible; for I saw in this little-known mountain all that I had read about the others."

Thus did Francesco Petrarca, known in English as Petrarch, describe his arrival at the summit of Mount Ventoux which he reached on April 26, 1336. For the first time since Antiquity, a landscape experience was turned into literature. The limitless landscape allowed the poet to reflect on the mortality of his earthly life. Spiritual holiness wins over the esthetic sense and in silent awe, Petrarch descends.

Petrarch (1304-74) was born in Arezzo, but grew up in Provence, mainly in Avignon and Carpentras, because his family had to flee from Florence and Pisa before settling in Avignon. In 1316, the young Francesco started studying law in Montpellier, continuing in Bologna in 1320. He returned to Avignon, however, where he entered holy orders. In 1327, he met Laura, his beloved muse who appears in so many of his poems, for the first time in the church of Ste-Claire in Avignon.

There is no source of information about the real Laura, who may only have been an imaginary figure whom the poet caused to die in 1348. In 1356, Petrarch left southern France and lived at various Italian courts.

Petrarch was regarded as the greatest scholar of his age and his interest in classical culture and Christianity strongly influenced contemporary literature. However, it is for his poetry, especially his sonnets, that his fame has endured. In his writing, he praises the Roman example and oscillates between duty and pleasure, enjoyment and abstinence, the medieval sensuality of the courts and the ancient Stoic meditations; these are some of the motivating factors behind his literary description of his ascent of Mount Ventoux.

Vaison-la-Romaine

From the 4th century BC, the Celtic tribe of the Vocontier inhabited the heights west of the Ouvèze. They were conquered by the Romans in the years 125-121 BC before the colony of Gallia Narbonensis was founded. To the east of the river stood the *Vasio Vocontiorum* which became the new center of administration, or *Civita*s, responsible for the districts of Die, Gap, and Sisteron, and receiving the special (theoretical) status of *Civitas Confoederata*. In a short time, Vaison developed into a flourishing community with Roman-influenced customs and buildings. Around the end of the third century the territory of the *Civitas* was divided, thereby creating the bishoprics of Die, Gap, Sisteron, and Vaison. A Christian community must have existed at this time, because Bishop Daphnus of Vaison attended the Council of Arles in 314.

A council held in Vaison in 529 proves the importance of the city, but it subsequently fell into decline. In the eleventh century, it experienced a revival. The cathedral was supplied with columns, capitals and numerous gifts under the bishopric. In the twelfth century, the bishop also functioned as the temporal ruler of the city. In 1160, Raymond, Count of Provence, seized the half of the city west of the Ouvéze and built a château. Over the centuries, the residents moved into this upper part of the city, while the old city fell into disrepair and even the cathedral was abandoned. A new church built in 1464 in the new city served instead. In the eighteenth century, the site of the old city began to be reinhabited, but since Gallo-Roman and medieval Vaison had crumbled, a new city took its place. This, in turn, lead to a loss in the significance of the upper city. The rise and fall of the two halves of the city led to the continual disintegration of infrastructure. The remaining Romanesque structures stand, therefore, like islands amidst a modern city background.

Remains of the Roman city, dating from the first and second centuries, were excavated in 1907, thanks to the life-long dedication of the Abbé Joseph Sautel of Avignon. The city experienced a further episode in its checkered history in September of 1992 when a flash flood swept thirty-seven people to their deaths and destroyed one hundred and fifty houses.

Excavation of the Roman City

The excavation of the Roman city opened up large areas on both sides of the Avenue du Général de Gaulle that reveal only the outer districts of the former city, because its center is buried under modern buildings.

The Romans, contrary to their practices in Glanum, built their new city on the green

Vaison-la-Romaine
Quartier de Villasse
Remains of the
Roman city

fields facing the Celtic settlement. Differing from the usual Roman foundation, the plan contains no uniform street pattern or a surrounding wall. Its expansion can only be guessed at by the size of the graveyards found in the outer districts. In 40 AD, the city was counted as being among the richest in Gaul.

Quartier de Villasse

The Quarter de Villasse has a Roman paved street once lined with stores. The terraced curbs of the sidewalk provide access to deep recesses that contained stores and workshops. On the west side, these were covered with arcades. At the south end of the street, there are the ruins of a wide auditorium—the so-called basilica—whose entrance arch has been reconstructed with the original parts. Because extensive aqueducts were discovered in the same area, the building must be interpreted as being part of a thermal baths complex. Across from the building lie the extensive grounds of the *Maison au Buste d'Argent*. Proceeding through the colonnaded vestibule, one reaches an atrium surrounded by a colonnaded hallway. To the south there is a wider and larger peristyle with a long, rectangular pool in the center. This colonnaded courtyard, surprisingly large for a private residence, was most likely the original *Palestra* of an older public baths. This would also explain the public latrines on the eastern side of the courtyard. To the west is the *Maison au*

OPPOSITE:
Vaison-la-Romaine
Quartier du Puymin
Roman statues of the
Emperor Hadrian and
his wife Sabina
(These are replicas,
the originals of which
are in the Théo-Desplans
Archeological Museum
in the Cemetery of
Puymin, see p. 49)

Vaison-la-Romaine
Archeological Museum
Mosaik der Pfauenvilla, Late 1st century AD.

Dauphin which derives its name from a fragment of putto riding a dolphin that was found on the site. On the East-West axis, there are a smaller and a larger atrium. The larger atrium has rooms leading off it in a North-South direction. This perspective frequently appears in Roman architecture. In the northeast corner, there are the ruins of the house baths. To the south, a colonnaded portico extends along the whole width overlooking the garden which has a surrounding moat. The ability of water to cool the air and reflect the light as well as its gentle splashing sounds were among the pleasures afforded by these ornamental lakes and pools. The villa was built in the second century on top of an older structure.

Quartier du Puymin

The House of Messii (so named after its inscription) with its large atrium, in the southwest corner of the district. The integration of the atrium into the space is characteristic of the period. In the peristyle to the east an ornamental pool separates the columned portico from the garden as in the Maison du Dauphin. This leads into a larger colonnaded courtyard on which there is an inscription on a frieze naming it as *Porticus Pompeiana*. In the middle, there is an ornamental pool with an apse-like curve at one end. The function of the building is unclear, though it was probably a public one. The niches in the northern surrounding wall held statues, but not the casts taken from the the theater which occupy them today.

The tour continues to a reconstructed building that is hard to interpret, but may be

a spring temple (*Nymphaeum*). To the east lay the ruins of the so-called "Peacock Villa." Halfway up the hill, the Théo-Desplans Museum displays the statues that have been excavated, including those of the emperors taken from the theater. Among others are the badly damaged figure of Claudius (43 AD) and the statue of Emperor Domitian (81-96 AD) wearing his armor. The pose and the relief on the breastplate are a copy of the earlier statue of Augustus (the statue from the Prima Porta). The reliefs depict the *Gorgoneion* and a Pallas-Athenian cult image accompanied by two victories. The statue of Hadrian is quite different from that of Augustus. He is depicted as a naked athlete with his *Paludamentum* (commander's cloak) thrown over his shoulder, reflecting the Hellenistic ideal of a ruler. The statue of the Emperor's wife, Sabina, serves as a companion piece (see right). The copy of Diadumenos by Polycletes was sold to the British Museum in 1896, so he is present here only as a cast. The floor mosaics from the Peacock Villa can also be viewed in the museum (see left).

The cavea of the theater to the north is tilted upon the steep slope. This is largely a reconstruction. Only the stone base of the stage front is preserved. The depressions on the stage for machinery and curtains are clearly discernible.

North of the Avenue Cevert, more Roman baths have been excavated (late first century). There is yet another in the southern part of the city, showing once more what an important place Vaison was under the Romans.

The Cathedral of Notre-Dame-de-Nazareth

The cathedral stands upon Roman foundations. When the diocese became more prosperous under Bishop Pierre de Mirabel, the eastern apse and the lower part of the nave were laid in 1040. The upper parts were

Vaison-la-Romaine
Archeological Museum
Statue of the Empress Sabina from the 2nd century AD.

Vaison-la-Romaine
Archeological Museum
Grave adornment in the form of a theatrical mask.

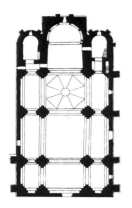

Vaison-la-Romaine
The 11th-12th century Cathedral of Notre-Dame-de-Nazareth
Interior view looking east (right) and ground plan (above)

built between 1150-60 before the dispute arose between count and bishop. The eastern section is executed in clear geometric forms: the side-apses are round while the choir is rectangular in shape. The masonry work consists of irregular, and in some cases, reused stones that are skillfully cut. In the nave, there are signs of early Romanesque windows which were later walled up during extensive building in the twelfth century. At the same time, buttresses supporting the newly planned pointed barrel-vaults were added. The masonry work and the richly ornamented window soffits as well as the frieze under the roof line of the side aisle are in good condition.

Inside, there is a high, three-aisled nave (see right), accompanied by deeply stepped pilasters and wall paintings. Although there is no transept, there is a quadrilateral cupola that rests on a trompe adorned with symbols of the evangelists. The choir apse is the most richly decorated, surrounded by arches whose early Romanesque, Corinthian capitals can be compared to similar ones in Venasque and in the Tour Izarn of St-Victoire in Marseille. There are three seats around the semicircle, in the middle of which stands the bishop's stone throne (also in Lyon and Vienne) in accordance with an old Christian arrangement.

The cloister on the north side that was built during the second phase of construction has an architectural system comparable to those in Arles and Moutmajour where three arches are connected to a massive arch. Unlike Arles, where the middle and corner pilasters contain large figures, Vaison's main supports consist of a series of small pillars. The decoration on the capitals are of two types. One uses sober lancelet leaves, while the other elaborates on the basic Corinthian style with entwining leaves and ribbons. From the cloister the large hexameter inscription on the church wall aligned along the compass points can easily be read, a symbol constantly reminding the canons of the fact that the cloister was seen as a part of God's order, leading to redemption.

The Chapel of St-Quenin

The small chapel of St-Quenin (see right) dedicated to the bishop of Vaison (556-578) is a curious structure in the area north of the cathedral on the site of an ancient graveyard. The eastern section is of a triangular foundation dating from the late twelfth century. From the outside, the building looks like a ship with a pointed bow. Beautiful classical columns and capitals accentuate the edges. Inside, the bow-shape covers the central apse which is ornamented with blind arches and adjoining side-apses. The exceptionally compact basic form provides enough space for a three-apse construction.

Vaison-la-Romaine
Late 12th-century chapel of St-Quenin, looking east (right) and ground plan (above).

A Papal State for A Hundred Years

Avignon, Villeneuve-lès-Avignon, and Barbentane

1 Cathedral of Notre-Dame-
   des-Doms
2 Palais des Papes
3 Petit Palais
4 St-Nicolas

5 Theater
6 Hôtel de Ville (city hall)
7 St-Agricole
8 Théodore-Aubanel Museum
9 St-Pierre

10 Calvet Museum
11 Requien Museum
12 St-Didier
13 Lapidarium
14 Convent of the Celestines

15 La Visitation
16 Augustinian Clocktower
17 St-Symphorien

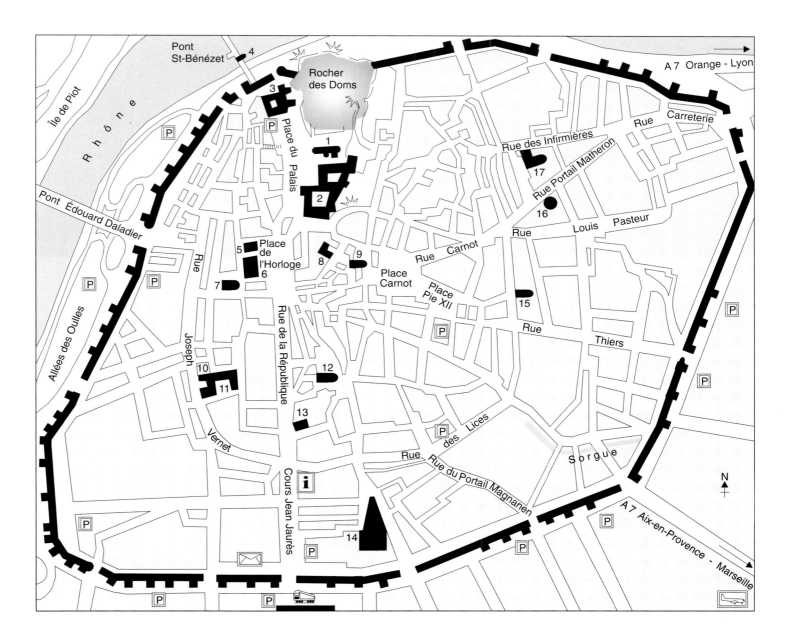

OPPOSITE:
Avignon
Pont St-Bénézet
»Sur le pont d'Avignon ...«

Avignon

Celtic tribes first settled on the limestone cliffs along the banks of the Rhône, close to the mouth of the Durance. Because of its strategic location on a main trading route, the settlement was extended by the Romans, who called it Avenio. But it was only during the reorganization of the Roman Empire in the 3rd century that the city became the capital of a *Civitas*. The first bishop to be mentioned, as late as 439, was one Nectarius. Trade and commerce, helped the city expand, and, as in Marseille, Arles, and Italy, a largely independent city regiment, the so-called consulate, developed under the political leadership of the episcopate and the local gentry. In the Albigensian Wars, the city sided with the local counts of Provence-Toulouse, who were themselves supporters of the heretics. As a result, Avignon was besieged by the northern French in 1226, surrendering after three months. The city walls, as well as 300 fortified city houses, were

razed to the ground. Because it refused to acknowledge the rule of Charles of Anjou, who ruled Provence through marriage, the city was besieged and taken again in 1251. In 1274, the Pope acquired the Comtat Venaissin, promised to him after the Albigensian Wars, which had previously belonged to the Count of Toulouse. When political turmoil in Rome caused Pope Clement V to leave the Vatican, he followed the advice of the French King and established a provisional residence in Avignon, ruling the city and a substantial area around it. Under Clement's successor, John XXII (1316-1334), Avignon became the official papal residence. A period of rapid economic expansion was the result. Both clerical and secular dignitaries built lavish residences in the city, which were known as *Livrées* or *Cardinalices*. Old churches were replaced by newer and more elaborate ones. Merchants, diplomats, jurists, and craftsmen flocked to the rapidly growing city from all over Europe. Pope

Boniface VIII established a university in 1303. The economic regeneration was made possible by the papacy's lavish spending, which in turn depended on the ruthless enforcement of tithe payments from the dioceses. Nepotism and simony were also rife, while clerics often held numerous offices. The decadence of the papal court in Avignon was criticized early on by authors such as Petrarch and Jan Hus and was one of the deciding factors in the start of the Reformation. When Gregory XI moved the papal court back to Rome in 1377, he allegedly heaped ironic praise on his predecessors for having reduced the number of brothels in Avignon to just on, which, however, encompassed the whole city!

The splendor of the papal city contrasted greatly with the general circumstances of the time. The Black Death of 1348 is alleged to have claimed 11,000 lives in Avignon alone. A few years later, the city had to pay huge sums in ransoms, to protect it from marauding

Avignon
Stream in the Park on the
Rocher-des-Doms

OPPOSITE:
Avignon
Palace of the popes
General view from the
northwest.

Avignon
City wall,
14th and 19th century

mercenary bands, the so-called Grandes Compagnies, which had formed after the Hundred Years War. The city wall was extended and greatly reinforced. The rapid development of the city also led to the uncontrolled growth of the suburbs and to indescribable sanitary conditions.

Even though Gregory XI returned to Rome in 1377, this was not the end of Avignon's time as a papal residence; the antipope pretenders Clement VII and Benedict XIII resided there up until 1409. Later, Avignon became the seat of a papal legate, and the city's prosperity was thus maintained. Following the Wars of Religion, however, Avignon lost much of its previous importance. This was also due to the fact that after 1481, when the French kings acquired Provence, the Comtat Venaissin was surrounded by French possessions on all sides. This had the effect, however, of furthering the development of certain types of commerce and industry, such as the silk and tobacco trade, which could not be subjected to by French taxes and duties, and flourished as a consequence.

There was another surge of economic growth in the eighteenth century, when many new mansions were built for the bourgeoisie. The roads were widened and street lighting was introduced. France made several unsuccessful attempts to annex the Comtat Venaissin, but this objective was finally achieved in 1791, during the French Revolution. The papacy acknowledged the annexation in 1814.

The nineteenth century saw new developments in agriculture. The mulberry trees introduced earlier to the area fostered silk production, and the city also became one of the world's leading centers for the export of red dye. In the long term, however, these industries

Avignon
View of the Rocher-des-Doms
from the opposite side of
the Rhône

could not withstand competition from Asian fabrics and the development of chemical dyes.

Only in the course of the twentieth century did Avignon, now the administrative seat of the Département of Vaucluse, once again become an important center of trade and industry. The city holds an international theater festival every summer in the papal residence and other historical venues in Avignon and district, which attracts visitors from all over the world. It was initiated in 1947 by Jean Vilar, whose initial intention had been to perform just three plays in the city.

Those tourists who are short of time will be forced to restrict their visit to the papal palace, especially since Avignon's main street, the Rue de la République, which intersects with the Place de l'Horloge, leads right up to its gates. Numerous other impressive monuments are partially hidden among a maze of little narrow streets, such as the Rue des Teinturiers, the Rue du Vieux-Sextier, the Rue du Roi-René, and the Place du Change, to name but a few.

The Palais des Papes

The palace built by the Popes in the fourteenth century was one of the largest châteaux of its time. Today, its labyrinth of rooms is mostly empty, making it impossible to guess their former function. Pope John XXII (1316-1334), formerly Bishop of Avignon, used his former bishop's palace as the papal residence, which is located to the south of the cathedral of Notre-Dame-des-Doms. Only under his successor, Benedict XII (1334-1342), was construction begun on the new, impressive papal château around the Palais Vieux in the northern part of the city. The palace originally consisted of a diamond-shaped, four-winged building surrounding an inner courtyard. Another separate wing was

The Grandes Compagnies
Following the temporary peace agreement of Bretigny-Calais in 1360 during the Hundred Years War, many soldiers decided, after five years of war, to continue fighting on their own behalf. The marauding bands, which were given the name of the Grandes Compagnies, plundered, destroyed, overpowered, and murdered their way through mainland Europe in the course of the following decade. They started in northern France, moving down to southern France and beyond. This caused many towns to strengthen their defenses in order to defy the robber bands.

ILLUSTRATIONS ON P.55:
Avignon
Palais des Papes, North
Sacristy of the
Palace chapel (above)
Murals in the Chambre des
Cerfs, ca. 1343
Fishing scene (Center)
Hunting scene (below)

Avignon
Palais des Papes
West façade (above)
Audience room (below)

located to the southeast of the main building, ending in the so-called Angel Tower. Clement VI extended and regularized the palace layout by building two large additional wings onto Benedict's separate wing, thus creating a second interior courtyard, the so-called Grande Cour, at the southern end of the palace. Among the later extensions to the building, the large gardens added by Urban V (1362-1370) deserve a mention, though they no longer exist today.

When the Popes returned to Rome in 1377, the antipope pretenders of the Great Schism continued to reside in the palace. Then, from the fifteenth century onward, the building was inhabited by papal legates. During the French Revolution, the palace was looted, and the Bastille du Midi was almost destroyed. The use of the palace as a prison and archive caused substantial damage to it. Extensive restoration work on this historic building did not commence until 1906.

The financing of the construction of the palace is well documented, and many of the craftsmen involved are mentioned in documents. Pierre Poisson from Mirepoix, near Carcassonne, has been identified as the master builder for the construction of the old palace, while Jean de Louvres, who is said to have come from northern France, may have been in charge of the extensions under Clement, indicating both southern and northern influences.

The names of the master builders, however, are no key to their functions and the historical importance of the building. Its massive walls and towers were made to withstand a siege, because, as a temporal ruler, the Pope also required adequate military protection. But the expensive fortifications also served a representative function, as in the case of similar buildings, such as the papal château in Villandraut, the city palace of John XXII in Cahors, and the palace of the archbishop of Narbonne. As in most of these residences of church dignitaries,

Avignon Palais des Papes
Ground plan of the lower palace:
1 Chapel of St. Jean 2 Consistory 3 Large treasury
4 Salle de Jésus 5 Papal robing room 6 Lower treasury
7 Treasury 8 Large Audience Room 9 Small Audience Room
10 Guardrooom. 11. Cour d'honneur 12. Cloister of Benedict XII

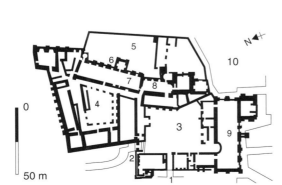

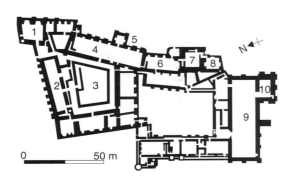

Avignon Palais des Papes
Ground plan of the upper palace:
13 Kitchen 14 Large refectory
15 Chapel of St. Martial
16 Robing Room 17 Pope's room 18 Chambre des Cerfs
19 North Sacristy 20 Cardinals' robing room 21 Large chapel
22 Loggia 23 New treasury
24 Chambre des Notaires
25. Terrace

strict symmetry was not considered important for Benedict's palace. This was in marked contrast to many of the châteaux of the French kings (the Louvre, Vincennes, Carcassonne). The representative aspect of the palace in Avignon becomes most obvious in those parts of the building which were extended under Clement VI, and especially in the east façade (see p. 54). The blind arcades in the lower part of the building are combined with symbols of temporal rule, such as the turrets with their pointed pyramid-shaped roofs, which draw attention to the main gate. Turrets of this kind can be found on the entrance gates to many châteaux of the temporal rulers of this time. The additions to the building under Clement VI also made the palace more symmetrical in layout, centering it around two large interior courtyards.

The style of the palace as a whole is sober, although some individual features are exquisitely worked. The vaulted ceilings of some of the huge rooms, such as the so-called Great Chapel of Clement VI, which is 53 ft (16 m) wide, are technical masterpieces. The individual features of the wall profiles and tracery are mostly sturdy and rounded, which is surprising because square-cut columns and elaborate tracery were among the architectural forms which predominated in southern France from the late thirteenth century onward. The architecture of the papal palace is primarily a functional one. Its main innovative achievement was that within an amazingly short time span it provided the necessary facilities for the ceremonial of the papal court.

When the Popes returned to Rome at the end of the fourteenth century, they continued to employ the same architectural style for the building of their new residences and even for extensions to the Vatican itself. In the old palace of Benedict XII, the most important court functions—the conclave wing in the south wing, the papal quarters in the west wing, and the papal chapel in the north wing—are all grouped around the inner courtyard with its open loggias. The so-called Trouila Tower, which housed storage facilities and the fuel supplies, and most importantly, the armory, stand on a slight elevation or mound. It was from here, also, that the enormous kitchen was supplied, which in turn supplied the main reception rooms in the east wing, the Great Consistory and, above it, the Great Banqueting Hall. The curia met in the Great Consistory, while the banqueting hall was used for large gatherings.

Private apartments were of course also required, and these were located in the southern annex which was built onto the Great Banqueting Hall, also housing two small meeting rooms, the Parament Chamber and the Small Banqueting Hall. The Pope's private quarters were located in the so-called Papal or Angel Tower (Tour des Anges); they included

the bedroom and private office, his last refuge, which was called the *Studium*. The Papal Tower was a self-contained unit, whose other stories housed the papal treasure and the library, all of which were connected by staircases. The private quarters were thus located on the periphery of the main building complex; from here, each successive room became more elaborate, culminating in the Great Banqueting Hall. This was a new development and marks a more differentiated ceremonial at the papal court from this time onward. Another innovation was the loggias which directly surround the inner courtyard and which are accessible via an elaborate low staircase. Representation and ceremonial gained further importance under Clement VI, who extended the private quarters by an enormous audience chamber and a new papal chapel in the south wing. The audience chamber was also the meeting place for the ecclesiastical court, which met around a huge round table, the so-called *Rota*. A new, elaborately designed office, the famous *Chambre du Cerf* (Deer Room), linked the private quarters to the chapel. The Great Chapel on the upper floor leads into a loggia facing out onto the inner courtyard. It contained the largest and most elaborate window within the palace, the so-called Absolution Window, which has since been replaced. This benediction loggia is where the Pope was crowned, and from here he gave his blessing to the faithful and announced indulgences. A wide ceremonial staircase led down into the courtyard.

The enormous hall of the chapel is one of the most perfect examples of a hall church with a single nave and relatively small windows, a style typical of southern France. The excessive load from above on the portal leading into the loggia soon destroyed it, leading to its replacement in 1359. The badly-damaged statues once depicted the Last Judgement.

The papal palace was richly decorated, but few remnants have survived to the present day. Of these, the frescos by Matteo Giovannetti are probably the most significant. The artist was summoned to Avignon from Viterbo, probably by Benedict XII, and between 1336 and 1368 was in charge of the decorative painting of the palace. The fact that an Italian painter, probably of the Sienna school of painting, was called in, is an indication of the growing internationalism of art appreciation. Unfortunately, the large frescos which Matteo and his assistants created for the Consistory and the Great Banqueting Hall were destroyed as early as the Middle Ages. Today, only the paintings in the adjacent chapels of St John and St Martial, and those in the papal apartments, survive. The fresco in the Great Audience Chamber was never completed, but two sections of the vault depict scenes from the Books of the Prophets and the Sybile of Erythrea. Sketches of a Crucifixion scene are faintly discernible between the windows of the

OPPOSITE:
Avignon
Palais des Papes
Murals in the pope's sleeping
quarters, 1343

east wall, while the north wall shows remnants of a depiction of the Last Judgement. The two chapels mentioned above contain frescoes depicting the lives of the saints named. It is noticeable how often Matteo incorporated a painted frame into the frescos, with the suggestion of a space in the background that invites anecdotal narration. In the chapel of St Martial, one field depicts the churches founded by the two saints as Gothic buildings in a landscape of trees. These imaginary buildings combine elements of southern French Gothic architecture.

More famous still are the frescoes in the so-called Deer Room (see p. 55), for which Matteo probably enlisted the help of French *collèges*. They depict courtly past-times, such as hawking, deer-hunting, and fishing in a pond, all of which seem to be taking place in a spacious forest setting containing different species of trees. The observer feels drawn into the picture, as if he were taking part in the scenes. Similar illusions are at work in the frescoes in the bedroom (see opposite). Above a painted plinth which suggests that draperies have been drawn, the walls are covered with painted vines and leaves and the birds which inhabit them. In the window embrasures, painted birdcages can be made out. These are mostly empty, as if awaiting the return of the birds that are enjoying the air in the palace gardens.

Hôtel des Monnaies

Opposite the entrance to the papal palace is the mint (*Hôtel des Monnaies*), which was built in 1619, possibly by an architect from Bologna for the representative of the papal legate Cardinal Borghese, who himself resided in Rome. The three-story façade has a rusticated ground floor, while the two top stories are decorated with extravagant reliefs of garlands, eagles, and dragons, the heraldic beasts of the Borghese family (see left and above).

Cathedral Notre-Dame-des-Doms

Avignon's cathedral, situated on high ground next to the papal palace, almost appears to be an annex to the residence. That is because the Popes at first took up residence here, later beginning construction of the papal palace on the adjacent site.

The cathedral is the last of the city's Romanesque buildings. It was part of a larger ensemble of church buildings extending northward, which also included the parish church of St-Etienne—later incorporated into the palace—and a small baptistry that no longer exists. The cathedral was replaced in three stages during the course of the twelfth century. The nave was erected at the beginning of the century, between 1130 and 1140 a dome was added, and the building was completed in the second half of the century when the portico was built.

LEFT AND ABOVE:
Avignon
Hôtel des Monnaies
Façade, detail of the relief
decorations (1619).

Avignon
Cathedral of Notre-
Dame-
des-Doms, tomb of Pope
Benedict XII in the north
chapel. The tomb had
been smashed and has
been reconstructed.

Avignon
Cathedral of Notre-Dame-
des-Doms, interior view of
cupola (above)
Ground plan (below)

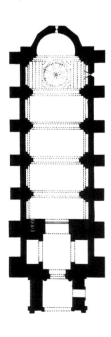

The west tower was destroyed during the siege of the palace in 1405, but replaced shortly thereafter. The side-chapels leading off the nave were added between the fourteenth and sixteenth centuries. A new apse was built by Louis François de Royers de La Valfrenière in the late seventeenth century. The tower was not completed until 1859, when the inordinately large statue of the Madonna was added.

The portico, with its round-arched portal and triangular gable, masterfully replicates classical building tradition, to the extent that in the past it was sometimes mistakenly considered a genuinely antique building. Some of its details are an exact reproduction of features of the Roman arch in Orange. The proportions of the corner columns, which are placed on pedestals, the shape of the Corinthian capitals and the entablature could all have been taken from a textbook on classical Roman architecture. The remnants of frescoes painted by Simone Martini between 1340 and 1344 have been removed and are now on display in the Consistory; only one preliminary sketch remains.

The church interior has been altered substantially by the addition of the Baroque galleries. In the twelfth century, the church was one vast chamber, with five bays and a choir bay whose narrowing walls terminated in an apse. The steep proportions and the traverse arches supporting the barrel-vault are characteristic of the time. Richly ornamented columns support the imposts of the blind arcades. The cupola (see above left) is a masterpiece of medieval building technology. In order to be able to mount its square base onto the rectangular bay, the architect added four arches at each side of the bay which terminated in the square platform. Above these, the diagonally set, funnel-like vaults in each corner of the base created an octagon on which the cupola itself was set.

The front of the twelfth-century high altar is decorated with small Corinthian columns. An example of the cosmopolitan taste in art of the Popes of Avignon is the altar tomb of John XXII in the southernmost chapel. The richly ornamented sarcophagus is covered by a large, finely worked canopy. Despite the clumsy restoration work, similarities with

OPPOSITE PAGE ABOVE
Avignon
Façade of the Petit Palais (last quarter of the 15th century) from the main square of the Palais des Papes

OPPOSITE PAGE BELOW:
Vittore Carpaccio
Sacra Conversazione, ca. 1500
Poplar 39 x 51 in (98 x 127 cm)
Avignon, Musée du Petit Palais

contemporary tombs in England are clearly recognizable both in the tomb type and in individual features, such as the ogival arches. The same is true for the tomb of Benedict XII in the north chapel (photo see p. 58, right).

North of the cathedral, the rocky landscape has been developed into an attractive park (Illus. pp. 53 and 60), which offers visitors a sweeping view of both the city and the opposite bank of the Rhône.

The Petit Palais

The great square, on one side of which stands the rock on which the papal palace is built, is bordered on the north side by an elegant palace, the so-called Petit Palais. In 1317, Cardinal Bérenger de Frédol built his residence here. In 1323, Cardinal Arnaud de Via, a nephew of John XXII, bought it and altered it substantially. After the death of its owner, this palace became the new bishop's seat, the old one having been incorporated into the papal palace. The main complex, grouped around two interior courtyards, was completed in 1364-65. The palace was damaged substantially during the conflict with the antipope pretender Benedict XIII but was subsequently restored, an additional story being added to some parts of the building. Bishop Giuliano della Rovere (1474-1503), later Pope Julius II (1503-1513), built a new south façade, which still exists today (see right). In the mid-eighteenth century, the southern wing was extended eastward.

The battlements and corner turrets are an indication of the defensive character of medieval palaces. The regular layout of stories and windows, however, as well as the size of the windows, show clearly that the main aim was to display a symmetrical façade to complete the square.

Since 1976, the Petit Palais has housed one of the most remarkable museums in France. The medieval art treasures, as well as Italian painting from the thirteenth to the early sixteenth century are almost all from the collection of the papal tax collector, the Marquess Giampietro Campana di Cavelli, which the latter had amassed in the years prior to 1857.

When the Marquess was revealed to have embezzled and committed other financial irregularities, he was forced to hand over his collection to Napoleon III. The paintings consisted of rare medieval art, including works by the Italian artists Carpaccio, Ghirlandaio, Botticelli, Gaddi, di Bicci, etc.

The collection was at first divided up among sixty-seven French museums allegedly for the purposes of research. Only after extensive efforts was the main part of the collection reunited with important works from the Late Middle Ages, here in Provence, in the Musée du Petit Palais.

Pont St-Bénézet

According to legend, St. Bénézet (a diminutive of Benedict) a young shepherd in 1177—acting on divine inspiration and mocked by the population of Avignon—began to build the bridge which, thanks to the song *Sur le pont d'Avignon* has become the hallmark of the city. In reality, the foundations of some of its piers are of ancient origins. A wooden bridge that had been restored at the end of the twelfth century was badly damaged during the siege of 1226. After the siege, a new stone bridge was built, which was completed in the late thirteenth century. At around the same time, on the French side of the Rhône, King Philippe le Bel built the tower which bears his name (see p. 65, Tour Philippe le Bel). The bridge was mended many times, but after it was badly damaged again in 1660 it fell into disrepair. The last four arches, with the chapel of St-Nicolas, were then restored as a monument in the nineteenth century (ill. below). The bridge, which could carry pedestri-ans and horses, was 1,000 yards (900m) long, consisted of 22 arches, and spanned both arms of the Rhône as well as the Ile Barthelasse. The sort of folk festivals and fairs, like those mentioned in the song, were often held on this island. The four eastern arches date from around 1345 and were originally round. The level of the road was then somewhat higher because of this. The small chapel of St-Nicolas dates from the twelfth century, but during the thirteenth century, when the stone bridge was built, it was split by a ceiling into two levels.

To the west of the Rue de la République

The city church of St-Agricol was built between 1321 and 1326, with substantial financial assistance from Pope John XXII. During the fifteenth century, it was extended by one bay and newly vaulted. The west façade with the portal, which is framed by an enormous ogival arch, is worth mentioning. Between the city hall and the church, Roman remains have been

OPPOSITE:
Avignon
Flights of Steps
Park on the Cathedral Mount

Avignon
Pont St-Bénézet
with the chapel of St-Nicolas

Avignon
Musée Calvet
The museum specializes in
French art from the 16th to the
19th century.

Baroque, but its direct model is the Chapelle de la Vieille Charité in Marseille. In the Rue Joseph-Vernet the most grandiose mansion is the Hôtel de Villeneuve-Martignan, built by Jean-Baptiste Franque (1683-1758) and François II Franque (1710-1793). Since 1833, it has housed the Musée Calvet (see left). The single-storied three-winged building is one of the most beautiful examples of Baroque architecture in Avignon. Jean-Baptiste Franque was one of Avignon's most important architects in the first half of the eighteenth century. His buildings are characterized by their original layout, both in terms of groundplan and façade, but also in their technical superiority, which is evident above all in the stone-cutting techniques and in the other rounded architectural shapes he used.

A collection by the physician François Calvet as well as one from a museum of church art, founded in 1792 and stocked with artifacts taken from churches abolished during the Revolution, form the basis of the present collection. The Musée Calvet also houses displays of ancient artifacts and especially French art from the sixteenth to the nineteenth century.

discovered. They consist mainly of three parallel walls that formed the foundations of a two-stepped portico surrounding the forum.

The Chapelle de l'Oratoire was begun in 1730 by Ferdinand Delamonce. A cupola rests on the oval church interior that is hidden within the rectangular walls. The groundplan of the round choir crosses into the oval nave. The complex design of the entablature with its incorporated arches (serliana) draws the observer's attention to the longitudinal and lateral axes of the building. This highly original building is modeled on examples of Roman

East of the Rue de la République
In 1356, Cardinal Pierre de Prato donated the money for the building of the collegiate church of St-Pierre. In the late fifteenth century, the architect Blaise Lécuyer from Geneva extended the building westward. The west façade (see p. 63) with its two mighty towers, its two-storied layout and its main portal, whose archivolt flanked by pinnacles extends toward the roof, has much in common with the portals of the cathedral at Carpentras, which was also

Avignon
St-Pierre
Details of the carved wooden
doors of the west portal by
Antoine Volard, 1551

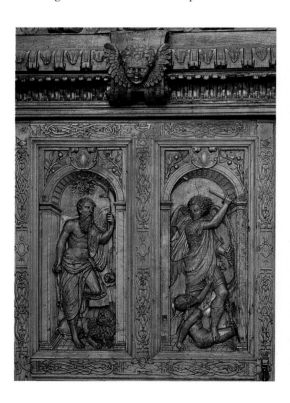

Avignon
West façade of St-Pierre
(late 15th century) (left)
Statue of the Virgin Mary in the
west porch (below)

Avignon
St-Didier
Carrying of the Cross
by Francesco Laurana, 1478

built by Blaise Lécuyer. Inside, the vaulting also displays some specifically Late Gothic characteristics with ribs resting on large consoles and cross over each other in a complex pattern. The choir-stalls, which were built in the mid-seventeenth century, harmonize well with the elaborate design of the paired columns of the choir.

In 1356, another cardinal, Bertrand de Deaux, provided the funds for the construction of the church of St-Didier. The builder's contract lists the names of the master builder and the stonemasons, some of whose work can also be seen in other buildings in the city. St-Didier is the largest of Avignon's Gothic churches and was consecrated as early as 1359. The minimalism of the single nave and the sparse forms are noticeable. The window frames, moldings, and ribs have mainly very simple slanting profiles, which required less work and expenditure than the cutting of more complex stonework. This thrift in the building of the

church is also apparent in the choir windows, in which no tracery is used.

The first chapel on the south side contains a fragmented group of sculptures by Francesco Laurana depicting the carrying of the Cross. These were commissioned in 1478 by King René for the Celestine church (see above). The vivid two-group composition is modeled on Tuscan Renaissance sculpture. Its architectural background combines some of the most modern building features of the time. The chapel opposite contains frescoes, created in ca. 1360 in a Florentine workshop. The same workshop probably also painted the tomb of Cardinal de Déaux, who died in 1355. This tomb, located on the north side of the choir, has partly been destroyed.

In 1564, the Jesuits opened a college in Avignon. In 1620, work was begun on a church, based on the plans of Etienne Martellange; the building was completed by François Royers de La Valfrenière in 1655. The church is of a type commonly used by the Jesuits, consisting of a large hall extending into numerous chapels on both sides, with upstairs galleries for the students. The church is adorned with heavy stucco ornaments depicting teeming, fertile plant life (see also p. 57, Hôtel des Monnaies). Since 1938, the building has housed the Musée Lapidaire or Lapdarium, which contains finds from Provence's Celtic, Gallo-Roman and medieval past.

The Celestine monastery

After Cardinal Pierre de Luxembourg, renowned for his saintliness, was buried in a pauper's grave after dying in 1387 at the age of 19, the Celestine Order, prompted by the antipope pretender Clement VII, built a large monastery on the site. Between 1394 and 1402 the architect Pierre Morel erected the choir, transept, and two bays of the nave. The work carried out later on the nave was never completed. Although the building was used for other purposes and later fell into disrepair, its interior is one of the greatest architectural and sculptural achievements in Avignon. The choir is longer than in any of the city's other churches and, unusually for the time, was separated from the nave by a transept. The choir ceiling is richly decorated. Subordinate vaults lend structure to the building's crowns, while the ribs are supported by suspended arches with step-like curvatures. A representation of Christ in Majesty, surrounded by a ring of cherubs, is suspended from the pendant. The building's purpose in the context of the Great Schism was obviously to serve as a symbol of the power of the antipope pretender.

Villeneuve-lès-Avignon

A separate city stands on the opposite bank of the Rhône. Villeneuve-lès-Avignon has its origins in a bastion (*bastide*). Shortly before the year 1000, the Benedictine monastery St-André had been founded here. After the Albingensian Wars, when the county of Toulouse, which had previously belonged to Provence, fell to the French crown, the King built a military outpost there, with the blessing of the monastery. This was to secure access to the Rhône and to control Avignon, which nominally belonged to the German Empire. The situation here can be compared to that of Tarascon or Beaucaire. When Avignon's walls were strengthened to protect the city from attacks by the Grandes Compagnies (see p. 53), King Jean le Bon (1350-1364) took care that Villeneuve, too, received equal protection. At this time, Villeneuve was already a kind of suburb of Avignon, with forty cardinals residing there in large mansions surrounded by extensive gardens. Today, Villeneuve is an unassuming city very much overshadowed by the more famous Avignon. Still, it boasts a number of art treasures of world standing and offers a spectacular view of the former papal city.

Villeneuve-lès-Avignon
Fort and 14th century Abbey of St-André. In Merovingian times the abbey was fortified

Tour Philippe le Bel

Between 1293 and 1307, King Philippe le Bel (1268-1314) built the tower that carries his name (Illus. right) as a French bridgehead of the Pont St-Bénézet. The rectangular Tower with its large cubical bosses, like the château at Aigues-Mortes, is a good example of northern French military architecture, which was introduced in the late thirteenth century following the French conquest of the country. The top story was probably added on during the fourteenth century. The view of Avignon from the tower platform is spectacular, especially in the evening when the walls of the papal city glisten in the evening light.

The château and Monastery of St-André

Access to the château on the hill is through the so-called gatehouse, which is framed by two mighty round towers. Some interesting work rooms have survived, such as the chamber from which the portcullis was operated, and the bakery with its carved baking-pans. The ruins of the monastery of St-André lie within the château itself, whose grounds offer a good view of the surrounding area. When it came into the possession of the reformed congregation of St-Maur in the seventeenth century, like Montmajour, it was extended on a grand scale during the following

100 years. The buildings were abandoned during the Revolution and quickly fell into disrepair.

Parish church of Notre-Dame

In the 1320s, Cardinal Arnaud de Via, a nephew of Pope John XXII, built a spacious summer residence here, which he converted into a college for canons in 1333. This involved substantial alterations to the building. The interior courtyard became a cloister, and the palace chapel was enlarged. Like many other Gothic churches in Provence, the church has a single nave to which large side-chapels have been added. As stipulated by the city council, the tower on the east side of the church incorporated an arch which allowed street traffic to pass under it. In 1350, the clerics—heedless of the citizens' protests—bricked up the openings and integrated the interior into the monastery. From the inside, the narrow, second-story windows within the wide façade are notable. Prayer-books rest on large consoles adorned with figures. A barrel-vaulted passage leads to the asymmetrical choir chapel inside the tower.

The Rue de la République leads northward. Some of the mansions of the cardinals are still extant at nos. 1, 3, 45, and 53. One of them is the former residence of Pierre de Luxembourg,

Villeneuve-lès-Avignon
Notre-Dame
Ivory madonna, 14th century

Avignon, Villeneuve-lès-Avignon, Barbentane

which today houses the city museum. Apart from some important medieval sculptures (ivory Madonnas and Laurana's death mask of Jeanne de Laval, wife of King René), the collection contains one of the great monumental French paintings of the Late Middle Ages, the Coronation of Mary by Enguerrand Quarton painted in 1453 (see above).

Enguerrand Quarton's Coronation of Mary

This large picture was painted in 1453 through 1454 by Enguerrand Quarton, who probably came from Picardy in northern France. The artist, who was born around 1420, worked both in Aix (1444) and Avignon (1447-1466), and together with Nicolas Froment and Barthélémy d'Eyck is one of Provence's foremost painters. The *Coronation* was commissioned for the Carthusian church by canon Jean de Montagnac, who gave the painter detailed instructions about the composition.

The center of the painting shows the coronation of Mary by God the Father and the Son, who—in accordance with the contract—are completely identical. This illustrates a compromise found in 1439 between the Roman catholic and Greek orthodox churches, in answer to the question of whether the Holy Spirit is of the Father alone or of both Father and Son. This temporary agreement between the two churches is also referred to in the depiction of Jerusalem and Rome in the bottom part of the picture, which resembles an altar base and also completes the comprehensive theological theme of the painting with a depiction of the Last Judgement. The city portraits show specific churches which are depicted as Provençal buildings.

Quarton's artistic achievement lies in the fact that he combined the various subjects so harmoniously and to scale, imposing a clear structural relationship and bright colors.

Enguerrand Quarton
The Coronation of the Virgin,
1453-54
Tempera on wood, 73.2 x 88 in
(183 x 220 cm)
Villeneuve-lès-Avignon
Musée Pierre de Luxembourg
de Villeneuve-lès-Avignon

Villeneuve-lès-Avignon
The Val de Bénédiction charterhouse (third quarter of the 14th century).
Cloister and monks cells (above)

Tempera wall paintings in the chapel showing scenes from the life of John the Baptist, including Salome presenting her mother with John the Baptist's head, and the laying of St. John in his grave (school of Matteo Giovanetti)

The Carthusian monastery of the Val de Bénédiction

Cardinal Etienne Aubert, later Pope Innocent VI (1352-1362) built a summer residence in 1342 which he converted—like the palace of Arnaud de Via (see p. 66, "Parish church of Notre-Dame")—into a Carthusian monastery, also meant to contain the papal cemetery. The enormous complex, bigger even than the parent monastery of La Grande Chartreuse near Grenoble, was built in stages, reaching completion in the late fourteenth century.

Crossing several courtyards, one reaches a walled-in section and then the church itself, which is badly damaged. It contains the tomb of Innocent VI, dating from 1360, whose canopy consists of three open tabernacles resembling contemporary tower reliquaries. The immediate model for the grave was probably the tomb of John XXII in the cathedral in Avignon (see p. 58).

The cells of the monks are arranged around the larger of the two cloisters. As usual in Carthusian monasteries, the stone huts are arranged in rows. Each contains a study with a fireplace, a bedroom, and an attic for storage. Meals were provided for each monk in a small anteroom.

In the chapel of the dining hall, the refectory, wall-paintings have survived from the workshop of Matteo Giovannetti (see p. 68, below). These are not frescos, which are painted on the still-wet plaster, but tempera, which is applied to dry plaster. Where the plaster has been damaged, the brown preliminary drawing becomes visible. In addition to the apostles, the paintings depict several scenes from the life of John the Baptist and there is a Crucifixion above the altar. On the northeast wall, the patron, Innocent VI, can be seen kneeling before the Madonna.

The style of the paintings is characterized by restrained gestures and courtliness, while the depictions are full of carefully observed details. It is clear that the paintings resemble those in the St. John's Chapel of the papal palace. However, they were probably not painted by Matteo Giovannetti himself. The painters were probably members of the same workshop, who were entrusted with the task of filling in the sketches. If the patron's identification as Innocent VI is correct, the latter's coming into office marks the earliest possible date of origin of the paintings.

A third cloister, the Cloître St-Jean, was altered in the eighteenth century.

Villeneuve-lès-Avignon
Church of the
Val de Bénédiction Monastery
Tomb of Innocent VI (ca.1360)

Barbentane was originally the property of the Archbishop of Arles, but in the twelfth century it passed into the hands of the bishop of Avignon. He built his château, whose mighty tower, the so-called Tour Angelica, still exists today. It was built on a clifftop in the 1360s and was unmistakably modeled on the Tour Philippe le Bel at Villeneuve-lès-Avignon. The existing château, built in the third quarter of the seventeenth century, was decorated in Italianate style, with elaborate marblework. That is because the then owner, the Marquis de Barbentane, was the French envoy at the court of the Grand Duke of Tuscany. The flat roof, whose outline is broken by strange candelabra-shaped moldings, also seems to have been influenced by Italian originals. A beautiful formal French garden surrounds the château.

Roman Provincial Capital and Van Gogh's Refuge

Arles, St-Rémy, and the Alpilles

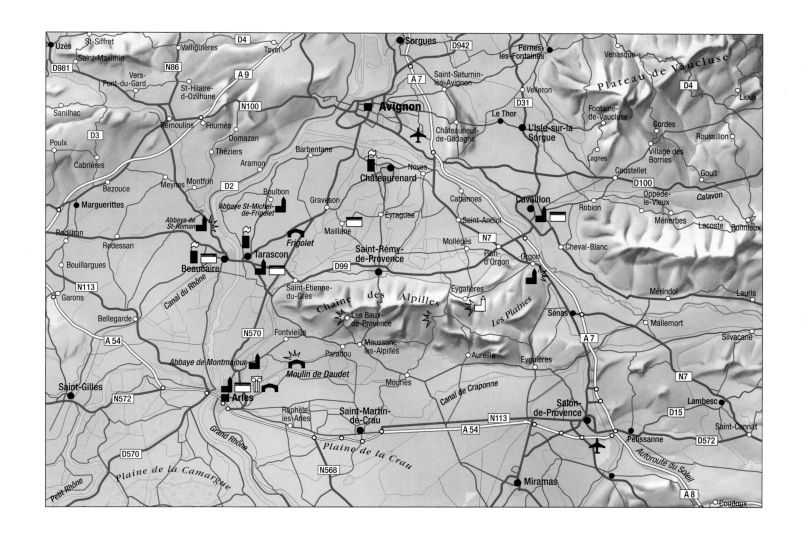

Rooftop view of the landscape of Arles

The history of Arles
4th century BC: Arelate, a Greek trading post
46 BC: Arelate becomes a Roman colony.
254 AD: first mention of a bishop, by the name of Trophimus.
307-337 and 395-423: Arles becomes the capital of the western provinces of the Roman Empire, as well as First City of Gaul (417).
855: Capital of the Kingdom of Provence-Burgundy, becoming part of the German empire, as Arelat, in the 10th century.
11-12th century: Seat of the Count of Provence-Barcelona
1131: Self-governing city, ruled by the Consulates
Mid-13th century: After the Albigensian Wars, the Counts of Anjou become the rulers of Provence, and Arles is incorporated with Aix and Marseilles into their county and loses its erstwhile importance.
1481: Upon the death of the last Count of Provence, Charles III of Maine, Arles becomes part of France.

Arles

As early as the sixth century BC, there was a Celtic-Ligurian settlement known as Theline perched on a limestone cliff in the marshy Rhône delta. An important Greek trading center, Arelate, grew up here in the fourth century. When the Romans conquered Gaul, their first intention was to secure the *Via Domitia*, the road linking Italy to Spain. Soon, however, a separate Roman province, *Gallia Narbonensis*, was established in southern France, stretching from the Pyrenees to the Alps. Its principal cities were Narbonne (the provincial capital, founded 118 BC) and Marseilles. Arles initially gained in importance under the Romans when the Consul Marius connected it to the Gulf of Fos (near Marseilles) via a canal in 104 BC. When Arelate was given the status of a colony in 46 BC, the veterans of the sixth legion settled there, and the surrounding countryside was placed under the rule of the city. This was a political maneuver on the part of Caesar to stem the influence of Marseilles, a city which had opposed him. Arles immediately became an important shipbuilding center, and from the first century BC the city received its fortifications and public monuments which can still be seen today, as well as a bridge

of boats which gave rise to a suburb, Trinquetaille, on the right bank of the Rhône. A meeting point of waterways and land routes developed here, leading to rapid economic growth. This also explains why the city became such an early center of Christianity. As far back as 254 AD there is mention of a bishop, and important synods took place here during the fourth century (314 and 396). Under the Emperors Constantine (306-337) and Honorius (395-423), Arles even briefly became the Roman capital of Gaul, Spain, and Britain! Accordingly, the city also obtained the primacy over numerous dioceses in southern France in 417 and 450.

With the campaigns of conquest of the Ostrogoths, Visigoths, Normans, and Franks from the fifth century onward, decline soon set in. With the division of Charlemagne's empire in 855, the city became the capital of the "Kingdom of Burgundy", which encompassed Burgundy and parts of Provence, also named "Arelat" after the capital. Three counties were established here: Provence-Barcelona, Provence-Forcalquier, and Provence-Toulouse. Arles, which belonged to the county of Provence-Barcelona, formed a powerful self-governing city in the twelfth century, the so-called consulate. From the eleventh century onward, the city was nominally part of the German empire, but with the dismissal of the last imperial administrator by the Count of Provence-Barcelona, Raymond Bérenger, and by means of astute French marriages, the city came into the possession of the House of Anjou, a dynasty which governed Provence in the latter half of the thirteenth century.

The Anjous suppressed the city's strivings for autonomy and the worldly political activities of its Archbishop, and established their seat in Aix. Thus, the autonomous political power of Arles waned from the thirteenth century. The silting-up of the Rhône harbor also contributed to a decline in its economic importance.

Until the eve of World War II, the city remained a mere regional trading center. It is thus easy to see why the local mixture of tradition and originality attracted world-weary artists like Gaugin and Van Gogh. The city has managed to preserve a great deal of its special Mediterranean atmosphere to the present day, especially in the Place du Forum, with its plane trees and cafés.

The city has recently begun to regain economic importance thanks to its medium-sized enterprises, administration, and culture. The Centre International de la Photographie et de l'Image, founded in 1965 in the Musée Réattu, has become a cultural center of international standing, thanks to its exhibitions, conferences, and the school of photography. The opening of the Musée de l'Arles Antique in 1995 once more emphasized the importance of the city in its heyday, and this has proved an additional boost to tourism.

The Roman City

Of the Roman road network, the two main streets—the *Cardo*, running in a north-south direction, and the *Decumanus*, running from east to west—are still clearly recognizable in the present-day street plan as the Rue de l'Hôtel de Ville and the Rue Jean Jaurès, and is still discernible in the Rue de la Calande. As in the majority of Roman urban developments, these main thoroughfares, which intersected at right angles, were supplemented by a checkerboard system of side-streets enclosing the larger blocks or *insulae* which measured 83 x 116 ft (25 x 35 m). In the middle stood the forum, part of whose later expansion can still be seen in the house on the south side of the Place du Forum, in the form of a temple front (second and fourth centuries). The underground substructures of the original forum are still evident. The *Cryptoporticus* (entrance by the former Chapelles des Jésuites in the Rue Balze) has barrel-vaulted double galleries (pictured right), laid out over a rectangle, of which three can still be seen. These served as a foundation for the forum building above, and were used for storage.

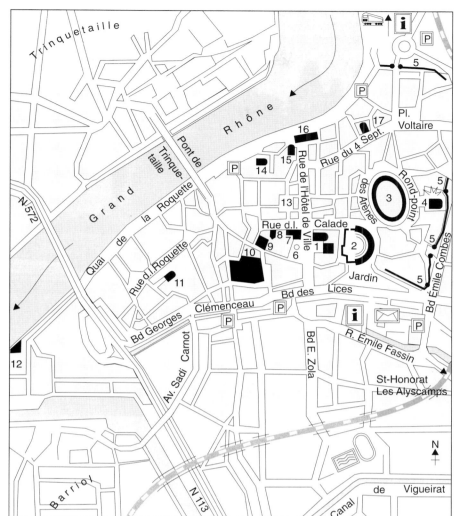

1 St-Trophime with cloister
2 Roman Theater
3 Amphitheater
4 Notre-Dame-la-Major
5 Ruins of the medieval city walls
6 Place de la République and town hall
7 Lapidarium (Musée lapidaire d'Art paien)
8 Arcades
9 Museon Arlaten
10 Espace Van-Gogh
11 St-Césaire
12 Musée de l'Arles Antique
13 Place du Forum
14 Dominican church
15 Baths of Constantine
16 Musée Réattu
17 St-Julien

Arles
These arcades are underground double galleries beneath the old Forum.

Arles
Ruins of the Roman theater
ca. 15 AD.

Arles
Musée de l'Arles Antique:
Statue of a female dancer

To the north, the city stretched up to the Constantine baths; to the east, as far as the west wall of the theater; as to its extension in other directions, however, we know very little. An aqueduct supplied the city with an abundance of water from the Alpilles. Toward the Rhône— as in Orange—an arch commemorating the founding of the city, built under Augustus and torn down in 1643, graced the landscape.

The theater is also one of the early structures erected under Augustus in ca.15 AD. As in most Roman theaters, the auditorium was subdivided into three tiers, which had four, nine, and 20 rows, making a total of 33 steps. Between the cleverly designed support system of the semicircular *Cavea*, lay the access stairways and stores, workshops, etc. There were three levels of arcades on the external structure, corresponding to the three tiers. Only those at the Tour de Roland on the south side have been preserved. The orchestra pit, the semicircle in the center of the rows of spectators, was originally paved with red cipoline marble and green marble slabs. The actual stage was about 20 ft (6 m) deep and was terminated by the stage wall which was 233 ft (70 m) wide. The two columns still standing were part of its lower story. There were another two stories above it, which contained numerous columns, niches, and openings.

The "Venus of Arles" which is now a permanent exhibit in the Louvre museum (there is a cast in the Musée de l'Arles Antique), as well as the group of three dancers, and a colossal statue of Augustus, probably all originated from this site

The theater owes its good state of preservation to its conversion into a fortress back in the early Middle Ages. The towers, which are still standing, actually belong to that fortress and were not part of the original theater architecture. Later, dwelling houses were built inside the theater, so that an entire neighborhood grew up.

The Amphitheater

In Flavian times, the late first century AD, the city was substantially enlarged and adorned with further ambitious structures, most notably the amphitheater and the hippodrome. The Hippodrome, located southeast of the Roman city beyond the N 113, which is over 400 ft (100 m) long, as well as the tombs in its vicinity, are still being excavated. The obelisk which has stood in front of the Town Hall since 1675 originated from this site.

The amphitheater has been the symbol of the city since time immemorial (pictured opposite). In its dimensions, as well as its outer wall, it is very similar to the one in Nîmes (453 ft (136 m) long, 360 ft (108 m) wide). Outside, the oval building is encircled by a two-story arcade with 60 arches, as well as an attic story which has not been preserved. While the lower section consists of simple piers with impost moldings, more elegant Corinthian half-columns were used for the next story. Behind the outer arcades, a corridor-like passageway encircles the entire construction. This corridor was paved

OPPOSITE:
Arles
Internal and external views of
the Amphitheater
Late 1st century AD.

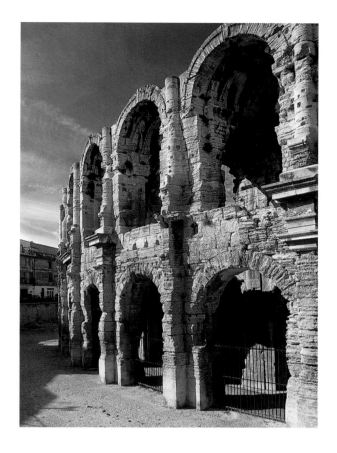

Arles
The Constantine baths
4th century

Arles
St-Trophime, west portico
Group of figures on
west front

with flat stone slabs, some of which remain, while in Nîmes vaults were built on this location. Circular galleries and numerous exits onto all tiers enabled the crowds of spectators to be channeled smoothly in and out, despite the huge size of the auditorium, which contained 34 rows of seating divided into four tiers, offering 20,070 seats and 800 standing places. A high circular wall divided into two sections kept spectators at a distance from events in the arena. In Roman times there was probably a wooden floor over the base of this wall. On the north side, an underground corridor, through which the wild animals and gladiators passed into the amphitheater, leads away from an opening in the circular wall. The amphitheater was probably built in the last two decades of the first century. This not only links it closely with its sister amphitheater in Nîmes, but also to the Colosseum in Rome. The design and construction also emulate the Colosseum. Like the Roman theater, the amphitheater was remodeled for defense purposes in the Middle Ages. Three towers still bear witness to this today. Until well into the nineteenth century, there were two churches within the residential area which grew up within its walls. The uncovering of the *Arènes* (arena) since then has enabled the revival of the ancient gladiatorial tradition here, in the form of the famous Arles bullfights (in April and September).

The Constantine baths
The thermal baths in the northern part of the city (illus. above) formed a stepped, palace-like complex, about 800 ft (200 m) deep which was possibly connected with the Emperor Constantine's residence adjoining it on the south, meaning that it was probably erected in the fourth century. The Roman baths possessed certain similarities in the sequence of the various rooms, and the way in which they were

used. Vaulted and closed bathing-rooms alternated with open-air facilities. The heating of the baths was accomplished via underfloor heating (hypercausts) in which the hot air circulated under the floors which were laid on top of pillars, and rose through vertical shafts in the walls. In addition there were gymnasia, changing-rooms, dressing-rooms, restrooms, a library and reading room. As public meeting places the baths gained in importance over the forum, which also explains why they were built in Arles like a large annex along the same axis as the forum. Of the baths complex, the *caldarium* (warm bath) and the *tepidarium* (lukewarm bath) adjoining it to the south are still accessible today; the rest of the baths was destroyed during later building work. Despite this, the baths of Arles are the best-preserved of their kind in Provence. The *caldarium* consists of a large, transversely rectangular, formerly barrel-vaulted room, opening out to the north into a large exedra with the original vaulting of *opus mixtum*, reinforced with rib-like bands of brick. The exedra contained a pool, as did the short sides of the *caldarium*. Part of the lining of the east pool is still present. Between the marble slabs and the brick core of the wall, there are vestiges of the hypercausts, the hollow bricks used for central heating. Fragments of the brick pillars which supported the floor can be seen and one of the lower heating rooms to the east still exists. The *tepidarium*, a wide, transversely rectangular room, adjoins the *caldarium* on its south side. The foundation walls of its western exedra can still be examined closely from the outside. An old exedra of the adjacent cold bath or *frigidarium*, is only traceable in the bulge of the wall line in the Rue D. Maïsto.

Cathedral of St-Trophime
The oldest diocesan church probably stood close to the city walls on the site of a temple. In 449, a church dedicated to St. Stephen was moved to its current site in the town center, between the forum and theater—perhaps as a consequence of the primacy of Gaul being granted to Bishop Patroclus in 417. In 972, the relics of St. Trophimus were brought from the Alyscamps to the cathedral, where he was soon revered as the sole patron saint and missionary for all of Gaul. In 1152, the removal of St. Trophimus and other relics to a new site was recorded. This probably denotes the completion of a new chancel. The tower, nave, and doorway were built in the second half of the twelfth century. Construction of the Gothic chancel dates from the third quarter of the fifteenth century, when the miracle-working tomb of Archbishop Louis Aleman (1423-50) became a lucrative pilgrimage center. Archbishop Adhémar de Monteil de Grignan (1689-97) extensively remodeled the entire building in the Baroque style, incorporating galleries and a painted crossing cupola. The church's treasure and furnishings were for the

OPPOSITE:
Arles
St-Trophime
west portal, second half of
12th century

most part lost during the French Revolution. In 1801, the bishopric was abolished. From 1870-75, sweeping restoration work took place which reversed the Baroque alterations.

The church stands at the southeast corner of the former forum, over vaulted chambers which even out the differences at ground level and probably date back to Roman times. The west front, dating from the early eleventh century, is plain, but ornamented with a magnificent portico whose design is based on the Roman triumphal arch, and which, next to that of St-Gilles, is the most important Romanesque figurative portico in Provence (illus. p.79). The two groups of three columns in the front plane recall the ancient arch of Orange. As in St-Gilles, the portico is almost a separate feature, whose recesses contain large statues. The portico merges into the wall via several archivolts.

The iconographic plan is grouped around a tympanum of the Last Judgment with the detailed, almost monotonous portrayal of the rewarding of the good (to the right of Christ on the tympanum) and the punishment of the wicked (on his left). The theme of judgment is combined with the theme of the incarnation of Christ, which is portrayed in great detail on the register, level with the capitals, with remarkable narrative concentration on the story of the three Magi: the Adoration of the Magi, the Magi before Herod, and the Massacre of the Innocents. From the repeated amassing of figures on the upper register as well as the turbulent scenes on the lower register, it is plain to see that one of the overriding concerns in the design of the portico was to revert to the tradition of the late-Classical sarcophagus fronts. The four apostles and patron saints of the church in the recesses illustrate the Redemption and the history of the church of Arles. On the left side, from the portico outward, there are St. Peter, St. John the Evangelist, St. James the Greater, and St. Bartholomew. To the right stand Paul, Andrew, James the Lesser, and Philip. The two local saints, Trophimus and Stephen, are portrayed on the interior face of the outer frontage. St. Trophimus is being crowned with his bishop's miter by an angel; St. Stephen's soul is being borne up to heaven by angels. The large portico figures of Arles do not stand in their recesses as if freely movable, but rather, together with the relief background and the lateral pilasters, they form a closely structured unit which renders the sculpture a part of the architecture. The significance of the lions at the base of the intrados recesses is unclear. Comparable motifs can also be found in St-Gilles, and above all in Italy.

The portico sculptures were created in a workshop which was inspired by the superb sculpture in the north wing of the cathedral's cloister and in St-Gilles. For this reason, the portico is thought to have been built in the last quarter of the twelfth century, ca. 1190.

The interior of the three-naved basilica (illus. opposite) is the largest, and at the same time the tallest, Romanesque ecclesiastical interior in Provence (length of nave 133 ft (40 m), height 66 ft (20 m)). The side-aisles give the impression of narrow corridors. Otherwise, the nave is extraordinarily sparse; the standard blind arcading is missing from the side-aisles; in the central nave, only the area of the line of the ceiling vault is emphasized by the placement of columns in the wall panels and by an acanthus molding running along below the spring line of the pointed barrel-vaulting. The ambitious nature of cathedral construction is thrown into relief by the high, wide transept, seldom found in Provence.

The cathedral's history is complex. The stonework of the west wall and the nave walls, which is divided into small sections, belongs to an early eleventh-century construction. The transept (in central ashlar stonework without the stonemason's symbol) followed at the end of the century. Originally, three apses were probably joined to it on the east; the original level was 13 ft (4 m) higher than today; among other things, it contained a crypt. Gradually, they carried on building the last nave bay from the east, whose barrel vaulting was only included in the plans during the actual building work. Around 1152, at the time of the transportation of the relics of St. Trophimus, the construction was probably concluded in architectural terms. The inscription honoring the Saint on the north side of the last bay corresponds stylistically with this theory. The letters at the beginning, middle, and end of the verses yield the acrostic TRO(phimus) APO(stolicus) GAL(icanus). The remaining four bays, with their large ashlars and stonemasons' symbols, as well as the nave vaulting, were probably built in the two decades after 1152. The chancel, dating from the third quarter of the fifteenth century, is the only Gothic ambulatory chancel with chapels in Provence. The overall structure follows the pattern of the large classical cathedrals of the thirteenth century, although the sharp rib profiles and complicated ambulatory vaulting clearly speak the architectural language of the fifteenth century late Gothic period.

The north side-aisle contains the sarcophagus of St-Honorat-des-Alyscamps (ca. 350, illus. below). The front depicts Christ, the Apostles, the miracle of the loaves and fishes, the healing of the blind, the miracle on the cliffs, the healing of the Bleeding and the miracle in Canaan. The narrow-side panels on left show the sacrifice of Cain and Abel, Christ cursing the barren fig tree, three Jews

Arles
St-Trophime
Detail of the 5th-century tomb of Geminus

OPPOSITE:
Arles
St-Trophime
View looking eastward

Arles
St-Trophime
The tomb of St-Honorat-des-Alyscamps (ca. 350) inside the church, beneath two columns.

The most impressive feature is the carved decoration. The two older wings are both subdivided by two thick intermediate pillars, between which quadrilobed arcades extend over twin columns. Corner and intermediate pillars as well as the arcade capitals are richly adorned with sculptures. The corner pillars are carved with relief figures of the most important saints of the Arles church, to wit, Stephen in the east and Trophimus in the west. There are the two Apostles, Paul on the northeast pillar (illus. left) and Peter on the northwest pillar (illus. opposite). The scenes on the solid corner pillar are dedicated to the themes of the Resurrection and St. Stephen. The pillar of St. Trophimus depicts Christ's empty tomb with angels and guardians, as well as the three Marys buying spices; the pillar of St. Stephen shows the Ascension of Christ and the stoning of St. Stephen. Of the more simply adorned intermediate piers, the one on the west of the north wing shows Christ on the road to Emmaus with the two disciples, while the one on the east shows him with Thomas and James.

The east wing contains statues in landscape settings which were probably only carved in the early thirteenth century. On the northern pillar, there is the figure of Jesus being beaten, flanked by a flagellator, and probably Judas. The southeastern corner pillar depicts Gamaliel, teacher of Paul, reputed to have himself taught St. Trophimus. The relief ensemble in the north wing was undoubtedly the work of several sculptors. The treatment of the garments differs, and the relationship between figure and framework or relief background varies. While the corner figures are very rigid and axially emphasized in the "corner recesses," other figures, such as St. Peter, or statues on the intermediate pillars, such as Atlas, protrude and their heads and limbs are more mobile.

Arles
St-Trophime, cloister
Northeast pillar (above)
Gallery and details of the capital decoration (above right and center)
Double columns in the colonnaded cloister (below right)

refusing to bow down to idols; those on the right show the adoration of the magi and the entry into Jerusalem. The tomb of St. Geminus of Cologne is in the chapel of St-Sepulcre; here, Christ is portrayed with Peter and Paul in bas relief, typical of 5th-century metaphorical language.

The Cloister of St-Trophime

The cloister is reached via the archiepiscopal buildings to the south of the cathedral. Of the 17 Romanesque cloisters in Provence, this is the most lavish and important. The dating is uncertain, despite an epitaph on one of the pillars dating it to 1188. Since it is the oldest section, the north wing must already have been built ca. 1180, while work on the east wing probably extended into the beginning of the thirteenth century. As at Montmajour, the other two wings were executed ca. 1370 in a Romanizing style. The length and width of the Romanesque cloister wing are surprisingly large.

Arles, St-Rémy, and the Alpilles

Arles
Hôtel de Ville (town hall)
Ground floor hall, 1676

The Hôtel de Ville/Town Hall

The north side of the cathedral square was laid out in the seventeenth century. It is flanked by the new town hall to the north, and the east side was closed off by the rebuilding of the façade of the archbishop's palace in the eighteenth century. In 1657, the city council sponsored a competition for the rebuilding of the town hall. The winning Arles architect Jacques Peytret was, however, obliged to allow royal master-builder Jules Hardouin-Mansart and the latter's brother Michel to make alterations to his plans, particularly in the area of the vestibule vault and the façades. In terms of the structure of the façade, the three-story building (illus. opposite), completed in 1676, emulates the garden façade of the Palace of Versailles, designed shortly before by Louis Le Vau. On the west side, part of the previous late fifteenth-century construction is still preserved. The broad-spanned flat vaulting of the ground-floor hall (illus. above), extolled as a masterpiece of stereotomy and masonry, deserves special attention.

Arles
Place de la République
Detail of fountain

OPPOSITE:
Arles
Place de la République with view of the façade of the town hall and St-Trophime
The obelisk is from the ruins of a 2nd-century Roman circus

Les Alyscamps and St-Honorat

As in other cities, the Romans laid out the cemeteries in Arles outside the city walls along major arterial roads, in this case in the southeast near the extension of the Via Aurelia leading from Rome via Marseilles. The name of Champs-Elysées (Alyscamps), the Elysian or holy fields, was already in use in the Middle Ages for the huge necropolis, only part of which still exists today. Here, the dead were laid to rest at various levels between the fourth and thirteenth centuries. The necropolis suffered its first decline when the body of St. Trophimus was transferred to the rebuilt cathedral in 1152.

Today, a tree-lined avenue leads through the former burial ground, most of whose sarcophagi have ended up in museums. Nevertheless, sarcophagi of different eras still line the avenue leading to the church of St-Honorat (illus. opposite). The basilica erected over the tomb of St. Gènes, who was executed in the third century, formed the center of the cemetery. A section of the basilica has been uncovered to the west and north of the church. There is a walled-in area immediately surrounding the church, in which the graves are arranged in a strict east-west orientation, so that the dead can look to the east when they are resurrected.

In 1040, the church passed to the powerful abbey of St. Victor in Marseilles, and accepted St. Honoratus, the fifth-century archbishop of Arles, as its patron saint. The vestiges of the wall built of rubble on the north side of the nave, which may have extended in front of the existing Romanesque façade, probably also dates from this time. The present construction was begun in the second half of the twelfth century, but owing to the wars against the Albigensians, it was never completed. As early as the sixteenth century, the crossing piers had to be reinforced with sheathing, since they were in danger of collapsing.

LEFT:
Arles
St-Honorat, interior view of the choir and two side-chapels

OPPOSITE:
Arles
Les Alyscamps with a view of St-Honorat

Arles
Henri Ciriani
Musée de l'Arles Antique
Exterior

Musée de l'Arles Antique

In 1983, a competition was held for the design of a single building to hold all the ancient art treasures of Arles, which had previously been distributed among various collections in the city. The winner was the Peruvian-born architect Henri Ciriani whose bold design was based on a large triangle with a triangular inner courtyard. The building was completed in 1995. The new Museum, a stone's throw from the Roman circus, combines an overview of the ancient culture of the city, and numerous important works of art. These include a statue of Augustus and two sculptures of dancers dating from the late first century BC, originally in the Roman theater. Two recently discovered mosaic floors are displayed here, the late second century Annus mosaic and the Orpheus mosaic dating from the third or fourth century. The transition to Christianity can be understood from the many sarcophagi, the most lavish of which is the Trinity sarcophagus dating from the second half of the fourth century. It is decorated with numerous scenes from the Old Testament (illus. p. 89, below, right).

Musée Réattu

When the Grand Priory of the Order of the Hospital of St. John of Jerusalem was transferred from St-Gilles to Arles during the Wars of Religion in 1583, a prebendary of the Order moved into the building which had been there since the fourteenth century. The building, which was extended on several occasions, was acquired by the Arles painter Jacques Réattu (1760-1833), and today houses a museum named after him. The museum features locally produced art up to the present day, as well as 57 of Picasso's drawings from 1970-71, which the ninety-year-old painter donated to the city.

Museon Arlaten

The Provençal poet and rediscoverer of Occitan tradition, Frédéric Mistral, founded a museum of regional folklore in the Hôtel Laval-Castellane, a late-Gothic nobleman's palace with an inner courtyard dating from the early sixteenth century. The extensive collection features daily life in old Provence, as well as Occitan art, handicrafts, costumes, and more.

OPPOSITE:
Arles
Musée de l'Arles Antique
Interior with the Trinity sarcophagus, second half of the 4th century.
The decoration is divided into three zones featuring scenes from the Old and New Testaments. The dead couple are shown framed by a cockle shell.

The sculpted sarcophagus first came into being when Roman burial customs underwent a change in the late first century. The deceased were no longer cremated, but buried in coffins. In contrast to the simple sarcophagus, devoid of sculpted decoration, the lavishly embellished tombs were status symbols for which the marble was usually imported from Italy or the Pyrenees. Some of the sarcophagi were produced in Rome, but often without the final treatment. Until well into the fourth century, the themes owed much to Roman mythology, occasionally mixed with Christian content, as in the Dioscuri sarcophagus. Christian metaphorical language was only introduced gradually, often in the form of the juxtaposition of scenes from the Old and New Testaments (Suzanne sarcophagus). Pagan images were also provided with new Christian content. Columnar sarcophagi became more common from the middle of the fourth century; these broke down the earlier frieze-like compositions into just a few highly stylized individual scenes, some of which were only a slight variation on the formula. In the fifth century, the tendency toward symbolic simplification of metaphorical language increased. Carving was in shallow bas-relief. Sarcophagus production in Arles ended before the mid-fifth century, but the Romanesque sculptors of the twelfth century readopted the medium. In terms of Christian themes, expectations of the hereafter and Christ's redemption were of great importance, but the intention was also to effectively portray the chief protagonists of the new religion, Christ and St. Peter. The sculpting of sarcophagi was by no means the secret means of expression of a persecuted religion, but quite the contrary—a thoroughly "official" art form which was commissioned in particular by the senatorial upper class in one of the capitals of christendom at that time.

Vincent Van Gogh
Café Terraces in the
Place du Forum in Arles,
Evening, 1888
Oil on canvas, 32.4 x 26.2 in
(81 x 65.5 cm)
Otterlo, Kröller-Müller Museum

Vincent Van Gogh
Self-portrait, 1888
Oil on canvas, 16 x 12½ in
(40 x 31 cm)
Private collection, Switzerland

Van Gogh in Arles

The painter came to Arles in February 1888, fleeing from what he considered to be decadent Paris Salon society, and in search of "the future of the new Art." He lived initially in the Hôtel Carrel on the Rue de la Cavalerie, then shortly thereafter in the so-called "Yellow House" on the Place Lamartine. Both buildings were destroyed during World War II. Van Gogh painted like a man possessed, "like a locomotive." Many of his most famous paintings marking the further development of the Post-Impressionist and Japanese-Parisian influences, were produced at this time, including *Les Alyscamps, La Maison de Vincent, Le Café d'Arles* (illus. opposite, today rebuilt on the Place du Forum), *Le Pont de Langlois* (above; the original drawbridge erected over the Canal du Fos, no longer exists but there is a copy, about a mile (3 km) south of Arles, on a side-road off the D 35). A total of 200 paintings and 100 drawings were produced by the artist. Van Gogh's idea of establishing an artists' colony in Arles only succeeded in attracting Paul Gauguin to the city in December, 1888. Soon, however, irreconcilable differences arose between the two painters, and Van Gogh cut off his ear in a first nervous breakdown. With the increasing frequency of his crises, the painter retreated into Dr. Peyron's sanatorium in St-Rémy. The memory of the painter is perpetuated by the Fondation Vincent-van-Gogh-Arles (in the eighteenth-century Palais de Luppé), whose collection is dedicated by contemporary artists to the pioneers of modern art.

Vincent Van Gogh
The Bridge of Langlois in
Arles with Lady, 1888
Oil on canvas, 19.8 x 25.6 in
(49.5 x 64 cm)
Wallraf-Richartz-Museum,
Cologne

Arles
Place du Forum with
"Café Van Gogh."

Montmajour

The massive building complex of the former Abbey of Montmajour stands on a limestone outcrop on the road to Les Baux, a few miles northeast of Arles. Until the Middle Ages, the Abbey formed a sort of island surrounded by marshes. A cemetery was established here and tended by hermits. In 949, Teucinde, a Provençal noblewoman, purchased the island belonging to the cathedral chapter of Arles and donated it to monks for the founding of a monastery. The strict organization of the new community and its direct subordination to the Pope made it attractive for pious donations whose purpose was to ensure that the community of monks would pray fervently for the salvation of the souls of the deceased. Several Counts of Provence arranged to be buried here for just this reason. Moreover, a special indulgence, the *Pardon de Montmajour*, which the Pope had granted in 1030 during a visit to the monastery, assured a steady stream of pilgrims. The first church was built here in the eleventh century, soon to be replaced by the existing Romanesque building, between 1130-40 and 1170-80. The monastery lost its independence in the thirteenth century, and Montmajour was further weakened by a dispute with the then priory of St-Antoine-en-Viennois over the possession of the true relics of St. Anthony. The Abbey was taken over by the Benedictine Reform Congregation of St-Maur but this only briefly halted further decline. Nevertheless, great Baroque extensions were made to the building between 1703 and 1736 by the Avignon architects Pierre Mignard and Jean-Baptiste Franque. The abolition of the Abbey in 1790 followed the partial dismantling of what had just been built, until Henri Révoil initiated the first restoration in 1872 and prevented the further sale of Romanesque capitals and columns. Montmajour now appears as a massive, imposing complex of buildings whose unfinished Romanesque church is surrounded by immense Baroque ruins. On the south side, at the edge of the rocky outcrop, the Chapel of St-Pierre is built into the rock, east of which stands

Montmajour
Ground plan of the southern aspect of the original, 12th-century abbey

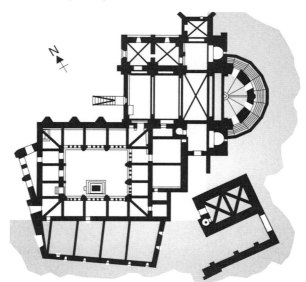

a massive dungeon; 833 ft (250 m) further east stands the small Chapel of Ste-Croix.

Built at the highest point of the rock, the abbey church was architecturally very ambitious, despite the fact that its nave was never completed. The building consists of a twin-bayed nave—which should actually have five bays—a sharply projecting transept, and a chancel, broken into polygons from the outside. The nave is built over a lower church or crypt whose radial chapels give the impression of a highly projecting plinth. All of the wall openings are small and the only decoration is to be found on the embrasures between two windows. The outside of the building consists of a series of sharply angular shapes, the quality of whose stonework is also exceptional.

The crypt extends under the nave, transept, and chancel. The domed apse represents a sort of central chamber which communicates with the ambulatory via round-arched openings (illus. right and below). The corbels remaining in the ambulatory wall carry the falsework for the bricking-up of the annular barrel vault. The carefully hewn ashlars were engraved by the stonemasons with large symbols—generally letters of the alphabet—so-called stonemason's marks, which made it easier to calculate how much work had been done.

The layout of the crypt as a whole is reminiscent of chancel ambulatories with a chapel crown, a style used in many of the most ambitious monastery churches of France and Spain from the late eleventh century onward, and which was later readopted in Provence by the abbey-church of St-Gilles. The precise functions of the ambulatory crypt in Montmajour, however, are unclear. From a technical viewpoint, it achieved an ingenious leveling of the ground for

the church above. The central rotunda could have contained the relics of the Holy Cross, past which the pilgrims would have filed via the west corridor. The radial chapels were probably distinguished burial places and side-altars located in the immediate vicinity of the main relic, such as, the Counts of Provence might have wished for themselves.

The interior of the upper church (illus. p. 94) is surprising in its breadth and height, an impression that is reinforced by the absence of decoration on the walls. The crossing is deeper than the bay; before ribbed vaulting was inserted there in the thirteenth century, there was probably a typically Provençal squinch cupola. Rib-like bands are also to be found in the apse vault, and the capitals of the half-columns of the entrance to the chancel already have a Gothic appearance. Circular chapels are set into the very thick east walls of the transept. Thus, just as the chancel is rounded on the inside but polygonal on the outside, round internal forms are also enclosed in straight, external walls

Montmajour
Crypt of the abbey-church
View to the east (above)
Ambulatory (left)

elsewhere in the building. Both the crypt and the upper church undoubtedly date from the twelfth century, though they were not built continuously. The transept and east sections were probably added immediately after the crypt. The news that the monks moved into the upper church in 1153, which must thus have been partially completed, bears this out. Accordingly, the nave would have been built somewhat later, together with the cloister, while the crypt, as the oldest part of the building, must have been begun around 1130-40.

Thanks to its pilaster structure, diagonally belted barrel-vaulting in the cloister corners, and, the style of the sculpted decorations, the cloister on the south side of the church (illus. above) gives the impression of being based on the cloister at Arles. When contemplating the outstanding decoration, however, it should be borne in mind that when the cloister was uncovered and restored in the nineteenth century,

many objects could no longer be assigned to their old place, and in the north wing in particular, many capitals underwent extensive restoration. Nevertheless, the original sculpture falls into two basic types, namely, capitals with corner volutes and heads in the middle of the slabs, which can be traced back to classical forms and carvings of palmettes, tendrils, branches, and plant stalks, which are organically adapted to the capital block. Several parts of the building, especially the columns and capitals on the south side, were created or added in the fourteenth century, which is also true of the cloister at Arles. The basic features of the Romanesque order were preserved, but the fluting on the pilasters, for instance, was replaced by Gothic tracery. The wall tomb of the Counts of Provence belongs to the late Romanesque works in the cloister. A connection has been established between it and the tomb of Count Raymond-Bérenger (d. 1166).

FAR RIGHT:
Montmajour
11th-century
Chapelle de St-Pierre
interior looking eastward

RIGHT AND BELOW
CENTER:
Montmajour
12th-century
Chapelle de Ste-Croix
Interior and exterior

BELOW:
Montmajour
Northern aspect
of the original abbey;
on the left are the abbey-
church and dungeon, added
in 1369.

The Chapelle St-Pierre (illus. above) which stands south of the church on the slopes of the rock, is one of the earliest Romanesque buildings in Provence. Despite its small size, transverse walls and arches divide up various parts of the church. The western end of the front part was used for burials; from there, a doorway leads into the nave. A separate bay was built in the east in front of the apse. The ceiling is circular barrel-vaulting throughout. The wall plan of the north side with its small columns embedded in wall is a forerunner of a design used in the twelfth-century Provençal Romanesque period. The capitals are of particular interest. With their volutes and rosettes, they adopt rudimentarily basic classical forms, though the body of the capital is decorated with palmettes and interwoven bands. Consequently, the capitals of St-Pierre represent an important basic type of early Romanesque sculpture which, unlike the portico capitals of St-Victor in Marseilles, do not strive to emulate the Corinthian capital, but rather intend to achieve a combination of basic classical form with geometric elements.

The keep or dungeon (illus. below left) is 86 ft (26 m) high and was built by the Abbé Pons de l'Orme in 1369 as protection against the Grandes Compagnies. The battlements offer a panoramic view of the Camargue to the south and the Alpilles to the north.

The little chapel of Ste-Croix (illus. center left and opposite) was built on a cloverleaf-shaped plan, probably designed specially for the *Pardon de Montmajour*, in order to take some of the strain off the crypt. In addition, the building served as a funerary chapel, the dead being brought from far and wide (see also p. 86, Les Alyscamps). The building, with its sober interior, is an architectural anomaly, with its basic geometric forms and symmetry.

OPPOSITE:
View from the dungeon of Montmajour looking east;
the Chapelle de Ste-Croix is in the center.

Tarascon

The origins of the city lie on a nearby island in the Rhône, known as Narnica or Jovarnica, which the Romans made into a *castrum* or camp to safeguard the river crossing. When the inhabitants of Ernaginum, near present-day St-Gabriel, sought refuge from the Visigoths in 480, they fled to the vicinity of the *castrum*. The castle came into the possession of the Counts of Provence in the eleventh century, while the riverside settlement evolved into a largely independent community. The cult of St. Martha spread the city's fame throughout the whole of Provence. According to the legend, the saint—one of the biblical figures who were supposed to have traveled by sea from the Holy Land to Provence—had tamed a terrifying monster known as the Tarasque. The creature was said to live in an underground grotto and had turned up time and again to devour children and cattle with impunity. The saint had so subdued the monster with the sign of the Cross that the people were then able to chop off its head, so the story went.

The strategic importance of Tarascon was mainly due to the proximity of the French administrative center of Beaucaire, which had stood facing it since 1229. When Charles of Anjou, son of the French King Louis VIII, inherited the estates of the Counts of Provence in 1246, the fortress in Tarascon constituted an important connection between the territories of the French crown and those of its lateral lines. Nevertheless, urban privileges remained almost completely intact. Under "Good" King René I, the second Anjou dynasty also extended the fortress to include rooms of state. King René also revived the old traditions in as much as he organized a great festival in 1474 in honor of St.

Martha and the victory over the Tarasque, held to this day in the form of a major procession every year on the last weekend in June. Another literary figure, well-known in France, also continues to be commemorated. He is Tartarin of Tarascon, a quixotic French character whom Alphonse Daudet, in 1872, made into the boastful and naïve protagonist of his novel of the same name, and to whom the inhabitants of the city only gradually warmed.

The Château

The symbol of Tarascon is its château, one of the most important of its kind, in which the typical medieval fortress is transformed into a Renaissance château. The château complex, which had existed since the early eleventh century on the island in the Rhône, was rebuilt by Charles II of Anjou in 1291. The present-day château was begun under Louis II of Anjou around 1400 and completed under René I in 1449. The latter used the château complex as a splendid backdrop for glittering tournaments, and as one of the most important royal residences, in which the artistic King composed his poetry. The château was never used solely for military purposes. The complex of buildings covering almost the whole island is clearly divided into two separate areas, a complex of outbuildings to the north (illus. opposite, top) and a higher, four-winged area of state apartments to the south (illus. top of p. 100). Strangely, round towers which offer better protection against artillery, alternate with militarily obsolete square towers on the landward side. Presumably, the design of the round towers dates back to the previous building, but the differently shaped towers served to highlight the main château with its round towers against the

OPPOSITE:

Tarascon
Château, ca.1400-49, exterior looking east (above)
Pharmacy of the Hôpital St-Nicolas (below left) (shown on ground plan as no. 10)
Reception room or banqueting hall on the first floor (below right)

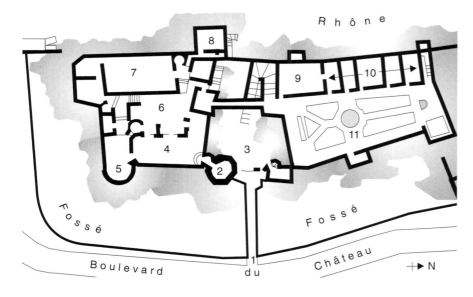

1 Entrance
2 Tour de l'Horloge
3 Residential tower
4 Gallery
5 Under-chapel
6 Cour d'honneur
7 Banqueting hall
8 Tour de l'Artillerie
9 Reception room
10 Pharmacy
11 Garden/lower courtyard

Tarascon
Château, Cour d'honneur

Arles, St-Rémy, and the Alpilles

René I

King René I, whose long rule over Provence lasted from 1434 to 1480, was transformed into a quasi-legendary figure in the 19th century. At the same time, he was rather a tragic individual, politically speaking. René was unsuccessful in the attempted reconquest of the Angevin territories in southern Italy, and after his death Provence finally fell to the French crown. Historically, this was part of a process which reversed the rise of the powerful French principalities of Burgundy, Berry, Orleans, and Anjou in the late 14th century and the simultaneous weakening of central power during the Hundred Years' War. René was descended from the second line of the House of Anjou, which began in 1368 with the investiture of Louis, son of the French king Jean le Bon, in the appanage of Anjou and Maine. Through cunning, the county of Provence also soon fell once more into the Angevin territories, as did the northern territories of Barrois and Lorraine. But an unfortunate line of succession and the unyielding French King Louis XI prevented Provence from developing into a strong, independent principality under René I. Upon the death of René in 1480, Provence passed to his nephew René II, and to France when the latter died in 1481. René I was nicknamed "the Good" for his promotion of a glittering courtly culture. This included tournaments lasting for several days in, for instance, Tarascon, and a magnificent court in Aix and Tarascon, as well as the extensive promotion of poetry, music, painting, and sculpture. The King himself composed an allegorical romantic novel, the "Book of the love-inflamed Heart", and attended poetry recitals. With his court painters Barthélémy d'Eyck and Nicolas Froment, he engaged artists who had learned the new metaphorical language in the Netherlands. Lastly, the King successfully persuaded Francesco Laurana of Naples to build a large Lazarus altar in the cathedral of Marseilles in the new Italian Renaissance style.

Arles, St-Rémy, and the Alpilles

OPPOSITE:
Tarascon
The château, viewed from the
Rhône in the southwest
(above)
Audence room with two ogival
ceiling-vaults (below)

outlying buildings from the outside as well. These outer buildings contained the guard-rooms and the accommodations of the château garrison. By contrast, the main château consists largely of rooms of state. In the very narrow inner courtyard (illus. p. 98), a projecting cir-cular staircase containing many windows leads to the upper floors—a design which was to acquire especial significance in sixteenth-centu-ry château architecture. The staircase leads directly into two chapels which are built on top of each other. The lower one, whose architec-ture bears comparison with that of the church of Ste-Marthe, probably dates from the time of the previous château, begun in 1291. The upper chapel with its side-oratories served as a royal chapel to king René and his wife. In the northeast tower (the Tour de l'Horloge), the walls of the lower room are decorated with large graffiti, especially representations of ships, witness to the numerous prisoners incar-cerated here between the fifteenth and eigh-teenth centuries. Of the furnishings, six tapes-tries with scenes from the life of Scipio deserve particular mention. The wall hangings were made around 1660 from originals created in Brussels in 1532-35 by Giulio Romano. The roof terrace of the Tour de l'Artillerie offers a panoramic view over the Alpilles, the Rhône, Beaucaire, and Mont Ventoux.

Ste. Marthe

This saint was identified in the eleventh century as being the sister of Lazarus, whom Jesus raised from the dead. In reality, she was probably a martyr of the same name, executed in the fourth century. In the high Middle Ages, cults flour-ished around Mary Magdalene, Martha, Lazarus, and Maximin, who had allegedly reached Provence straight from the Holy Land. The tomb in Tarascon also benefited from this

legend. In 1184, Martha's relics were "rediscov-ered", and a new church building was conse-crated as early as 1197. The continuously extended building was badly damaged in 1944. The church (illus. above), which from the out-side gives the strong impression of being a single unit, actually developed in many stages. The oldest sections are the foundations of the tower, built around the second quarter of the twelfth century, and the crypt (later renovated). The building which was consecrated in 1197 is still recognizable in the two west bays from the grad-ed, and in some cases slightly sharpened, blind arches and the Romanesque capitals (the ceiling vault and side-chapels were added later). The portico (illus. below right) also undoubtedly belongs to this late Romanesque period. What still remains of the sculptures which were chis-eled out during the Revolution, are some of the most exquisite examples of Romanesque sculp-ture extant, and recall those of St-Gilles and Arles. The the arch contained, as here, a repre-sentation of the crown with the surrounding symbols of the Evangelists. The lintel depicted the entry into Jerusalem, with scenes from the story of Martha and the New Testament on the side-friezes. The triforium-like gallery of pilasters and miniature columns above the por-tico block also corresponds to the late phase of Romanesque art in Provence. The gallery clearly distances itself from classical precepts and can be compared with the triforium motif in St-Paul-Trois-Châteaux.

The third, Gothic construction accounts for the main part of the present-day church. The late Romanesque building which was not yet completed in 1197, was probably continued in a modernized version; this is indicated by sever-al early Gothic bud capitals. This Gothic

Tarascon
Ste-Marthe, consecrated 1197
General view (above)
Interior (below left),
ground plan

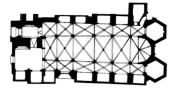

Tarascon
Ste-Marthe, south portico

Beaucaire
Ruined 13th-century battlements with tower

building is a basilica with three naves, no transept, and a low chancel apse (illus. left). The small clerestory windows, for instance, are in keeping with southern French tradition. The elegant sheaf pillars are quite remarkable, and were probably developed from the composite pillars of the late Romanesque building. The octagonal west tower (ca. 1470) with its four turrets recalls similar towers in Avignon. The two octagonal chapels to the side of the chancel date from 1683. The twelfth-century crypt in the west section of the church was altered in the seventeenth century. As early as the Middle Ages, it was supposed to convince the observer that it was the actual burial chamber of St. Martha, whose fourth-century sarcophagus from Arles, can be seen in the apse.

The tomb of Jean de Cossa (d. 1476), Seneschal of Provence and friend of King René is located in front of the entrance. The Neapolitan origin of this officer of the court also seems to extend to the choice of the sculptor whose style is similar to that of Francesco Laurana, summoned by René from Naples to Marseilles.

Beaucaire

Until into the eleventh century, almost nothing was known about this city, which bore the name of Ugernum in Roman times, and was settled no later than the second century. Only in 1097 does the fortified town of Belicadrum turn up in the sources as a border town of the county of Toulouse. Deprived of its walls in the Albigensian Crusades (1217), in 1229 the town became one of the three important royal administrative centers in southern France, the others being Carcassonne and Toulouse. In the seventeenth and eighteenth centuries in particular, the town, a free port since the fifteenth century, was an important trading center and held several fairs. Each street was devoted to a particular trade as shown by the name. There was a Rue du Beaujolais (vintners), a Rue des Bijoutiers (jewelry), a Rue des Marseillais (oil and soap), etc. The city's wealth in its heyday—nowadays it is a backwater barely spoiled by tourism—is attested by the lovely mansions and a splendid Baroque church (illus. below). The latter, the former collegiate church of Notre-Dame-des-Pommiers, was built around 1734 by J.-B. Franque and G. Rollin. Based on Roman design, its façade curves strongly forward in the center, with concave sides. The church, whose silhouette is stepped like a basilica, terminates in the east with a three-conch complex, in which the transept has the same shape as the chancel. There is a triaxial nave, and the galleries, elsewhere built into the arcades, are omitted from its central axis; the central colonnade is framed by double pilasters and crowned with a large cartouche. This centering of the nave gives the façade the look of a triumphal arch.

Outside and above on the right transept arm are the remains of a long relief frieze, which is unmistakably Romanesque. It is a series of scenes from the Passion: the Prediction of Peter's denial, the Washing of Christ's feet, the Last Supper, Peter cutting off Malcus' ear, Judas before the high priest, the Arrest of Christ, Christ before Pilate, the Flagellation, Carrying of the Cross, the Women at the grave, and the Women buying spices. Although the individual figures are often portrayed stereotypically, the reliefs still clearly belong to their surroundings as part of the late Romanesque sculptures.

Beaucaire
Three-cornered fortification tower

Beaucaire
Notre-Dame-des-Pommiers, ca. 1734
West façade

The town hall, erected 1678-84 by Jacques Cubizol of Nîmes, is in a style developed in Montpellier. The three-winged complex encloses a courtyard with an open staircase in the central section. In front of it, a two-story loggia surmounts a double pair of columns. The heavy decoration is in keeping with local customs of the period, but is old-fashioned compared with northern French building decorations.

In the Rue de la République, several other lovely houses of this period have been preserved. The Maison des Cariatides (also known as the Hôtel Margailler) has a caryatid porch built by Antoine Camartine in 1675-80; the great ground-floor colonnades lead to salerooms and storerooms. Next to it stands the eighteenth-century Hôtel Clausonnettes, with its lovely inner courtyard, whose low, curved garden frontage improves the view from a minaret-like belvedere.

The former Franciscan church of St-Paul, is flush with the houses as in the Middle Ages, and is only seen from a distances thanks to its tower. The building is a typical southern French hall construction with accompanying mid-fourteenth-century chapels; the chancel was built in the fifteenth century. In its structure, the high tower corresponds to the tower of Ste-Marthe in Tarascon.

The Château Ruins

The steep cliffs over Beaucaire were already fortified back in Roman times. A château which had probably been built in the eleventh century was badly damaged during the Albigensian Crusades when it was retaken by Count Raymond VI in 1216. The bulk of the fortress was rebuilt in the thirteenth century, after Beaucaire became the royal administrative center in 1229. Louis XIII had the complex razed in 1632, following the Wars of Religion. Today, the Château (illus. top of p.102) has lovely grounds in which falconry is often demonstrated. Historically, the fortress represents an important example of southern French royal military architecture. The ground plan of the château is irregular as was usual in the thirteenth century, as this was dictated by the terrain. Even so, the upper complex, which is subdivided into a main château and outbuildings, is almost rectangular. The masonry is characterized by precise regular courses of ashlar. The most important elements are the gatehouse with its fortified entrance in the east, behind which stands a small late Romanesque chapel. The curtain wall in the northwest leads to the massive triangular tower, whose strange design is probably explained by the terrain. Next to the tower, the living quarters with interesting basements have been excavated. This section separated the main château from the outbuildings. Opposite, on the northwest side, several courses of stone suggest a massive round tower—perhaps the castle keep. There are also the remains

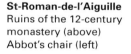

of several Gallo-Roman round towers. The Musée Auguste-Jacquet, a museum of the local history, is located within the eastern section of the walls.

St-Roman-de-l'Aiguille
Ruins of the 12-century monastery (above)
Abbot's chair (left)

St-Roman-de-l'Aiguille

On a rock about 3 miles (5 km) north of the city on the D 999, then along the footpath to the right, are the ruins of the twelfth-century monastery of St-Roman-de-l'Aiguille, hewn almost entirely from the rock (illus. above left). The monastery was converted into a château in the sixteenth century. About 2 miles (4 km) west of Beaucaire (D 38), the Gallo-Roman wine-cellar of Mas des Tourelles can be visited. Don't miss the opportunity to sample the wine, made according to ancient Roman recipes.

Chapel of St-Gabriel

The small, remote chapel of St-Gabriel (illus. p. 105) is all that remains of a town named Ernaginum on the Via Aurelia, whose inhabitants fled from the Saracens to the site of

present-day Tarascon in 480. The village declined, but in the Middle Ages a fortification was once again erected there, from which perhaps date the remains of the tower over the actual chapel. Just what purpose the chapel itself served is uncertain. Although small, it is clear from the richly ornamented west front that it had some importance. The entrance side consists of an overgabled portico, not unlike a large recess. This encloses the round-arched portico, which is framed by a triangular gable with two half columns. The gable relief, which is shaped like a late early-Christian sarcophagus, depicts the Annunciation and Visitation. The tympanum shows Daniel in the lions' den, assisted by an angel of God, as well as the Fall. On the gable of the portico, the symbols of the Evangelists surround the richly ornamented oculus. Thus, in just a few images, the chapel saint, the Archangel Gabriel, is depicted as a harbinger of God's salvation, in its foreshadowing in the Old Testament (Daniel), through the Annunciation of the Incarnation, and in the testimony of the Evangelists.

Alphonse Daudet's Mill

Fontvielle, a picturesque village, still has its fourteenth-century watchtower. Alphonse Daudet lived a stone's throw away in the Château de Montauban. One of the mills on a plain in the southern part of the village is also dedicated to him (illus. above). Despite the fact that the poet neither owned nor occupied this mill, he pretended to have written one of his major works, Letters from my Mill (*Lettres de mon moulin*), in a Provençal mill— although it was actually written in Paris. The author narrates dozens of humorous legends and stories of life in Provence, some historical, some contemporary.

The Roman mills of Barbegal are a unique example of Roman industry (3rd-4th C). The watercourse from the Alpilles branched off here. One aqueduct flowed to Arles, the other into a reservoir from which two waterfalls with drops of over 66 ft (20 m) drove eight mill-wheels built into the hillside. This flour mill on an industrial scale was capable of producing up to 660 lb (300 kg) of flour per hour!

Les Baux-de-Provence
View from the northwest

Les Baux-de-Provence

Between the Val d'Enfer and the Val de la Fontaine, on a hill shaped like a ship's bow whose reddish rocks owe their color to their high bauxite content, lies one of the main attractions of Provence. This picturesque ruined city has an interesting past. This once-flourishing town was ruined by the gradual subjugation by the French crown of an independent, rebellious principality. In the eleventh century, the Lords of Baux made this town the capital of their extensive domain, from which they repeatedly opposed the Holy Roman Emperor, the King and the Pope, and terrified the local populace, "a line of noblemen who were vassals never," as Mistral described them. When the family died out in 1426, the town passed to the county of Provence, and with it becoming part of France in 1481. Since the town opposed the annexation, it was besieged and taken by French troops under Louis XI, and its walls were demolished. Demoted to a barony, it then became a dowry for favorites of the King. The town remained rebellious, however, and sided with the Protestants in the sixteenth century. In the early seventeenth century, this Huguenot refuge still opposed the King, and was yet again captured, this time by Richelieu, and its walls destroyed. It then passed to the princes of Monaco, but fell once again to France during the French Revolution. In the nineteenth century, the inhabitants left and it declined, and only tourism—occasionally in excess—discovered its charms. The vines grown on the calcareous soils

Bauxite
This sedimentary rock, composed of aluminum, ferric oxide, and silicon, derives its name from the town of Les Baux, where it was discovered in 1821. There are also deposits in Languedoc. It is made into aluminum. Geologically, bauxite is a product of clay exposed to the sun. In similar conditions, the sandier rock of the Luberon turns into ocher. The French bauxite deposits are largely exhausted, and quarrying is expensive; the mineral is thus mainly imported from abroad.

Les Baux
Place St-Vincent (above)
General view of the town with the village church of St-Vincent (below)

around the town, produce the wine known as *Les Baux-de-Provence*.

The château, with its thirteenth-century dungeon perched on the edge of a steep rocky cliff, dominates the town. The town itself occupies the western and southern slopes of the château rock and is said to have had a population of 3,000 in the thirteenth century, though this had dwindled to 220 by 1935. Most of the houses, some of which were destroyed and then rebuilt, date from the sixteenth and seventeenth centuries.

Now that Les-Baux de-Provence has become a tourist attraction, numerous restaurants, boutiques, galleries, and small museums have sprung up. The early sixteenth-century Hôtel de Brion contains the Fondation Louis-Jou, a

printing museum, and is worth seeing. Modern art is on display in the Hôtel de Porcelet (1569). Archeological and historical finds from Les Baux are on show in the medieval Manoir de la Tour du Brau.

The village church of St-Vincent belonged to the cathedral chapter of Avignon in the fourteenth century. Part of the twin-naved building, the core of which is Romanesque, was hewn out of the rock. In 1609, the nave was extended to the west, and the Romanesque portico was extensively restored in the nineteenth century. The Pavillon de la Reine Jeanne, a gem of a small Renaissance chapel in the Val de la Fontaine below Porte Eyguières, is believed to have been built by Jeanne de Quinsqueran, the wife of a Baron of Les Baux.

Les Baux
Ruins of the town with the castle keep (above)
Reconstruction of a medieval engine of war (below)

View of the Alpilles from Les Baux-de-Provence

The Alpilles or "little Alps" stretch eastward from Tarascon toward Durance. Geologically, this mountain chain is an extension of the Luberon range, but with their considerable height of up to 1,643 ft (493 m), the Alpilles give the impression of being a separate small mountain range. Olive and almond trees grow in the shale soil, with the occasional cypress, but more often than not the bare rock is exposed.

This is where the "stone of the Midi" was quarried, the grayish-to-pink limestone used since ancient times for large stone buildings. The calcareous sediments deposited during the Miocene are relatively easy to quarry and hew. Once exposed to the air, they harden into an extremely resistant material. This barren landscape, flooded with light, has been compared time and again to the Greek countryside, notably by the Provençal poet Frédéric Mistral. Some parts of the unspoiled mountains are nature conservation areas, populated by eagles, vultures, and owls.

The D 5 and the D 27 roads leading south from St-Rémy over the mountains, as well as the D 24 and D 25, not to mention numerous hiking trails, offer lasting impressions of the scenery, especially from La Caume, on the ridge south of St-Rémy.

OPPOSITE PAGE:
St-Rémy-de-Provence
Reliefs of battle scenes
on the plinth of the so-called
Julian monument.

St-Rémy-de-Provence
Commemorative arch,
ca. 20 BC (right)
and the so-called Julian
monument

St-Rémy-de-Provence

Like Tarascon, St-Rémy probably came into being when the inhabitants of ancient Glanum abandoned their homes toward the end of the third century, perhaps out of fear of invasion by the Teutons. As early as the sixth century, the Abbey of St-Rémy of Reims had property here, which is also reflected in the town's name. This small town was also the birthplace of Nostradamus. The lapidarium of the ancient city, including numerous archeological finds, is located in the Hôtel de Sade (fifteenth to sixteenth century). The Hôtel Estrine houses the Centre d'Art-Présence Van Gogh, a reminder of the Painter's one-year stay in the town (see p. 114).

Glanum

There was a spring here, and since time immemorial, the highway from Italy branched off here to the north and west. It is possible that Greeks from Marseilles built a settlement next to the native Celtic-Ligurians in Glanon (or Glanum I) and minted a few drachmas here as

early as the third century BC. At the end of the second century BC Roman rule was strengthened, and with the conquest of Marseilles in 49 BC, the Romans began to transform the whole landscape. In Glanum, this can still be seen today in the architecture. With the invasion of the Teutons in the fourth century, most of the inhabitants retreated to St-Rémy; the old city quickly declined, and was only rediscovered in the nineteenth century. Only the triumphal arch and the burial monument (illus. above) always remained well in evidence. In the eighteenth century they were frequently painted (Hubert Robert) as restored relics of the Roman past.

The monumental arch was presumably erected to commemorate the re-establishment of the town—as, for instance, in Orange. It was probably erected in ca. 25-20 BC, a date consistent with the wave of rebuilding which took place within the town. The road from the direction of Ernagi ran through the arch, which stood outside the town. The arch is impressive for its excellent carved decoration, resplendent with

St-Rémy-de-Provence
Bust of Nostradamus
above the Nostradamus
fountain (1503-1566)

heavy festoons of fruit, which is particularly well preserved in the coffered vaulting of its archway. Between the outside columns, trophies of war and prisoners can be seen depicted in high-relief carvings. Their attire of fringed cloaks and breeches shows them to be Celtic prisoners. Details on the weaponry make it clear that these are Gauls. Some of the powerfully modeled, reliefs are three-dimensional. This style of relief, and the emphasis on the bodies underneath the garments, as well as the lively arrangement of figures, is strongly reminiscent of Hellenistic sculpture, such as the Pergamon altar.

At some distance from the arch, but without any recognizable architectural connection thereto, stands the so-called Julian monument, a tower-like building, described as a "mausoleum" in the Middle Ages. A striking feature of this building is how the different architectural styles have been stacked right on top of one another. Above an altar-like base rises a four-sided arch, over which a small round temple encloses two statues of the deceased, in honor of whom the monument was erected. On the architrave of the mezzanine is preserved an abridged inscription which might indicate that Sextus, Lucius, and Marcus from the house of Julii erected this monument to their parents. It is also possible, however, that the monument was built in honor of their adopted sons and grandsons of Augustus, Caius, and, Lucius.

The large reliefs at ground level (illus. right) are not easy to interpret. In the east, there is the fight for the body of Patroclus; in the north, mounted soldiers in battle; in the west, embattled Amazons; and in the south, the hunting of the Caledonian boar and the killing of Niobe's daughters. The composition, which at first glance seems rigid, is rendered subtly rhythmic by the use of masks and cupids on the festoons above, each one of which marks an important compositional axis. The contour line surrounding all the figures which raises the composition as a whole away from the ground is typical of this school of southern Gallic sculpture, which has hardly any successors. The commemorative arch already reveals a more severe style, even though Hellenistic traditions are still at work here.

The excavation site opposite (illus. p. 112), reveals three phases of the city's development. Glanum I is the Greek settlement with large ashlars set without mortar; Glanum II represents the Roman superstructure from the second century, with buildings made of small ashlar blocks. Finally, Glanum III characterizes the period from the end of the 1st century onward, in which the city was provided with its large public buildings. When touring Glanum, it is best to start quite far to the south, on the slight rise accommodating the shrine to the spring of the original inhabitants, reached by a flight of steps. Even the Greeks

St-Paul-de-Mausole
Romanesque cloister in the old monastery.
In the 19th century, the monastery was a nursing home and it is here that Vincent van Gogh stayed as a mental patient from May 1889 through May 1890, when he had a nervous breakdown.

remodeled these steps, by paving them and the pool with marble. The Romans, in turn, extended the complex with a temple which they erected to the north of the site and dedicated to Valetudo, goddess of health. Heading toward the excavation site, one reaches the former portico to the shrine of the spring, the large ashlar blocks of which testify to the fact that it was erected under Greek rule.

Further to the north and left, there are two temples dedicated to the Imperial cult, situated on a high base and within a courtyard-like surround. The smaller temple was only subsequently incorporated into this courtyard, which was built ca. 30 BC. To the east of both temples, on the other side of the old main street, stood a semicircular fountain, and further to the east, the Hellenistic theater. In Roman times, the forum stood to the north. It was a colonnaded, arcaded square closed on the north side by the so-called basilica, a transversely rectangular building with three naves, the foundations of whose internal columns are still there to be seen. The orientation of the axes indicate that the forum and temple were related to each other. Nothing is known about the function of the "house with apse" adjoining the basilica. This area stands on the rubble of older buildings which were torn down to serve as the foundations for later ones.

The same holds true for the Roman baths complex which date from the late first century BC and are situated north of the apsidal house. The classic sequence of caldarium, frigidarium, and tepidarium was completed by a swimming pool which was later moved to the south in order to make room for a palestra or gymnasium. The foundations of a peristyle house from Glanum were discovered at the southwest corner of the palestra. In Glanum II, a house with two-columned halls, called the *Maison de Capricorne*, after its mosaic floor was built on the top of the peristyle house. On the other side of the street stands the so-called *Maison des Antes* with its large interior courtyard. Adjoining it is the Greek house of Cybele and Atys, which is actually two houses connected via a passageway. With the establishment of a place of worship to the goddess Cybele in the northern section, however, the passageway was walled up, and part of the large peristyle court destroyed.

It can be seen that the Romans regulated the whole of the old town center, and erected monumental public buildings when the town was re-established. At the same time, the Hellenistic character of the town declined. The old, trapezoid agora, for instance, was buried under the southern section of the forum. The pre-Roman complex was characterized by smaller buildings which stood in irregular relationship to one another. The city's point of reference, the shrine of the spring, was nevertheless always retained. Without intervening greatly here in the stock of buildings, the Romans integrated the shrine by aligning the city's main axis with it, and by erecting their own temples in this part of the city.

St-Paul-de-Mausole

Toward the town of St-Rémy near the ancient remains stands the former monastery of St-Paul-de-Mausole. In the eleventh century, it fell under the control of the bishop, and from 1317 came under the jurisdiction of the Chapter of Avignon. The complex is unusual in its completeness. The church, cloister, and collegiate building are almost intact, although partially remodeled. In the cloister (illus. above) the decoration of the capitals recalls the late Romanesque sculpture of Montmajour or Arles. The cloister is also famous for housing the asy-

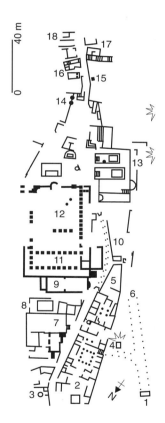

1 Entrance 2 Maison des Antes
3 Fountain 4 Shrine to Cybele
5 Maison d'Atys
6 Old main street
7 Baths 8 Spring 9 House with an Apse 10 Water course 11 Basilica 12 Forum
13 Temple 14 Monumental arch
15 Monument
16 Nympheum 17 Gallic shrine
18 Altars

OPPOSITE:
Glanum
Views of the ancient mausoleum near St-Rémy looking toward the site of the Roman forum (above and below right) and a modern reconstruction of a corner of the temple (left)

Frédéric Mistral, the man who rediscovered Provence, was born the son of a farmer in Maillane in 1830, and died there at an advanced age in 1914. After studying law in Aix, he devoted himself entirely to the revival of Provençal literature and culture, which under centuries of French rule had been sorely neglected. In epic and narrative works frequently dealing with ancient traditions, he describes in modern Provençal the life and loves of the people of Provence (Mirèio, 1859; Calendau, 1867; Lou pouèmo dòu rose, 1897). As the leader of this cultural renaissance – the Félibrige – he published an unabridged dictionary of the modern Provençal language, Lou tresor dou félibrige.
In 1904 he received the Nobel Prize for Literature, whereupon he founded the Museon Arlaten, the model for all folklore museums in Provence.

Maillane
Bust of the poet
Frédéric Mistral
(1830-1914) (above)
The Mistral House
and memorial (below)

lum to which Vincent Van Gogh retreated between May 3, 1889 and May 16, 1890 after his nervous breakdown. The painter had his own studio on the ground floor, where he continued to paint like one possessed.

Maillane

Frédéric Mistral, the Provençal poet and rediscoverer of the Occitan tradition, was born in 1830 in Maillane, a charming village on the fertile plain of Petite Crau de St-Rémy, where he lived most of his life until his death in 1914. Today, the house that he moved into in 1876 serves as a memorial to him (illus. below). His grave is marked by a mausoleum which is a copy of Queen Jeanne's pavilion in Les Baux.

St-Michel-de-Frigolet

St-Michel-de-Frigolet, a small abbey founded in the eleventh century by the monks of Montmajour and taken over in the following century by the Augustine canons in Avignon, was resettled by the Premonstratensians in the nineteenth century. The small cloister dates from the late twelfth century. The chapel of Notre-Dame-du-Bon-Remède was included as the apse of the north aisle of a neo-Romanesque complex in the nineteenth century. Unfortunately, it is a gothic fantasmagoria, overflowing with crenellations and turrets.

The word *frigolet* is derived from *férigoulo*, the Provençal term for thyme, which is processed here into a medicine. Alphonse Daudet's story of the Elixir of R.P. Gaucher, which is about the medicinal herbs processed in St-Michel-de-Frigolet, is set here.

Boulbon

Like St-Gabriel, the chapel of St-Marcellin (illus. above) in the cemetery of Boulbon is a small gem of Romanesque architecture. The interior of the single-naved church is remarkably steep. East of the tow, there are the imposing ruins of the fortress, erected ca. 1400 by the Counts of Provence to protect the road from Avignon to Tarascon. The battlements are topped with merlons, machicolations and other defensive devices and seem to grow out of the steep cliffs which they overhang.

Salt, Rice, Horses, and Bullfights

The Camargue, St-Gilles, and Aigues-Mortes

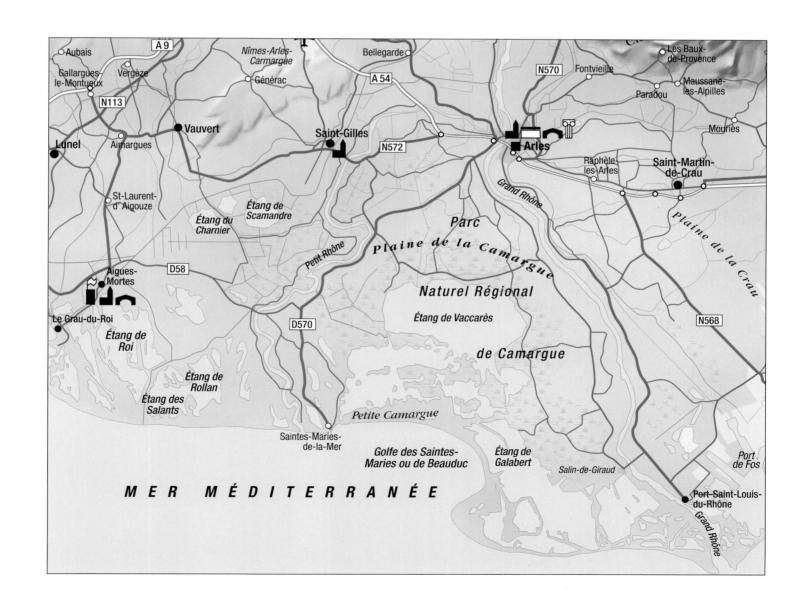

The landscape of the Camargue

The Camargue is the region between the two branches of the Rhône, which divide at Arles into the smaller western Petit Rhône and the Grand Rhône. The delta covers an area of some 187,500 acres (75,000 ha). The huge amounts of silt that the river brings down with it—some 66 million cu. ft (20 million cu. m.) a year—mean that the coastline is in a constant state of flux. In the west especially, the land is growing into the sea. The town of Aigues-Mortes which was founded as a seaport now lies five miles (8 km) inland. The currents from the Mediterranean are stronger in the east; Saintes-Maries-de-la-Mer, an inland town in the seventeenth century, is today sometimes threatened by the incoming tide.

This completely flat landscape, only 5-15 ft (1.5-4.5 m) above sea level, is dotted with saltwater lakes and, at least in the past, was regularly flooded, while its rivers constantly changed their courses. All this has created highly specific geological and botanical conditions. Only certain types of plants can live here, because the salt concentration is so high. A wide range of small sea-fish live in the warm waters of the area, such as shrimp, eels, and mullet. The shallow waters with their abundance of fish and the absence of natural enemies make the landscape a paradise for numerous species of birds, including migrating birds, that overwinter here. The wealth of zoological and botanical life was recognized and valued from the early twentieth century, and since 1928 more of the area has been designated as a nature reserve.

Near the coast, in the Basse Camargue, the salt is harvested in large salt-pans. Wild horses and the famous semi-wild bulls roam the marshes. The herdsmen, who are called *Gardians*, still wear the traditional black,

The Camargue
Etang (above)
Camargue horses (center)
Paddy-field (far left)
Flamingos (left)
Camargue bullrunning
(p. 119 below)

The Courses Camarguaises
The small black bulls with their lyre-like horns were bred as early as the Middle Ages. Their meat is a great delicacy, but the animals are bred mainly for the *Courses camarguaises*, the French variation of bullfighting. The bulls are first brought into the bullring when they are between three and five years old, carrying a white paper flower, the cockade. So-called *Razeteurs*, usually clad in white, then try to capture the cockade. If they do not succeed within 15 minutes, the bull is released into the peaceful pastures of the Camargue for another year, after which it will again take part in a bullfight. If the animal proves to be too tame, however, it ends its life in a local dish, such as *Gardiane*, a beef ragoût in which the meat is simmered slowly in red wine and whose quality is measured by the thickness of the sauce.

A *Course camarguese* is not always a public affair, however, but also serves to amuse the guests at private functions, especially weddings (Illus. right). Here a man is trying to capture the cockade from a young cow, in the expectation that she will defend her honor.

broad-brimmed hats. They are outstanding horsemen, who herd their horses and bulls, called *Manades*, on horseback. The famous white horses are very small; they are only about 14 hands or (4½ ft or 145 cm) at the withers. In the past, they were mainly used in agriculture, today they carry tourists. Their wide, hard hooves are well adapted to the marshy ground and do not have to be shod. The coat is black at birth, but at around six months its color changes to the characteristic silvery-gray.

The bulls, with their lyre-shaped horns, are mostly reared for the Provençal *Férias*, also called *Courses camarguaises*, the local bullfights in which no blood is shed (see above). When the bulls are about one year old, the *Gardians* drive them toward groups of young men who wrestle them to the ground and brand them in a kind of folk festival.

In the upper Camargue, there have been increasing efforts in the last decades of the twentieth century to convert the land to agricultural use, for growing fruit, grain, and wine. Along the Grand Rhône, the conditions are favorable especially for the growing of rice (see p. 118). This was very useful when France lost its colonies in Indochina in the 1960s. Today, however, rice production amounts to only a third of its former volume. Still, the Carmargue remains Europe's largest rice-grower.

For travelers approaching the Camargue from Arles via the D 570, the Musée Camarguais, housed in an old farmstead, offers an extremely useful introduction to the history and geography of the region. The Château d'Avignon lies on the same road. It is a large eighteenth-century manor house that was extended in the nineteenth century into a splendid château by Louis Noilly-Prat, an industrialist from Marseille. The road continues through the bird sanctuary of Pont de Gau, which also houses some rare species of birds kept in aviaries. The nearby information center at Ginès-François-Hüe has an exhibition of fauna and flora of the Camargue. There is a wax museum further south which contains realistic portrayals of local scenes and legends, such as the Arrival of the three Marys or Van Gogh at the beach with his easel.

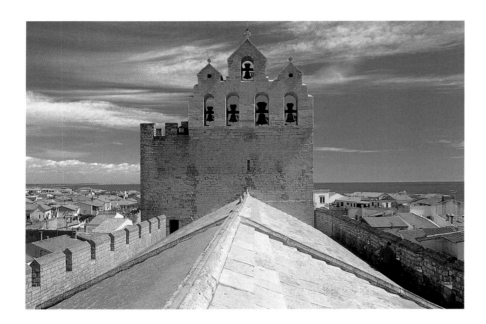

Les Saintes-Maries-de-la-Mer

The village of Les Saintes-Maries-de-la-Mer, which today lies on the coast, was originally located inland. When painted by Van Gogh in the nineteenth century, it was still a small fishing village, but, due to its coastal location, it has suffered much from the mass influx of tourists seeking beach holidays. The village has a long history, as is shown by the ruined Roman walls, vaults, and columns found under the local church. They were discovered as early as 1448, when René I, Count of Provence, instigated a search for the remains of the three Holy Marys, after whom the church is named: Mary, mother of the apostle James the Younger, and Mary, wife of Zebedee and mother of James the Elder and John, along with Mary Magdalene, accompanied by their servant, Sarah. According to legend, Sarah was a gypsy. For this reason, every year gypsies hold a colorful festival which takes place in the village on May 24 and 25. Women from Arles in local costume, Spanish dance groups, and many *Gardians* join in the festivities. The highlight of the festival is a procession in which the statue of Sarah is carried from the church down into the sea and back (see right), and then dressed in new clothes.

From the outside, the village church looks like a strong bulwark, while the whole village is surrounded by a fourteenth-century battlemented parapet (see below). A second story above the choir gives the appearance of a tower, but is actually a chapel. The main building consists of a single nave and a choir that narrows into an apse and was probably built in the twelfth century. The chapel above the choir, originally dedicated to St. Michael, was probably also built at that time. The shrine of the three Marys was only opened here in the nineteenth century. After the relics had been rediscovered, they were placed in a crypt in the choir to keep them accessible. The apse contains an

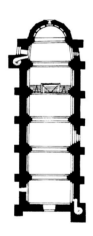

The Provençal saints
Since the 11th century, Provençal legend has linked all the local saints, whose origins lie in the Holy Land, into one group sharing a common destiny. This group includes the three Marys and their maid Sarah already mentioned above, as well as St. Martha, Lazarus, Sidonius, and Maximinus, among others. Some of the biblical figures here blend into each other. The cult of Mary Magdalene, for instance, combines in one saint the Mary of Magdala to whom Christ appeared on Easter morning, the Mary of Bethany who washed and oiled his feet when he visited her house, and finally Mary, the sinner who dried his feet with her hair. According to legend, all these local saints were not martyred in Palestine but abandoned at sea in a rudderless boat, which through God's grace was washed ashore in Provence. Here Christ's contemporaries immediately started to proselytize (see St-Maximin, Aix, Marseilles). From the 12th century onward, the search for the remains of these prestigious saints promptly led to relics being found, first in 1184 in Tarascon, then in 1279 in St-Maximin, and finally in 1448 in Les Saintes-Maries-de-la-Mer, making these places centers of pilgrimage.

Les Saintes-Maries-de-la-Mer
Pigrim church
View looking east (above)
Crypt (right)

OPPOSITE PAGE:
St-Gilles
West façade of the original
Abbey-church, second half of
the twelth century.

holy sites in Palestine and Rome. The stream of pilgrims was certainly the most important reason for building the church. It was been estimated that the festival of St. Giles, which lasted for three days, brought about 50,000 pilgrims into the town to visit the saint's grave. St-Gilles also prospered due to its harbor, which contained the local headquarters of the two great orders of knights, the Knights of St. John and the Knights Templar. The silt deposits in the harbor began to build up in the early thirteenth century, while at the same time Montpellier and Narbonne emerged as important transshipment centers. This, along with the dwindling in the number of pilgrims, led to a rapid decline of the town and its church. In 1208, the papal legate, Peter of Castelnau, was murdered in the town, on the orders of Raymond VI, leading to the crusade against the Albigensians. In 1226, the monks submitted themselves to the rule of the French king. In the sixteenth century, the Huguenots pillaged and almost burned both town and church. Today's St-Gilles is a small and rather uninteresting provincial town, located in the middle of barren plains.

The abbey-church
The opulent sculptures adorning the façade of the abbey-church, making it one of the most significant examples of Romanesque sculpture anywhere (see opposite) are thus all the more outstanding. Dating the church and its west façade has proved difficult. A church was consecrated here in 1096 by Pope Urban II, but it was probably an earlier building. The oldest part of the present church is without doubt the large crypt beneath the nave (see below). According to an inscription, its construction probably commenced in 1116, but continued for several decades. Both lower and upper church closely match the west façade, which was probably built in the second half of the twelfth century. Some parts of the extensive building project, such as the vault, may not have been completed by the year 1200. The church was badly damaged during the Wars of Religion in the sixteenth century, when both the

St-Gilles
Ruined choir with the *Vis de Saint-Gilles* in the original Abbey-church (above)
Ground plan (below)
Crypt (below right)

arcade whose capitals resemble those in the northern section of the cloister wing at Arles.

Roads running eastward around the Etang de Vaccarès, the largest of the saltwater lakes (D 37 and D 36), make it possible to tour more saltworks. One of these, the old royal salt-works at Salin-de-Bedon, lies in an area which is populated by numerous species of birds throughout the year. There is also a rice museum, the Musée du Riz.

St-Gilles
During the Roman era, the town of Vallis Flaviana was located on the site of the present St-Gilles, but nothing remains of it today. Around 700, a Benedictine monastery was founded, and around 925, a separate church seems to have been built beside the existing church of St. Peter and Paul, to house the relics of St. Giles, its legendary founder. The counts of Toulouse, the monastery's feudal lords, transferred it in 1066 to the powerful Abbey of Cluny, and before Raymond IV embarked on a crusade in 1096, he transferred all his rights to the land around it and the town to the abbey. From the eleventh century onward, the monastery became an important stop on the pilgrimage to the grave of the apostle James the Elder at Santiago de Compostela, as well as the

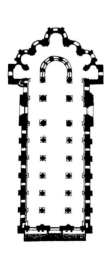

nave and the tower were destroyed. The present nave with its plain design was built between 1650 and 1655.

The main and oldest part of the 130 ft (40 m) long lower church building is the small, rectangular section of the crib containing the tomb of St. Gilles. The crypt was mainly used for the adoration of the saint's relics. Building proceeded in stages. First the bays around the tomb area were built, then those to the west of it, with their elaborate rib vaults, and finally those to the east.

Of the choir, which was probably built during the later stages of construction during the second half of the twelfth century, only ruins remain (see p.124, above). The choir was U-shaped with a surrounding ambulatory with five radial chapels. Such choirs are typical of many pilgrimage churches along the pilgrimage route to St. James of Compostela, and can be found at the cathedral of Santiago, at St-Sernin in Toulouse, and at Ste-Foy in Conques, to name but a few. This shows what an ambitious and, within Provence, unique building program formed the basis of the church's construction. The ground plan of the church can be reconstructed by looking at the part of the wall with the spiral staircase. The transepts of the choir and its longitudinal chapels were covered by elaborate rib vaulting, whose zigzag patterns mirrored those in the western part of the crypt.

The choir towers probably dominated the choir chapels. The famous *Vis de Saint-Gilles*, a spiral staircase within a barrel-vaulted passage led up to them. The individual stones used in the construction of this staircase had to be cut in such a way as to produce complex spherical forms with slightly convex or concave surfaces. This stonemasonry is among the most remarkable achievements of medieval architecture. The graffiti left by subsequent visiting master builders illustrates how even in the seventeenth century. This staircase was admired as a supreme example of the mason's art.

The sculptures of the west façade

The west façade is another prime achievement of the Romanesque, not only because of the opulence and quality of the sculptures, but also because it attempts—to a greater extent than any other Provençal work of art of the time—to make new use of ancient styles. The façade with its three portals and the relief design of the wall itself was certainly modeled on the Roman arch in Orange or on the Roman theater façades with their three entrances. The grand staircase, which has remained unchanged, leads up to an entrance façade which is set on a plinth in two sections. Above this, large statues stand in rectangular niches separated by fluted pilasters. To the side of the center portal, the structure is further emphasized by the inclusion of columns decorated with plant arabesques. Columns are integrated into the walls of the side-porticos while statues are integrated into the central portico. The pillars on which the entablature rest have all the classical characteristics one might expect, such as the Attic plinths, the broadening of the column shaft and the Corinthian capitals. The pairs of columns on both pedestals at the sides of the main portico are highly unusual. Nothing rests on them, as if they were never intended for use.

The large statues represent the twelve apostles along with St. Michael (left) and the three archangels in a group (right) in the outer niches. The passion of Christ is told in great and sometimes dramatic detail in the relief frieze. The sequence begins on the left portal with the preparations for and the entry into Jerusalem. The wall between the left and the main portal depicts two men in conversation, Judas is promised the thirty pieces of silver, the banishing of the moneylenders from the temple, and the raising of Lazarus from the dead with Mary Magdalene and Martha. The last two scenes do not really belong in the context of the passion; obviously an attempt was made to incorporate local saints into the narrative. The middle portal shows Christ among seven of his disciples,

OPPOSITE:
St-Gilles
West façade of the original Abbey-church, left (John the Evangelist, Peter; above Peter denying Christ) and right (James the Greater, Paul; above, Judas' kiss) on either side of the central portico

Peter's denial of Christ, the Last Supper and other scenes which are difficult to interpret. The wall to the right of the main portal depicts in moving scenes the arrest of Christ, followed by the Judas kiss, Christ before Pontius Pilate, the scourging at the pillar, and the carrying of the cross. The crucifixion is finally shown in the tympanum of the southern portal. The relief frieze shows scenes in the story of the resurrected Christ: the road to Emmaus, Christ as gardener, and *Noli me tangere*, as well as the washing of Christ's feet by Mary Magdalene and the three Maries at the graveside.

The Passion of Christ and the witness of the apostles are presented in a monumental style, and the depiction of the Last Judgement showing Christ in Majesty in the main tympanum complements this history of salvation. There are also scenes from the Old Testament on the side pedestals: Cain and Abel, Samson with the lion, and David and Goliath. They point to the impending salvation contained in the New Testament.

Stylistically, the sculptures of St-Gilles are in the Roman tradition of the region, but also owe something to those in neighboring Languedoc (Toulouse). It would be good to know more about their purpose. They seem to anticipate the goals of the pilgrims, as if they were meant to reinforce the concept of pilgrimage. The incorporation of the local saints into the Passion is an indication that these were linked to central scenes from the Bible, in order to enhance their prestige.

The so-called Romanesque House, whose façade dating from around 1200 still survives, stands opposite the west wall of the church. It houses a museum exhibiting sarcophagi from Arles as well as pieces of Romanesque sculpture.

BELOW AND OPPOSITE:
St-Gilles
West portal of the original Abbey-church, scenes from the bas-relief friezes: Peter washing the feet of Christ; Peter (below); Christ before Pontius Pilate and the flagellation (opposite)

The Camargue, St-Gilles, and Aigues-Mortes

Aigues-Mortes
In the harbor (above)
City walls (right)

OPPOSITE:
Aigues-Mortes
Tour de Constance,
mid-13th century
The ribbing of the vaulted
ceiling on the top floor.

Aigues-Mortes

Louis IX, called St. Louis, acquired land in the bay of Eaux-Mortes from the monastery of Psalmody in 1240 and established his own port on the Mediterranean coast. He built a harbor where in 1248 he assembled 35,000 men and 1,500 ships for a crusade against Cyprus. However, the royal army was soon overwhelmed, and the crusaders returned home. In 1270, Louis again attempted a crusade, and again the port of embarkation for his fleet was Aigues-Mortes. On arrival in Tunis, however, the king died of the Plague. The town was founded at the same time as the harbor, but only the Tour de Constance and a settlement on a checkerboard street plan were built at the time. This grid pattern can also be found in other contemporary settlements called *bastides*, mainly founded in the Duchy of Aquitaine which was claimed by both England and France. Like those settlements, Aigues-Mortes was made attractive to prospective settlers by waiving various taxes. Three churches ensured

the spiritual welfare of the settlers. These were the parish church of Notre-Dame des Sablons, a Franciscan convent, and the monastery chapel at Psalmody.

The massive city wall was only built as protection in 1272. The town was finally completed in the late thirteenth century under Philip IV, le Bel (1285-1314). Barely fifty years later, however, silt deposits built up in the sea-roads, and the harbor became unusable. The town quickly lost its importance. A positive side-effect has been that the ground plan of one of the most impressive examples of a thirteenth-century planned settlement has survived almost intact to the present day, although in the course of time most of the dwelling-houses were replaced by modest new buildings.

The so-called Tour Carbonnière, a square tower with a dome that was built as part of the fortifications of the harbor under Philip le Bel ("the Beautiful") in the late thirteenth century is about a mile (2 km) out of town. Aigues-Mortes also has its own isolated round tower, the Tour de Constance. Here the tradition of the *donjon*, or castle keep, lives on, as the tower is not only a single bastion, but also contains heatable living quarters roofed by elaborate rib vaulting, as well as a chapel. An upper story also has a rib vault (see right) and up to the eighteenth century, the tower was used as a prison for political prisoners. Many of these were Huguenots, such as Marie Durand, who carved her desperate motto "*recicter*" on the wall. She was eventually released in 1768, after 38 years of imprisonment, but died shortly afterward. Gertrude of Le Fort has described Marie Durand's fate in her novel, "The Tower of Constancy."

The town itself forms an almost perfect rectangle of about 1900 x 1000 ft (570 x 300 m). The whole complex resembles in many ways the rectangular castle at Carcassone which was built in ca. 1240. Protruding round towers (see p. 130 below) protect the walls; the distance between them is such that attackers are always within easy reach of archers mounted in the towers. The five main gates are also protected by round towers. Their irregular distribution is due to strategic considerations, but can be partially explained by the road layout. The stone of the walls has partly been bossified, both to reduce the effects of projectiles hitting it and partly to symbolize strength and the ability to defend the castle. Other characteristics of the castle are its crenellations along the battlements and the machicolations on the towers, which are not, however, systematically incorporated into the battlements, as was customary in fourteenth century buildings such as the papal palace in Avignon. A road runs along the town side of the castle wall to maintain the flexibility of the defenses. Wide flights of steps leading up to the gate and corner towers made it easy to

gain access to the battlements quickly. Although the emphasis appears to be solely on the military aspect, talented sculptors were also employed to decorate the château. Confirmation that artists from the north of France were sent down south for this major royal project can be seen in the structure of the keystones of the upper stories of the towers which flank the gate. These highly decorative keystones are ornamented with leaves. The carefully planned defense system, the regularity of the plan as a whole, and not least the high quality of the individual carvings, such as the rib vault and keystones, make Aigues-Mortes one of the earliest and most complete examples of royal military architecture introduced into the south from northern France, after the annexation of Provence.

There is an impressive view of the medieval château from the D 979 heading south. Here the saltworks, the *Salines du Midi,* can be visited and there is an exhibition on the history and methods of salt-harvesting.

Salt Harvesting

Along with life-sustaining table salt (sodium chloride), the Mediterranean also contains a high percentage of other salts such as magnesium sulfate and magnesium chloride. Between the ninth and fourteenth centuries techniques were developed for separating the various salts. In the Midi, however, the only technique used is evaporation through warmth and wind of the seawater which is channeled into the shallow salt basins. This produces the concentration, saturation, and ultimately the crystallization of the harvested salt.

As each of the salts precipitates at different degrees of saturation, those salts which precipitate before the table salt can be extracted as the salt concentration gradually increases. Then the liquid with dissolved salts, such as magnesium chloride and magnesium sulfate which remains when the sodium chloride has crystallized, can be removed. The degree of saturation is measured using the Baumé scale, a hygrometric measurement; table salt crystallizes at a very high concentration (25 Bé) and can be gathered using rakes. It is then dried and refined. It is essential for the process that the salt concentration is precisely controlled through the size and depth of the salt-pans and by correcting the effects of other sources of water, such as rain.

Salines-de-Giraud
Salt heaps

Two Thousand Years of High-Tech

Nîmes, Uzès, and the Pont-du-Gard

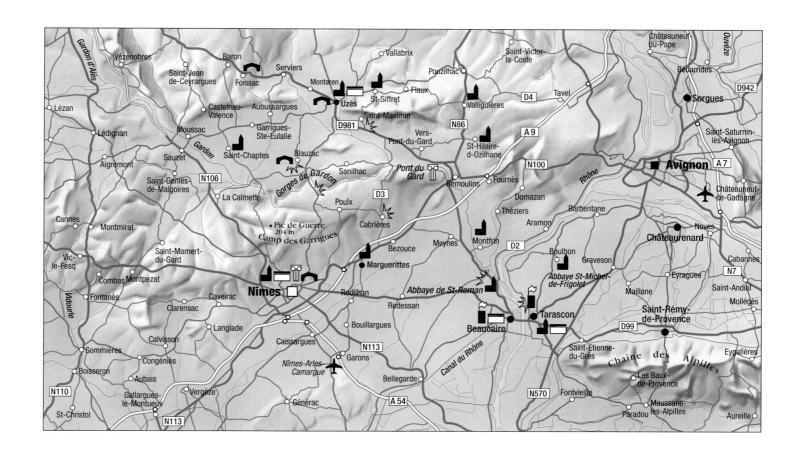

Nîmes

In the fourth century BC, the Volci tribe possessed a significant territory with 24 settlements and a capital city called Nemausus. When the Romans conquered the land, they did the same as in other large cities, in that veterans from the legions were settled here, some of whom had served in Egypt. Coins from this time period, depicting a chained crocodile, reflect the history of the new residents.

Augustus raised the settlement to the status of a colony in 27 BC, giving it the name of Colonia Augusta Nemausus. Under Augustus, the city also received an outer wall and a lavish infrastructure, complete with monumental public buildings. In the second century, the city flourished. The fact that the city was an important administrative center was one of the reasons why it had a bishop as early as the third century. The Teutonic invasions of the fifth century, combined with a general deterioration in the communal fabric, caused a number of residents to move into the countryside. The exodus from the city continued over the centuries. When the French crown annexed Languedoc in 1229, Nîmes became French, but fulfilled no administrative function; the administrative seats were set up in Beaucaire, Carcassonne, and Toulouse.

The Huguenots made for some of the city's best citizens in the sixteenth century. Like Geneva, Nîmes set itself up as a independent city of the Reformation which led to continuous fighting between Protestants and Catholics, and much bloodshed. In the fifteenth century, the city became a center of the textile industry.

Nîmes is currently one of the fastest expanding and most progress-conscious cities in France with a focus on high-tech industry and the tertiary sector. Numerous architects have received major commissions to build avant-garde projects, such as Jean Nouvel's Nemausus apartment complex in the south of the city, on the Boulevard du Général Leclerc and Norman Foster's Carré d'Art (see p.140).

Despite its excellently maintained monuments, Nîmes is not a great tourist attraction and has few places of interest dating from medieval or post-Renaissance times. The city is much more of a pulsating business center, yet one whose Mediterranean climate effectively prevents it from being devoted exclusively to Mammon. The bullfights which are held here three times a year (at Easter, the wine harvest in September, and in February) make it clear that the French capital is far away.

The Roman Nemausus was not built on the grid system, but rather according to the roads which meet here, all of which lead to the forum. The most important traffic route, the Via Domitia, stretched from Arles to Narbonne. Sixty towers were spaced along the Roman city wall that followed the contour of the landscape. In the twelfth century the wall was reinforced, but then leveled in 1786 and replaced by the boulevards.

The sights described below are listed in a clockwise direction, with the ancient monuments along the boulevards first, then moving into the narrow lanes of the old city.

The Amphitheater

The imposing amphitheater (see p.137), one of the best surviving examples of its kind, was built at the end of the first century AD, at the same time as the Arena in Arles and the Colosseum in Rome. With the decline and disappearance of Roman rule, it was occupied by the western Goths who expanded the giant structure into a fortress. During the Middle Ages, houses were built inside the arena, making it a distinct neighborhood of the city which even had its own church, Notre-Dame-des-Arènes. Charles VI built a castle here (in 1391) which was connected to the Porte d'Auguste. In the following centuries, many houses were built on the seating tiers of the arena. The immense building forms an oval 443 ft (133 m) long, 336 ft (101 m) wide and 70 ft (21 m) high. The 60 rounded-arch arcades are set off by massive Tuscan pillars on the ground floor; on the floor above, Tuscan pillars are placed on high pedestals. Only broken remnants remain of the attic, or top floor. In some places brackets remain with holes for the masts of sunshades. The whole

1 Amphitheater
2 Cathedral of St-Castor
3 Musée du Vieux Nîmes
4 Archeological Museum
5 St-Baudille
6 Porte d'Auguste
7 Birthplace of Alphonse Daudet
8 Building with Romanesque Façade
9 Maison Carrée
10 Museum of Contemporary Art (Carrée d'Art)
11 St-Paul
12 Musée des Beaux-Arts
13 Fontaine Pradier
14 Roman fortress
15 Tour Magne
16 Temple of Diana

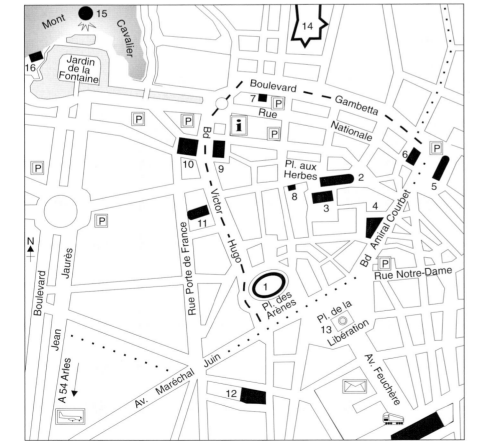

Nîmes, Uzès, Pont-du-Gard

building is reinforced by a cleverly designed system of barrel-vaulted radial tunnels. These lead to a total of 162 staircases and 124 entrances and exits, enabling a smooth flow of human traffic for the 25,000 spectators which the arena could accommodate. Depending on the social position of the visitor, the seating was divided into three levels. The first level, reserved for honorary citizens, consisted of four rows; ten rows made up the next level. The oval arena with a length of 230 ft (69 m) is separated from the spectators by a high wall. Beneath the sandy soil on which the arena is built, there are two intersecting tunnels that served for the erection and installation of scenery.

The amphitheater did not serve merely as a functional building. Its sheer size caused the city to expand radically, and was a concrete manifestation of the might of the Roman empire, proof of its achievement and ability to construct monumental buildings.

Nîmes
Amphitheater, late
1st century AD
Aerial view (above)
Detail of external walls (left)

Gladiator fights and Bullfights

In Antiquity, gladiatorial combat was staged in the amphitheaters. Beginning in the first century BC., under the Roman Empire, citizens were encouraged to attend these performances as a way of exercising control while offering the citizens diversions to keep them happy. The gladiators were mostly major criminals or prisoners of war, though a few freemen also took plart. The gladiators were kept in special barracks and trained in swordplay and other gladiatorial skills. Later, a variety of other types of gladiatorial combatants were introduced. The *Retiarii* used a net and trident and the *Laquearii* used a lasso and stave; they fought single-handed or sometimes in groups. The *Bestiarii* had to fight wild animals to the death. If the organizer of the games liked a combattant, he had a fighting chance of survival. The signal to end the combat, given by the organizer, was the "thumbs up" sign. Today, the ancient amphitheaters of Provence are used to stage bullfights. In the mid-19th century, Spanish-style bullfighting came to southern France, to such provincial cities as Nîmes and Arles, where it competed with the traditional bullrunning (*Bious*) of the Camargue. The bloodthirsty *corridas* follow a classic pattern. The mounted *Picadores* stick long lances into the bull then the *Bandilleros* place short staves in its back. The irritated bull then has to face the *torero*, who provokes it by waving the *muleta*, the small cape, in front of it, eventually killing it with his sword. In Provence, the less bloodthirsty version of the bullfight is generally preferred, where the aim is to remove the paper flower, the cockade, from between the bull's horns. The fighters are called *écarteurs* and *sauteurs* maneuver their way around the animal, usually a cow, or jump over it keeping as close to it as possible. The bullrunning *Ferias* are not limited to the arenas, the animals are allowed to run right through the town, sometimes in herds.

The Maison Carrée

The Maison Carrée adds an additional, exceptionally preserved Roman building to the city (see above). The temple was a part of the forum, connected to it by a three-winged colonnade on a rectangular plinth. The Roman curia may have stood at the far end of the rectangular site facing the Maison Carée. This former temple was called the Capitol in the Middle Ages and beyond, because it served from the eleventh to the sixteenth century as the administrative seat of the city fathers, who were called Capitouls. It was put to many other uses but during the French Revolution it was given to the city. The building was first renovated then converted into a museum. Today, many contemporary art exhibitions are held in the Maison Carrée. The holes in the stonework to hold the fixing for the bronze letters on the frieze of the façade make it possible to reconstruct the inscription which says that the temple was dedicated to the grandchildren of Augustus. A few years later, more text was added

to state that the two brothers had been deified. In light of this evidence, the temple must have been completed between 3-2 BC.

Although the absolute dimensions of the temple are small (51 ft (15.5 m) wide, 88 ft (26.4 m) long, 56 ft (17 m) high above the podium), the building has a significant and effective monumental quality combined with a plastic energy. It is an impressive example of a Roman plinth temple and demonstrates the skill of the architect and builders. The temple stands on a 15-step plinth. The façade consists of six fluted columns supporting a triangular pediment. There is a bas-relief climbing-frieze on the entablature and lavishly decorated consoles on the eaves. All of this is makes the Maison Carrée an outstanding example of early Roman Empire style, and shows that concepts and workshops were exported into the Roman province.

The plan of a temple framed by a colonnaded portico and raised on a plinth or podium has its

Nîmes
Maison Carrée
completed in 3 or 2 BC.

OPPOSITE:
Nîmes
Temple of Diana,
1st to 2nd century (above)
Tour Magne
1st century (below)

Nîmes
Norman Foster
Carré d'Art
Façade with forecourt (above)
and interior view (below right)

parallel in the Forum of Augustus in Rome. However, in Nîmes, the columned hall on the Cella walls continues only as a blind structure (*pseudoperipteros*). There are other similarities with the Augustinian building in Rome, for instance in the outstanding Corinthian capitals. However, local workshops who were not so skilled as those of Rome were also obviously trained to copy the Roman examples, explaining the poorer quality of some of the capitals.

Carré d'Art

Next to the antique temple, the Carré d'Art exhibition hall designed by the British architect Norman Foster is a successful, modern and innovative interpretation of the Roman masterpiece. The cubic structure, the plan of a high portico supported on slender pillars, and the monochrome coloring are all counterpoints to the design of the temple. The architect invites the public to enter, because the building appears to be composed of one gigantic, see-through, glass staircase running the entire height of the building as the central motif, leading to the exhibition and administration rooms. The permanent collection concentrates mainly on contemporary art (Martial Raysse, Arman, Jean Tinguely, Gerhard Richter, Christian Boltanski) and is supplemented by temporary

exhibitions which are frequently changed. The museum concentrates on three main subject areas: French art since 1960, the Anglo-American and German art scenes, and the *Identité méditerranéenne*. There is a magnificent view from roof terrace, including an usual view of the Maison Carrée.

The Temple of Diana in Jardin de la Fontaine

Around the Celtic holy springs of Nemausus at the foot of Mont Cavalier, the Romans constructed the building also used for the veneration of the water-sprites, which is now known as the Temple of Diana (see right). The buildings that were once responsible for the whole of the city's water supply have disappeared, except for the large auditorium. This served from the tenth through the sixteenth centuries as a church. In antiquity, the building was not a temple dedicated to Diana, but rather a part of the *nymphaeum*, that was built about 166 ft (50 m) east of the spring. The wings of the building extend to the left and right of it, but little is known of their purpose. The small, main auditorium was an architectural structure consisting of a row of columns on a pedestal. The wall, in front of which they stood, contains rectangular niches topped with porches. The barrel-vaulted ceiling rests on an entablature that is composed by five cross-vaults, between which stone paneling slabs were held in place in grooves. The Romanesque master-builders must have seen such vault construction and copied it in their cross-reinforced, longitudinal vaulting, a style that began in the eleventh century.

The spring to the north of the auditorium today supplies the parks and wells of the city with water. Between 1739-60, the engineers or architects, Jacques-Philippe Maréchal and Esprit Dardalhon, redesigned the area, which had hitherto remained intact, by landscaping it as a large park (see p.142-43), into which they integrated the ancient ruins. An important part of this beautiful and comprehensive remodeling of the city is the grand main street, the Avenue Jean Jaurés, that was aligned parallel with the Jardin de la Fontaine.

The Tour Magne

The Tour Magne (see right) is on the summit of Mont Cavalier. It is a four-sided tower originally standing at a height of about 120 ft (36 m), which was once part of the pre-Roman defenses. Under Augustus, the tower was reinforced, heightened, and included into the new city defenses, of which 30 defense towers around the old city still survive, though in poor condition. Earlier stairways, still visible in the bases, can be seen on the accessible ground floor. The pour-wall technique that holds broken stone masonry on the outside and inside is clearly visible. In addition to this, ashlar was also laid in order to reinforce the courses. From the top, there is a grand view of the city and the areas beyond. East of the Tour Magne, the so-called Castellum has survived, marking the terminus of the great Roman water course which ran from the Cévennes (Pont du Gard). A round cistern contained 10 lead water pipes of about 16 in (40 cm) in diameter and distributed water to various wells in the city.

Nîmes
Jardin de la Fontaine
In the 18th century it was
turned into a baroque garden
among the ruins. Rainwater
falling in the Garrigue runs underground and emerges here
as a spring. In antiquity, there
was a shrine here to the water-
sprite. This was the first public
park in France.

143

Nîmes
Cathedral of Notre-Dame and St-Castor, detail of the 12th-century façade

The Porte d'Auguste

The Porte d'Auguste in the north-east corner of the old city is a typical example of a Roman city gateway, such as the Porta Nigra in Trier. The Via Domitia passes through two large arches into a courtyard, from which there are two further entrances to the city. There were special entrances for pedestrians. Outside the gates of the city, two semi-circular watchtowers built into the wall protected the approaches.

The Jesuit Church

The Jesuits moved into the city in 1596, but due to the resistance of the Huguenots, were forced to leave in 1621. In 1629, a compromise was reached, whereby an equal amount of education was given to Protestants and Jesuits. In 1673, the engineer Mathieu de Morgues built the Jesuit church and college. The church is a typical single-aisle Jesuit church with recessed galleries and a flat cupola emphasizing the altar area. The former Jesuit college is now occupied by the natural history and archaeological museums. The archeological museum contains many finds from the city's Celtic and Roman past, as well as life-size reconstructions of a Gaulish and a Roman dwelling.

The Cathedral of Notre-Dame et St-Castor

The current building stands upon Roman foundations. In the seventh century, a group of three churches was built on the site, Notre-Dame, St-Etienne, and the baptistry of St-Jean. A new episcopal church was begun in the twelfth century and completed in stages. The church, heavily damaged in the Wars of Religion, was restored in the seventeenth century. In the 1890s, Revoil completely revamped the building in the Romano-Byzantine style so that almost nothing of the original building exists except for the façade on the west side. Only the lower half and the tower date from the original twelfth century construction. The portico was rebuilt in the seventeenth century. It is topped by a mutilated relief frieze depicting Samson with his lions, Zachariah with a sacrifice, and Alexander the Great riding on a gryphon. The upper part of the façade is decorated with a carved frieze containing 17 panels, six of which are medieval (see left). These show scenes from Genesis (the temptation of Adam, the fall from grace, the banishment from the garden, and Cain killing Abel). The city's local history museum is housed in the former bishop's palace.

Next to the amphitheater, there is a statue of the personification of Nîmes surrounded by the Esplanade de Gaulle (see below). The statue was sculpted by James Pradier (1790-1852) in 1848. Further south, the Musée des Beaux-Arts has a new exhibition room created by J.-M. Wilmotte in 1986. Roman mosaics, as well a paintings of the fifteenth through the nineteenth centuries, including works by Bassano, Rubens, and Seghers as well as numerous sculptures by James Pradier make for a large and interesting collection. Pradier was one of the most successful sculptors of the reign of the citizen-king Louis-Philippe. In addition to his allegorical figure representing Nîmes, the artist also produced similar statues for Lille and Strasbourg. The statues on the Place de la Concorde in Paris are also his work.

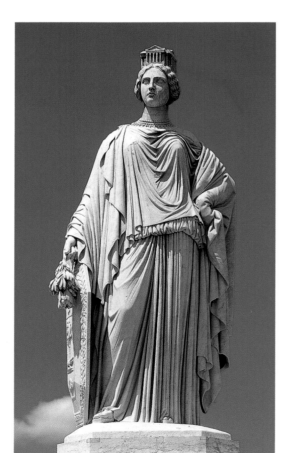

Nîmes
James Pradier
Personification of the city
Nîmes, 1848

OPPOSITE:
Uzès
Cathedral (mainly 17th century) with the 12th century Tour Fenestrelle

Uzès
Cathedral, exterior and interior (above)
View of the city and surrounding landscape (right)

Uzès

One of the most exciting cities of western Provence lies a little further away on a hilltop. The Roman city of Utetia was primarily a military outpost, raised to the status of a bishopric by the fifth century at the latest. The line of the medieval city wall can still be discerned in the line of the boulevards. This shows that Uzès was a rather large city, whose temporal administration was raised to the status of vice-dukedom under Philippe VI in 1328. In 1565, its status was raised once more to that of a dukedom, finally receiving the status of Pairie in 1572. The city had converted to Protestantism in 1546 and remained a Protestant stronghold until Louis XIII symbolically entered it.

With the abolition of the Edict of Nantes, a number of the Protestant residents were forced to leave and the city suffered the consequences. The Industrial Revolution of the nineteenth century largely passed Uzès by, nor did it benefit from the growing tourism industry. Today, the city has the advantage that its medieval structure, accentuated with large Renaissance and Baroque buildings, has been retained in good condition. The summer festivities, especially the musical events, are a particular attraction.

Uzès has played a major part in the history of French literature in two ways. In 1661 Jean Racine, at the age of 22, lived here for a year with his uncle who wanted him to enter into the priesthood. He returned to Paris, however, and resumed his career as a playwright. The father and uncle of the poet and playwright, André Gide (1869-1951) also hailed from Uzès.

The oldest and tallest building in the city is the 140 ft (42 m) cathedral belltower, the Tour Fenestrelle, which dates from the twelfth century (see p.145 upper left). Its walls gradually expand upward into double arcades of columns.

The tower itself was always a free-standing campanile on top of a circular foundation, pierced with openings right up to the top. Both these characteristics seem to have been imported from northern Italy or copied from similar buildings in the Pyrenees.

The church building itself was renovated between 1645-60. A transept divides the three-aisled main part of the church exactly in half. The central position of the transept is well accentuated by the connecting bays covered with rectangular ribbed vaulting, while the extremes of the apse and choir have intersecting rectangular vaulting. The middle transept and the simple ordering of the pilasters of this early Baroque structure is reminiscent of northern French architecture of the time, such as the church of Sorbonne in Paris. The ribbed vaults, however, perpetuate the medieval tradition.

The church of St-Etienne, at the edge of the old city, was based on the plans of Pierre Boudon and built between 1765-78, to replace an older building which had been damaged in the Wars of Religion. The tower on the north side of the rebuilt church is based on the design of its predecessor. The ground plan and facade of the new building resembles the Baroque church of Notre-Dame-des-Pommiers in Beaucaire.

The Ducal Palace (Le Duché)

The Ducal Palace, in the city center, has the air of being a frigid military fortification rather than a château. It is mostly medieval in construction. The oldest part of the château is the Tour Bermonde in the southwest corner, a 143 ft (43 m) high castle keep (*donjon*) the lower part of which may date from the eleventh century. To the east lies the Logis de la Vicomté which includes a late-medieval chapel tower that was refurbished in the nineteenth century. For architectural historians, the wing between the chapel tower and the Tour Bermonde is of the most interest (see above). Its façade was designed in the last quarter of the sixteenth century by Philibert de l'Orme, one of the most important Renaissance architects in France. The showy frontage is emphasized by wide windows with narrow columns and cartouches. It is three stories high and the columns are in the sequence required at the time, of Doric, Ionic, and Corinthian orders. This is the earliest façade in France to use the

Uzès
Ducal Palace (Duché)
Late 16th-century Renaissance wing, between the Tour Bermonde and the church tower.

ABOVE AND LEFT:
Uzès
Place aux Herbes

Nîmes, Uzès, Pont-du-Gard

classic arrangement of the orders. The clarity and plasticity of the regular design as well as the large size of the elements are based on north Italian and northern French models.

At the southern aspect of the palace, the vicomte erected another symbol of his temporal power next to the Tour Bermonde, the Tour de l'Horloge (see left)—the clock-tower whose bell regulates the life in the city. Not far away was once the symbol of the competing institution of authority: one of the king's châteaux. Today only the quadrilateral Tour du Roi is left. The city hall, built in 1773, adjoins the north side of the château courtyard. The courtyard thus links the Duché with the boulevards.

The town's central square is the Place aux Herbes, lined with seventeenth-century arcades (see p.148). In many parts of the city, the sixteenth-century Renaissance façades imitate the court façade of the Duché. These include the Hôtel de Joubert et d'Avéjan at the end of the Rue de la République, and the Hôtel Dampmartin in the square of the same name.

The Garrigue

The Garrigue is a geological formation in southern France that was once covered with forests, but today consists of almost entirely defoliated crags of sandstone and shale hills. Small islands of vegetation consisting of shrubs, wild herbs, lavender, and broom, grow between the hills, thus creating the spicy fragrance usually associated with Provence.

The Garrigue
near Pouzilhac

LEFT:
Uzès
Tour de l'Horloge from the south frontage of the Duché (the ducal palace)

PAGES 150-51
The Pont du Gard

PAGES 152-53:
The Gorges du Gardon

Pont du Gard

Because the Nemausus spring did not supply a enough water to the city of Nîmes, the Romans built a water course in 20 BC during the reign of Agrippa, the son-in-law of Augustus. This 31 mile (50 km) long aqueduct brought water from the Eure spring near Uzès into the Cévennes. A giant viaduct spans the Gard valley which cuts deeply at some points into the rocky cliffs at each side. The bridge construction is one of the most famous examples of the Roman art of engineering. Yet the viaduct is not the only amazing technical feat of the water system. In some places the water runs through tunnels up to 1333 ft (400 m) long (mostly between Vers and Nîmes), as well as over six additional bridges. The difference in height between the beginning and the end of the system is only 56 ft (17 m), making for a meticulously calculated gradient of 17-56 cm per kilometer (about 6-22 inches per half mile). The gradient is steeper the closer it gets to the Pont du Gard, thus making it unnecessary to construct a longer and higher aqueduct.

The construction has survived in such good condition, because it remained in use for such a long time despite calcification of the water basin and inadequate maintenance. The water first stopped flowing due to limescale in the ninth century. By the Middle Ages at the latest, a road was laid on top of the first tier of arches. The pillars on the second tier were drilled to make way for a highway. In the first half of the nineteenth century, it was planned to restore the entire water system, which produced an exact measurement of the Roman construction. The dimensions are staggering. The water is channeled over the Gard at a height of almost 163 ft (49 m) and length of nearly 1,000 ft (275 m). Three tiers of arches had to be built, the uppermost tier consisting of numerous small arches. The width of the tiers decreases from 21 ft (6.36 m) at the base to just over 10 ft (3.06 m) at the uppermost tier of arches through which the water was channeled. The lower arch directly above the flow of the river has the largest span: 81 ft (24.5 m). Not a single medieval vault spans such a width! The lower arches are made from giant blocks of drystone whose sheer weight holds them together. In the section above, the stone blocks are smaller but are stabilized with giant stones spaced at intervals of about four courses.

The brackets on the arches are of interest. This is where the scaffolding was attached for the construction of the arches; later these same brackets were used for attaching scaffolding for making repairs. The water trough was once 4 ft (1.2 m) wide and almost 6 ft 8 in (2 m) deep, but calcification significantly reduced the depth and diameter. When first put into service, the aqueduct could deliver 66,000 cu ft (20,000 cu m) of water to Nîmes every day.

From the Land of Ocher to the Wooded Heights

Cavaillon, the Vaucluse highlands, and the Luberon

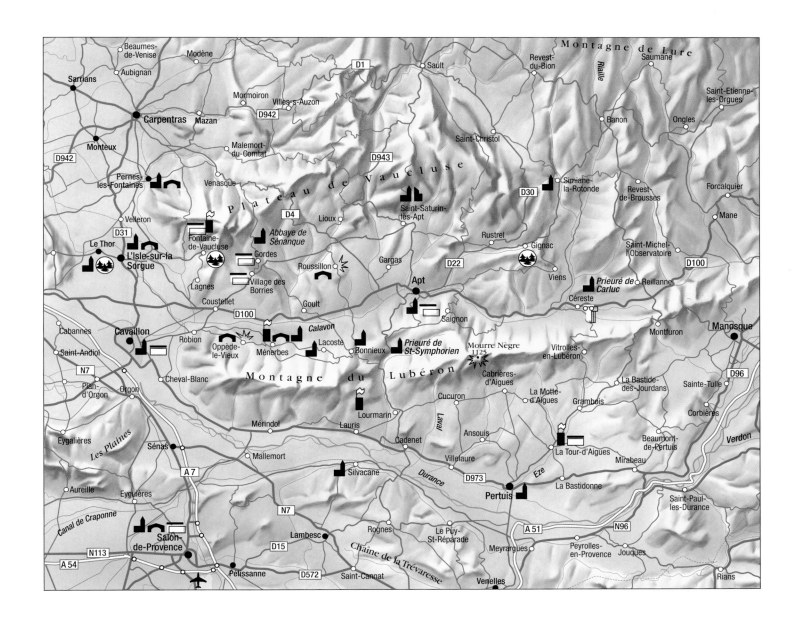

Cavaillon
Arched gateway, part of the original Roman monumental arches at the entrance to the city.

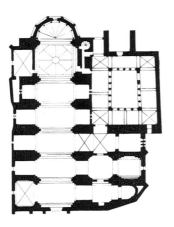

Cavaillon
Cathedral of St-Véran, first third of the 12th century. Apse and ground plan

Cavaillon

In prehistoric times the Celtic tribe of the Cavars lived on the hill of St-Jacques and traded with the Greeks in Massalia. The Romans settled at the foot of the hill in the 1st century BC and named the place Cabellio. The city converted to Christianity at an early date and from the fourth century had its own bishop. Since the city was part of the Comtat Venaissin, in 1274 it became a vassal of the Pope and was ruled up until the revolution by a bishop, together with a papal governor. The importance of Cavaillon has always lain in the surrounding orchards, and fruit production has been important since the Middle Ages. As early as 1235 the fields were artificially irrigated, and today the melons of Cavaillon are famous throughout Europe. The city today is more spread out, although the original town plan, consisting of buildings of several stories, has been retained to a seemingly uniform extent. The plane trees that turned the boulevards into shady avenues were cut down in the 1980s because they allegedly interfered with traffic—a mistake that will, hopefully, never be made again.

The Roman gate at the Place du Clos, stands as the singular proof of the antiquity of the site (see above). The two arches were originally made for a four-sided gate. The interior consisted of hip-vaulting made from two interpenetrating barrel arches. The arch originally stood in the forum but was moved to its current location in 1880. The decoration shows that the monument was completed in late Augustinian times, as were similar constructions in St-Rémy and Carpentras.

The Cathedral of St-Véran

The cathedral St-Véran was built in the first third of the twelfth century and has undergone few alterations or changes since then. Only a restoration in the nineteenth century introduced some pseudo-Roman sculptures and extensive painting. The apse (see lower left) is an impressive example of how the Romanesque master builders not only considered the decorative forms, but also combined the "classical" proportions of the blind arcades with the Roman building tradition. The classical model of the capitals is extensively varied in the leaf ornamentation. The quadrilateral tower above the cupola bay is set above a round tambour, unusual in Provence, in which the inside of the cupola is placed.

The interior (see below) also makes clear how exactly the Roman building was added to. The one-aisled structure is roofed with reinforced barrel-vaulting that originally rested upon stepped, blind arcades in the side-aisles. A Provençal peculiarity—as in Arles and Aix— is the siting of columns beneath the vaults. The blind arcades were opened up as early as the thirteenth century in order to add capitals. In the cupola bay, there are cartouches with (renovated) depictions of the Evangelists that continue into the quadrilateral tambour. The eight-sided cupola is outlined by ribbing, a style found elsewhere in Provence at this time. The small cloister on the south side is similar to a simplified version of the marvelous design in Arles, and Montmajour. The barrel-vaulting is replaced in some places by rib-vaulting.

The Synagogue

The synagogue was built in 1772-73 and is the third Jewish building to stand on this site. During the last alteration it received a beautiful Rococo façade. The rectangular prayer-room on the upper floor has an older foundation wall. The entire interior is elaborately furnished, much in the style of Louis XV salon. The ark is a niche containing a chest in which the Scrolls

Cavaillon
Cathedral of St-Véran
Interior looking east

OPPOSITE:
Landscape around Cavaillon

of the Law are kept. "Elijah's chair" on which the male children are presented before they are circumcised, stands raised on a large corner console. On the lower floor, there is the bakery where the *matzo* (unleavened bread) is baked.

The chapel of the hospital built in 1753 by J.H. Mollard is now a museum which not only contains beautiful works of art but also historical accounts of Cavaillon and its surrounding area. The climb to the small Roman chapel of St-Jacques (see right), on the site of a former Celtic settlement, is well worth the effort.

Le Thor

This little town possesses one of the most interesting church buildings of the late Provençal Romanesque period. Notre-Dame-du-Lac was build around 1200 and has hardly been altered since, except for the octagonal belfry which was added in 1834. The most striking features of the building (see left below) are its tall, narrow shape and extending buttresses. This is created by two ceiling vaults staggered on top of each other in the nave. The roof rests on the extensive pointed barrel-vaulting, intermixed with rib-vaulting, whose weight is absorbed by the massive buttresses.

The portico on the south side offers a rich expenditure of classical decoration whose deployment affects one differently as in other Provençal buildings. This is caused by the rib-vaulting made from powerful pointed, protruding ribs. The four-windowed interior (see left below) shows how well the rib's harmonize with the interior. The vaulting was certainly not added later, because the buttresses

are connected to the masonry work. The rib-vaulting is a sign of borrowing from the northern French gothic which stands out in an otherwise Romanesque building. Just how strongly the church relies upon local traditions is made evident by the basic attribute, such as the single-aisled nave, the quadrilateral cupola with trompe and depictions or symbols of the Evangelists.

The apse demonstrates how old building techniques were modernized. The blind arcades and the ribbed vaulting that adorn this part of the church are not unusual. However, the shaft rings on the extended columns and the finely profiled ribs that meet on a capstone decorated with the Lamb of God are innovations.

Fontaine de Vaucluse

The Sorgue spring winds through a steep valley containing a picturesque town containing a twelfth-century Romanesque church. It also offers a unique natural phenomenon that has yet to be entirely explained, a spring that gushes out of the earth, shooting upward like a manmade fountain.

The cliffs which overhang the valley are deeply fissured and potholed, with at one end of the valley, a cave on the lower face of the steep escarpment. The water level changes in the course of the year, rising rapidly in the Spring and pouring down the valley in a rushing cascade. Rainwater seeping through fissures, ravines, and cavities from a catchment area of 775 sq. miles (1240 sq. km), collects at the source of the spring, which lies

OPPOSITE AND RIGHT:
Le Thor
Notre-Dame-du-Lac (ca. 1200)
General view of the east part with transept tower and view looking eastward

Cavaillon
12th-century Romanesque chapel of St-Jacques

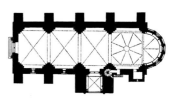

Le Thor
Notre-Dame-du-Lac
Structure of the choir
Viollet le Duc (above)
ground plan

Sénanque
Cloister (above); northern corner of the monastery cloister (opposite)
Ground plan (below)

ON PAGES. 162-63
Sénanque
Monastery church from the east (p. 162)
View of the transept (p. 163)

Fontaine de Vaucluse

deep down. The water filters through the porous limestone until it reaches a layer of waterproof clay 1026 ft (308 m) below ground level. The water at the bottom of this shaft is forced to the surface because it cannot flow out of the underground streams which feed it, some of which are 2223 ft (667 m) long. The spring which gushes out in a natural fountain was famous even in ancient times and Strabo, Seneca, and Pliny the Elder mention it in their writings. Petrarch chose the Fontaine de Vaucluse as his country seat and lived there for 36 years. The fountain has been scientifically researched. In 1985, Jochen Haselmeyer, a German diver,explored the spring, setting a world record in free diving by reaching a depth of 683 ft (205 m).

There are several interesting sights to see on the way to the fountain, such as a museum of the history of the German Occupation and the Resistance Movement 1940-45, as well as a cave museum, and a paper mill.

Sénanque

In 1148, bishop Alfant of Cavaillon was responsible for founding a Cistercian monastery on a large estate received from the local nobles of Gordes. The monks, who were brought from Mazan, choose a location in a wooded valley on the Sénancole stream which they dammed up. Supported by the lords of Venasque, the monastery rapidly flourished and became an important center in the midst of an agricultural district. After the thirteenth century, as the cities began to grow and the friars of the mendicant orders were less expensive for burials, the importance of Sénanque began to sink. In the fifteenth century, when some signs of prosperity began to return, the monastery fell victim to a revolt by the Waldensians (see p.179), a heretic sect. After the French Revolution, the monastery was sold, but in 1854 it was restored to the Cistercians. The anti-clerical policies of the French state forced them to abandon it again on numerous occasions before monastic life could finally be taken up again in 1989.

The Cistercian monastery, together with its fellow monasteries of Silvacane and Le Thoronet are among the most famous buildings in Provence (see right). The setting, among lavender fields on the heights of Vaucluse, is a perfect one; the clear arrangement and the geometrical proportions of the building, whose individual parts combine with a visible, technical perfection, is uncluttered by superfluous decoration.

This absence of sculpture and carving is not to be attributed to lack of financial resources. The reform order, founded by Robert of Molesme in the late eleventh century, revived the strict rule of St. Bernard with the monks living according to the Cistercian principles of asceticism. The structure also eliminates such unnecessary additions as towers and turrets and distracting pictorial or sculptural decoration. The perfect masonry of the cloister building, with its precisely fitting stones thereby guaranteeing a straightforward solidarity and longevity was at least as difficult to produce as elaborate carving and painting.

The monastery plan is ordered in such a way that the church points to the north. The plan allows the church to be at the highest point of the monastery and at the same time allows a part of the convent building to run alongside the stream in order to utilize the water. The church buildings were only accessible from the outside, through small porches intended for laymen, because the monks themselves had direct access to the church from the convent buildings via a pathway, almost identical with today's visitor's pathway from the monastery buildings to the church.

The monastery church is a three-aisled basilica with a transept crowned with a

cross tower from which the choir apse and four connecting apses extend. Transept, cross, and side- walls of the nave (see right) belong to the first building phase around 1160. During the work on the nave (see opposite) a change occurred in the design around the end of the twelfth century. The middle aisle was set higher than was planned in order to make way for windows on the wall of the high aisle. The pilasters had to be reinforced in order to make them thicker than the transverse ones. The barrel-vaults of the side-aisles tilt upward and start higher than those over the side-walls of the nave. The pointed barrel construction is predominant. The nave and transept are vaulted with pointed barrel-vaulting and the arcades of the middle aisle are formed by slightly ogival arches. The geometrical right-angled pilasters and the vault pattern are fascinating. The standard rounded base of the pillars were clearly of lesser importance.

The chapels of the transept contain niches for the ritual objects on the right side. The wall-niche grave in the eastern part of the transept served as a resting place for the Simiane family, who had donated funds to the monastery, and for whose salvation the monks prayed.

The cloister (see p.160, top) which is laid over an almost square foundation, is one of the best preserved in Provence. The good condition is especially impressive because all of the passageways are so similar to each other. The three small arcades above double columns are framed by a mighty arch. This static system easily carries the barrel-vaults in the passageways. In contrast to the church's interior, there is elegant decoration here. The columns set upon beautiful bases display flat reliefs on the capitals made of fronds and climbing plants.

The north wing contains the chapter house, used for meetings and legal proceedings. The vaulted ceiling rests on pillars. The room was originally unvaulted, but was redesigned in the early thirteenth century. A monastery outbuilding is connected at the east end, which served as a scriptorium and warm room. Above it is the dormitory, which takes up the entire north wing. Both doors of the west wall gave access to a washroom placed directly over the stream.

The refectory, in the west wing, was badly damaged in the Waldensian attack of 1544, was restored in the seventeenth century, and finally converted into a chapel in the nineteenth century.

A large building, used to house converts and the lay brothers who lived and worked in the monastery but who were not allowed to officiate in the religious rites, was also added in the seventeenth century.

Gordes
General view of the village and château from a neighboring hill

Gordes

The small city of Gordes whose houses and gardens cling to the slopes of the rocky mountains is dominated by the château and church. This is one of the most picturesque landscapes in Provence (see above). The château was built between 1537 and 1541 by Bertrand de Simiane as a replacement for a twelfth century structure. The long building, with its massive round towers, is in the tradition of medieval fortifications. The clear division of the courtyard side into separate floors with windows of equal width in the same axis and the Renaissance proportions reveal an attempt to produce a showy façade. The Renaissance style which is again used at Lourmarin (see pp.182-3), is among the earliest in all of France.

Inside the château, a spiral staircase leads through an old tower to a large room with an imposing fireplace. Somewhat to the west of Gordes lies the village of the *bories* (see p.165). There are about twenty of these strange huts, built in various shapes, both square and round and covering 2½ acres (1 ha). The drystone construction even covers the roof, achieving stability by means of the flat limestone slabs that underpin them. Mortar is not necessary for this type of building technique; if the spaces were filled with grass or similar material, it was only to prevent drafts or to keep out insects, rodents, and birds. The careful drystone construction also avoids the need for rafters.

This type of stone hut is to be found throughout the Mediterranean area. In Apulia these huts are called *trulli*, *orris* in the Pyrenees and *casitats* in Spain. The huts were used by farmers as outbuildings for storage and as bread ovens, and by shepherds as sheep-folds. However, in the distant past they were inhabited by all types of countryfolk.

In Provence, bories were isolated and not grouped into communities, having neither church nor cemetery. The building technique has been handed down from the Neolithic period and continued right into the nineteenth century.

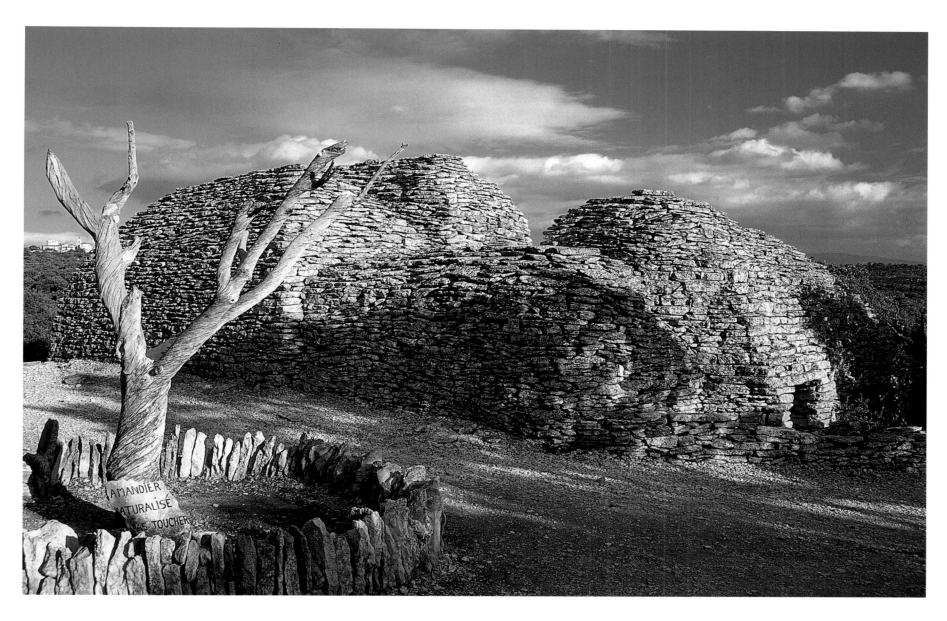

Les Bouillons

The D 2, D 103 and D 148 from Gordes to the south lead to the Bouillons oil-press. Preserved on a farmstead, this impressive structure stands in the middle of a park. Parts of it, such as the giant oak stump, date back to Gallo-Roman times.

Next to it, there is a museum devoted to the Glass artwork of Frédérique Duran where one can also learn about the history of stained glass.

Roussillon and the Surrounding Area

The beautiful village of Roussillon stands on a clifftop, surrounded by bright red and ocher slopes. These pigments are also reflected in the richly varied red and yellow tones of the plaster in the small hamlet. From the tiny eighteenth century city hall a street leads under the belltower to the cliff edge from which the view is magnificent. From Roussillon it is a short walk to the so-called "Provençal Colorado"–via Gargas, Rustrel, and Gignac–to see the way the ocher is constantly creating new formations (see also pp.174-75).

Les Bouillons
Oil press, part of which dates back to Gallo-Roman times

Ocher
Between St-Pantaléon and Gignac there is a 15-mile (25 km) stretch north of Apt where the ocher lies in strata 50 ft (15 m) wide. Ocher is a pigment of which ten per-cent is iron oxide, mixed with sand and clay. The intense color may vary through yellow, crimson lake, to reddish-brown, and even violet, making for a typically fantastic landscape. Ocher was exploited by the Romans and rediscovered in 1780 when a flourishing industry grew up here, to supply the textile and soap-making industries and the paper mills.
The processing of the sand is quite simple. It is first washed, to separate the sand from the oxides. The ore is then crushed, washed again and decanted into shallow basins. It is left to dry for a month, then crushed to fine powder. Ocher was replaced for most industrial purposes by chem-ical dyes after 1940.

OPPOSITE AND RIGHT:
Roussillon
Village with ocher cliffs

Pont St-Julien (near Apt)
1st century Roman stone bridge

Pont St-Julien

The Pont St-Julien is an almost completely intact Roman stone bridge spanning the river Coulon about 6 miles (10 km) west of Apt. The first century structure is still in use today. Three wide-span arches carry the road that climbs upward on both sides. The center arch is higher to allows boats to pass beneath it. The porthole-like openings in the arch spandrels allow water to flow away more quickly when the river is in spate.

Apt

Apt was a colony in Roman times, known as Apta Julia. In the third century, the city became a bishopric. It was completely destroyed by barbarian invasions between the seventh and ninth centuries, but began to recover in the eleventh century. Apt's history was fraught with difficulties, however. After a brief period of prosperity in the reign of the Avignon Popes, the town suffered greatly in the Wars of Religion and finally from the Plague of 1720. Improvements in agriculture in the nineteenth century were offset by the fact that the railroad did not come to Apt, dashing the hopes of the residents. Even though Apt is known today as the "capital of candied fruits," its painful past should not be forgotten.

The Cathedral of Sainte-Anne

The cathedral building stands to the north of the old Roman forum. At the beginning of the fifth century, a church was built on top of the old forum basilica but which fell into complete disrepair in the ninth century. The bishop's seat was located in the church of St-Pierre until the mid-eleventh century. At this time, rebuilding work recommenced on the cathedral but was soon postponed again after the completion of the current nave in the third quarter of the twelfth century. Around 1200, a side-nave was added to the south, matched by one to the north in the fourteenth century.

In accordance with Mansart's plans, a chapel of St. Anne was built on the north side around 1660. Unfortunately, the exterior of the building has been largely spoiled and the interior is an accretion of various styles from different periods.

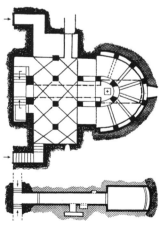

Apt
Cathedral of Ste-Anne
Ground plan of the upper and lower crypt.

In the eighteenth century, the Roman barrel-vaulting and apse vaulting were adorned with ribbed vaults and part of the building was covered with stucco. The original twelfth-century church is a one-aisled construction which originally had three window-bays, a transept (see below) and three east apses (of which the southernmost is preserved). Some exceptional features deserve to be mentioned, such as the fourteenth century stained glass in the apse, depicting Mary with the infant Jesus and Anne, flanked by Pope Urban V and Raymond Bot, the bishop of Apt. There is also a Romanesque altar in the south apse and a sarcophagus (ca. 400) from Arles in a chapel on the north side. The chapel of St. Anne contains a treasury, in which there are some valuable liturgical volumes.

Under the transept and center apse there are two interesting crypts (see below right). The original upper crypt, dating back to the mid-twelfth century, lies above a transverse anteroom that connects to a gallery crypt to the east. In the apse, there is a pre-Romanesque table altar. The ground plan, and the excellent masonry work which displays large stonemason's symbols show a link to the upper crypt, in a manner that closely resembles that of the underchurch of Montmajour. It is interesting to note that in Apt, worshippers once had access to the crypts through side-entrances.

To the east of the upper crypt there is an entrance to the lower crypt. A short tunnel leads to a rectangular chamber which is lined with Gallo-Roman masonry in the east, part of the basilica in the old Roman forum. The under crypt is one of the earliest Christian structures in Apt, possibly the burial chamber of the bishops Auspicius and Castor.

The former bishop's palace (ca. 1780) serves today as the seat of the Sous-préfecture and the city administration. The Porte de Saignon served as the city gate in the fourteenth century. The museum was built over the ruins of the Roman theater and contains Gallo-Roman sarcophagi and mosaics as well as faïence (earthenware) from Apt.

The Musée du Parc Naturel Régional du Luberon is on the Place Jean Jaurés. As the name implies, it concentrates on the natural history of the landscape, flora, and fauna of the Luberon.

Apt
View of the town and surrounding landscape

Apt
Cathedral of Ste-Anne
12th-century south transept (far left) and mid-12th century upper crypt (left).

ON PP. 170-71:
Vineyard in the vicinity of Apt

OPPOSITE, ABOVE,
AND RIGHT:
**Landscape with lavender field
near Sault**

PAGES 174-75:
Ocher cliffs near Rustrel

North and East of Apt

North of Apt the Plateau de Vaucluse rises, and extends to the Montagne de Lure range, an easterly continuation of Mount Ventoux. The highest point is the Signal de St-Pierre at an altitude of 4,186 ft (1,256 m). The plateau runs northward reaching altitudes ranging from 2000-3000 ft (600-900 m). Live-oaks, furze, and wild lavender cover this barren, underpopulated area with its karst soil. The scenery consists of countless rocky clefts, gullies, and ravines in which the rainwater collects before vanishing into the porous limestone. Some re-emerges in the spring that feeds the Fontaine de Vaucluse (see p.159).

The ocher-red cliffs and quarries of the famous Provençal Colorado lie between Rustrel and Gigna, along the D 22 (see pp.174-75). The ravines of Nesque, along with the rest of the natural beauties of the Plateau de Vaucluse, are a magnificent sight. To the east, there are numerous picturesque villages with narrow lanes and castle ruins: Sault, Aurel, St-Trinit, and St-Christol-d'Albion.

The church of St-Christol-d'Albion was built in the third quarter of the twelfth century, and originally had one-aisle. The choir is decorated with bas-reliefs, depicting animals and mythical creatures amongst grape vines, that blur the lines of the blind arcades.

Simiane-la-Rotonde
12th-century castle keep (above)
Carving of mythical creature centered above a capital (right)

Simiane-la-Rotonde

This hamlet at an altitude of 2,000 ft (600 m) used to have a medieval castle of which all that remains are a few ruins and a spectacular tower (see above). This castle keep was divided by a wooden floor into two stories. The lower story probably served as an armory and storage room while the upper served as elegant apartments. The tower is topped by a twelve-sided cupola supported by ribs (see p.177). The floor space of the former upper story is surrounded by twelve alcoves whose massive half-columns support the ribs. The architectural style and carvings are typical of Provençal work at the end of the twelfth century, and are similar to those of the monastery of Sénanque. The round castle keep of Simiane belongs to a rare building type in Provence, but the style is repeated in the Tour de Constance, the castle keep or dungeon in Aigues-Mortes (see pp. 130-131)

Prieuré de Carluc

To the south-east of Simiane-la-Rotonde lies the river Oppedette whose deeply-cleft Gorges d'Oppedette run southward. The ruined priory of St-Pierre-de-Carluc (see p. 154) stands close to the river Céreste. The priory is first mentioned in 1011, as part of a group of three church buildings dedicated to Mary, Peter, and John the Baptist. This is reminiscent of the early-Christian cathedral groups. Like the mighty Abbey of Montmajour, the Carluc priory enjoyed a period of prosperity between 1114 and 1118, thanks in part to the picturesque setting, surrounded by cliffs.

Simiane-la-Rotonde
Castle keep, interior of cupola
of the former upper story.

The Luberon

Between Cavaillon and Manosque, the Luberon mountain range stretches for 40 miles (65 km). A hollow near Lourmarin divides the range into two massifs. In the west there is the "Little Luberon" that climbs to an altitude of 2,333 ft (700 m) with bizarre formations that are occasionally reminiscent of the Alpilles. To the east lies the "Great Luberon" which rises to an altitude of 4,166 ft (1,250 m) at Mourre Nègre. The two aspects of the Luberon are in sharp contrast. The sunny southern aspect slopes gradually and has a Mediterranean climate suitable for cultivation. The north slope is much steeper and the ambient temperature is significantly lower. In prehistoric times, the Luberon was quite heavily populated, because the limestone contained numerous caves and shelters which were habitable. In later times, the population decreased and since the Middle Ages there has been a move to the large cities at the foot of the mountains. Small country mansions (*bastides*) developed in these areas and their estates were controlled from châteaux. In the sixteenth century, these landlords began a brutal persecution of the Waldensians. 19 villages were burnt, 3,000 people killed and 600 men sent to the galleys. Peace returned to the area which remained devoted to agriculture even with the arrival of foreign trade and the Industrial Revolution in the nineteenth century. Only after World War II did artists and intellectuals discover the quiet and beautiful landscape. To curb the destructive effects of mass tourism, a large part of the Luberon was made into a nature park in 1977.

ABOVE AND LEFT
Oppède-le-Vieux

OPPOSITE:
Ménerbes

In the twelfth century, a sect of wandering lay preachers, who rejected all Papal authority and demanded that people live in strict accordance with the Scriptures, was founded by the merchant Pierre Valdes from Lyon.

Valdes had abandoned his previous life in 1175 to preach the Scriptures. The movement was not rejected by the Church at first, but as early as 1184 some of its members were excommunicated. Nevertheless, the movement spread to Italy, France, Switzerland, Austria, and Germany as a result of its efficient infrastructure and hierarchy, which ensured that members were given instruction and travelers found shelter with other members. The strict reliance on Scripture in many aspects gives the Waldensians the appearance of a pre-Reformation movement. They rejected the adoration of the Madonna and the saints, the doctrine of Purgatory, and the system of indulgences. Accordingly, in the 14th century, many Waldensians joined the Hussite movement, and those living in the valleys of the southern Alps adopted the teachings of Calvin, the Protestant reformer, in 1532. In Provence, the Waldensians fell victim to the relentless persecution of Protestants by the members of the so-called Catholic League. In 1545, there was an appalling massacre of those Waldensians who had fled to the remote mountain villages of the Luberon. The persecution of the Waldensians did not end there. Like the Hugenots, they were affected by the repeal of the Edict of Nantes, in 1686, ending the toleration of other Christian sects in France. Up to the 20th century, repressive measures by the Catholic Church were directed against what is one of the oldest reform movements within the Church, and only recently have the Waldensians been tolerated by catholicism.

Oppède-le-Vieux

Oppède-le-Vieux is an historically rich and exceptionally scenic town set in the hollow of a bowl-shaped mountain (see p.178). The château perched on the hilltop was built by Count Raymond VI of Toulouse later passing to the Baux and then the Meynier family. It was a scion of this last, Jean Meynier d'Oppéde, who instigated the massacre of the unfortunate Waldensians. The château was burned down in 1789, during the French Revolution, and is now a picturesque ruin. The site itself was abandoned for a long time, but the rediscovery of the Luberon has given it new life over the last fifty years. the name *Oppède* is a gallicization of the Latin word *oppidum*, meaning a town. The Romans established many of these *oppida* in Provence, many of which have survived.

Ménerbes

Ménerbes sits like a large ship in the landscape with its thirteenth-century citadel perched on the "bow" like a figurehead to the east and an additional military structure on the "stern" (see above and left).

The sixteenth-century bell tower and four-teenth-century church are very attractive. Ménerbes has become a favorite with many French artists and intellectuals, including Picasso and his beloved mistress, Dora Maar, Albert Camus, and Nicolas de Staël.

At any event, Ménerbes has acquired the reputation of being the definitive Provençal artistic village, especially among foreign tourists.

Bonnieux

Bonnieux with its compact streets and houses surrounded by city walls (see below), was part of the papal territory until the French Revolution and experienced a fate similar to that of Avignon. Its hilltop location affords impressive view. In the little town there is an old church built on a former Celtic settlement. Some parts of this three-aisled church date from the eleventh century.

Lacoste

Lacoste is even smaller than Bonnieux (see opposite). It embraced Protestantism, which was a dangerous position with the papal state so close by, so it was frequently under attack. In 1716, the town fell under the rule of François Gaspard de Sade, the grandfather of the notorious Marquis de Sade (1749-1814). The Marquis de Sade himself lived here for 30 years on his extensive estate in which he had a theater built in which to perform his plays. He also fled here from Paris on more than one occasion to escape the threat of incarceration. The Marquis was finally arrested in 1778 and spent most of his subsequent years in and out of jail, a situation which remained unchanged by the French Revolution, ending his days in the Charenton mental asylum. While in prison, his château was destroyed in the excesses of the Revolution though it has recently been restored.

St-Symphorien

Outside of Buoux where the D 113 forks from the D 943, the old priory church of St-Symphorien (see right) stands alone in the middle of a forest. It has two Romanesque chapels that adjoin at right angles. The smaller chapel is, in effect, an arm of the transept due to the small apse that extends eastward from it. The high belltower, pierced with windows that fill rectangular niches, stands beside the church and is a simpler version of the tower of Notre-Dame-d'Aubune.

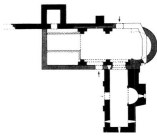

ABOVE:
St-Symphorien de Buoux
The priory church,
with tower (late 12th century)
and ground plan

Bonnieux
Southwestern aspect

OPPOSITE PAGE:
Lacoste
Southern aspect (above)
Fields around Lacoste (below)

Albert Camus

Albert Camus was born in Algeria in 1913 and grew up in a poor neighborhood of Algiers, former capital of the French colony. He soon followed his calling as a writer in order to "bear witness." Camus founded his own theater and worked as a newspaper writer and reporter in the late 1930s, with political allegiance to the Popular Front. In 1940, he left Algeria and joined the French resistance movement in order to fight against the German Occupation of France. These two experiences—the distance of the African colony from the French motherland and the self-destruction of the modern world through fascist barbarism—led Camus to put his philosophical reflections down on paper: "The Myth of Sisyphus" and "The Stranger" were published in 1942. Camus repeatedly describes the distance that divides the emotionally perceptive individual from the impenetrable and merciless reality of his environment which provides no ready explanations. From this position, life has no meaning or moral direction; much more, the constantly experienced confrontation between the individual and his environment may actually guarantee this absurd situation. From this, Camus derives his conviction that the dignity of the conscious, passionate, living "ego" should be the measure of life. The tirelessly active Sisyphus and the possessed, creative artist are transformed into the ideal conception of life. In 1957, Camus received the Nobel Prize for Literature. Shortly thereafter, he bought an old house in Lourmarin. On January 4, 1960 the author was killed in an auto accident near Sens.

Lourmarin

The château (see p.183, below) was constructed in different stages by the family of d'Agoult (see p.189, La Tour d'Aigues) between the end of the fifteenth century and 1542. The entire east wing is now missing from the original rectangular complex. The three-storied northwest wing with a square staircase-tower is the best preserved section and is in a very early, restrained Renaissance style (1525-42). The rooms contain beautiful mantelpieces. The lower section east of the staircase-tower, with its late-gothic galleries and windows, is part of the original building and dates from around 1500. The plans of the Italian architect Sebastiano Serlio (1548) to enlarge the château into a four-winged structure were never executed.

Lourmarin
General view (above)
Grave of Albert Camus'
in the Lourmarin cemetery
(left)

Lourmarin
Café terrace and olive grove
(above)
Château of Lourmarin
(left)

Silvacane
West façade of the monastery-church (late 12th century) (above), view looking east (right), Ground plan of the monastery (below)

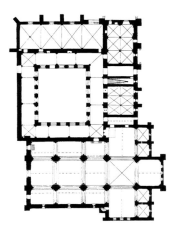

OPPOSITE:
Silvacane
Side and center aisles of the monastery church

Silvacane

Of the three Cistercian abbeys (the others are Le Thoronet and Sénanque), this is the last. It was founded in 1144 by the parent monastery of Morimond on the site of an existing priory built in the eleventh century by St-Victor de Marseille. The monastery remained relatively poor, until the last third of the twelfth century, when donations were made by the local nobility, including Guillaume de Fuveau and Raimond de Baux. They expected that, in return, the prayers of the monks would secure a pardon for their sins on Judgment Day. The money funded the construction of a church and a large monastery, begun in the 1160s and continuing into the mid-thirteenth century.

Like the other Cistercian monasteries of the region, Silvacane sank into obscurity in the fourteenth century. In 1443, the same thing happened to the cathedral chapter of Aix, when it became the parish church of La Roque-d'Anthéron. After the Revolution, the state acquired the building and restored the church; the cloister and the monastery buildings were first restored after 1945.

The complex follows almost exactly the same pattern as the Sénanque abbey (see p.160-61). Silvacane is an excellent example of how more modern building techniques allowed for innovation, especially in the vaulting system. As in both the other churches there is a basilica-like, three-aisled nave (see p.185) connected to an extended transept connected to the choir apse and four side-chapels. These eastern areas are square rather than round, enabling the choir to be lit by three clerestory windows and an oculus. The sides of the church are ornamented with typical Provençal blind arcades.

The rectangular ground plan enables the chapels to be covered with rib-vaults. The fact that this was an innovation which was still experimental can be seen in the development of the vault shapes from south to north. The older chapels in the south have thick torus ribs without a capstone, while in the north the ribs are thinner and meet in a capstone-like rosette. The rib-vaulting were only reserved for the most important areas, because the transept was covered with the usual ogives (the rib-vaulting in the transept is a later addition). The northern end of the chapel contains fragments of the grave of Bertrand de Baux, the grandson of the benefactor who built the monastery.

The nave built at the start of the thirteenth century is also roofed with pointed-barrel vaulting, interspersed with strong braces. Similar single-arch decoration can also be seen in the pilasters. Unlike those found in Sénanque and Le Thoronet, the half-round, pilasters on a plinth serve as supports for the hip-arches.

Silvacane
Chapter house (left)
Refectory (p. 187, above)
Cloister (p. 187, below)

Cavaillon, the Vaucluse highlands, and the Luberon

This strong emphasis on bay units and the application of modern rib-vaulting are an echo of the gothic skeleton construction that was practiced during the same time in northern France. It is no accident that the Cistercian architecture played an important role in the transition from Romanesque to gothic. In Silvacane, this is also confirmed by the appearance of bud-shaped decoration on the capitals, another example of the gothic repertoire of northern France.

The cloister lies at the far end of the church (see right). Its construction is similar to that of Le Thoronet. A double arcade of columns with an oculus in the spandrel is framed by a thick arch. However, when studied in detail, it can be seen that the cloister at Silvacane was built over a long period of time during the second half of the thirteenth century. Work began on the south wing that is adjacent to the church and continued in a clockwise direction to the east wing.

The monastery buildings to the east were erected at the same time as the church. The main area is on the ground floor whose six, rib-vaulted bays rest upon free-standing pilasters (see p.186).

There is a staircase at the north end leading to the upper floor, the garden (*parlatorium*), as well as the monk's chamber used as a warm room and the manuscript room (*scriptorium*) whose vaulting is similar to that of the main area.

Above that, the monks' dormitory covers the whole length of the east wing. The barrel-vaulted room is divided today into several smaller rooms. The ribbed-vaulted refectory in the north-wing (see above) was renovated in the fourteenth century or was one of the last parts of the monastic complex to be completed. Four ribbed vaults cover the rectangular space, which has suffered badly due to numerous changes of function. The tracery of the rose windows in the west has disappeared, for instance.

Cavaillon, the Vaucluse highlands, and the Luberon

OPPOSITE, ABOVE:
Ansouis
View of the château, 1630

LEFT AND P. 189,
BELOW:
La Tour d'Aigues
Portalvorbau (left) and remains
of the façade of the late 16th-
century Renaissance château

Ansouis

Ansouis is another small Provençal town that is dominated by its château (see right). Every local lord of the manor in the Luberon, of whom there were many, built their residences in the contemporary style. Ansouis was the seat of the Sabran family, descendants of the counts of Forcalquier who successively built on top of the highest point of the surrounding area beginning in the thirteenth century. The battlements and the foundation of the castle keep are both thirteenth century and thus the oldest parts of the complex. The parish church, behind it, is obscured from view. When the château fell into ruin, a new residence was built in 1630 whose uniform structure is built atop the first floor of the old fortress. The style is that of a seventeenth century mansion in Aix-en-Provence. The rococo styling and the small garden terrace were added in the eighteenth century.

La Tour d'Aigues

La Tour d'Aigues is one of the most important pieces of Renaissance architecture in France. In the early Middle Ages, the counts of Forcalquier ruled here, followed by the Sabran family in the thirteenth and fourteenth centuries, who started building the château. The estate passed to the d'Agoult family in 1410. One of their descendants, Jean-Louis-Nicolas Boulliers (died 1584), built the foundations in the Renaissance style. The château has largely been destroyed, first by fire and again by the French Revolution, but the ruins that remain are spectacular (see below right).

The château stands on an almost rectangular foundation (200 x 266 ft (60 x 80 m)) on the heights above the Lèze Valley. This square structure is a throwback to a medieval structure, but many French Renaissance elements have been incorporated. These include the entrance section on the inside of an open gallery with a pilaster outline whose bases are still visible. The side-wings, which were once two-storied, were accentuated by giant double porticos of colossal size, based on the example of the chateau d'Ecouen near Paris. The massive castle keep in the center is faced with rough stonework.

The west front facing toward the city was completely remodeled. The corner towers which once served defensive purposes were converted into residential pavilions, modeled after the Renaissance wing of the Louvre, built in 1546 by Pierre Lescot. The roof structure, whose windows were flanked by chimneys, is also copied from the château d'Ecouen. The porch of the portico (see p.188) with its rhythmically ordered colossal pilasters, its trophy reliefs, and its large, triangular-crowned gable is not a mere copy of Italian Renaissance examples, but echoes the classical monuments of the Provence (trophy reliefs), such as the monumental arch at Orange (see p. 25).

City and Mountain of Paul Cézanne

Aix-en-Provence, Montagne Ste-Victoire, and Salon-de-Provence

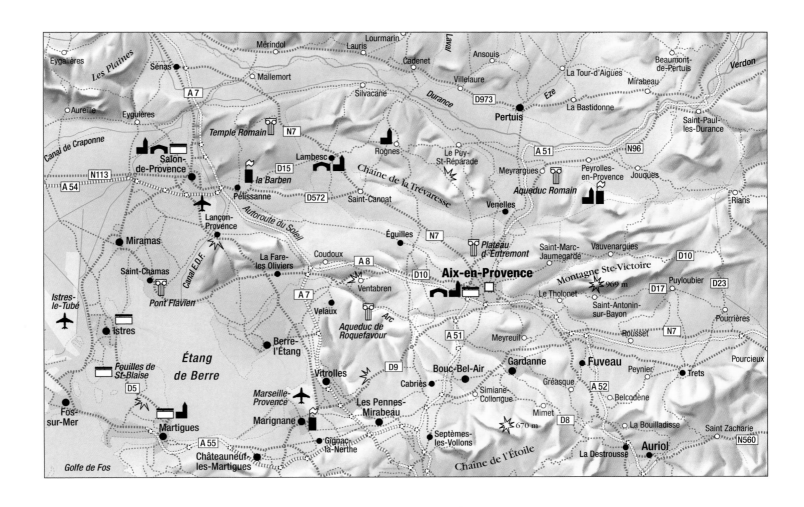

OPPOSITE PAGE:
Montagne Ste-Victoire
near Aix-en-Provence

Aix-en-Provence

The Celts settled during the third or second century BC in an extremely favorable position, in strategic terms, on a promontory north of present-day Aix. From this settlement—named Intermontes in the Middle-Ages, then Entremont—the Celts, referred to by the (Gallo-)Romans as Celto-Ligurians, repeatedly disrupted Greek trading activities in Marseilles. The Greeks finally appealed to the Romans for support, so the Romans totally destroyed Entremont in 123 BC. As protection against any Celtic campaigns of revenge, the Roman army commander, Caius Sextus Calvinus, founded the city of Aquae Sextiae Saluviorum, named after himself, to the south of the Celtic settlement.

The city was initially a luxurious villa-suburb of the wealthy Greek city of Massilia, but after the fall of the Greek metropolis, Aquae Sextiae acquired the status of a colony, and in the third century AD, under Diocletian, even rose to become the provincial capital of the second Narbonensia. This elevated status also had repercussions in relation to the position of Aix in the church hierarchy, since an archbishop governed the dioceses of the church province of Narbonensia II from the late fourth century.

The extent of the classical city is barely recognizable nowadays in a map of the city.

It stretched outward in a westerly direction like a narrowing trapezium from the present-day cathedral (only Avenue H. Pontier still follows the course of the Roman ramparts in the north). The cathedral district emerged from the sixth century onward, covering the area of the forum.

When the counts of Provence made Aix their headquarters during the second half of the twelfth century, they acquired the quarter to the south of the cathedral district. They built their château southeast of the Roman gates of the city. Charles of Anjou formed a royal alliance with the line of the Counts of Provence, by marrying Béatrice, the heiress to Provence in 1246, thus becoming Count of Provence. The couple built a royal residence here for their dynasty, which simultaneously also ruled over the kingdom of Naples. Despite their nominal presence in Provence, from the early fourteenth century, the Anjou line was totally preoccupied with its political activities in southern Italy.

Like most of the towns in Provence, Aix suffered severely during the Plague of 1348 and from the attentions of the Grandes Compagnies (see p. 53). Moreover, the second Anjou line under Louis of Anjou could only control the city by force and destroyed large parts of it.

The golden age of Aix-en-Provence was undoubtedly the reign of Good King René I,

1 Cathedral of St-Sauveur
2 Archbishop's Palace, now the Musée des Tapisseries
3 Musée du Vieil Aix
4 City hall
5 Ste-Marie-Madeleine
6 Baths of Sextius
7 Pavillon Vendôme
8 Musée Paul Arbaud
9 Fontaine des Quatre Dauphins
10 Musée Granet
11 St-Jean-de-Malte

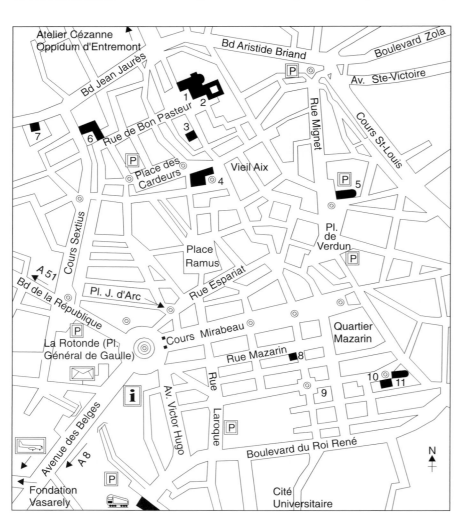

Aix-en-Provence
Fontaine des Quatre Dauphins
Fountain designed by J.-C. Rambot, 1667

OPPOSITE PAGE:
Aix-en-Provence
Cours Mirabeau (above)
Detail of the fountain in the Place-du-Général-de-Gaulle (below)

who built a royal residence here, where Italian sculptors, German singers and painters from the whole of France flourished under his patronage. Provence was annexed by the French king, Louis XI in 1481, and by 1501, Louis XII had created the Parlement de Provence, a system of representatives. This new state of affairs elevated the city to becoming the political capital of Provence; the mansions of the nobility and extensions to the city, which took account of its need for greater prestige at the start of this new era, testify to this even today.

The French Revolution signaled the end of this scenario. The former administrative center was downgraded to a Sous-Préfecture, and the economy of neighboring Marseille flourished as a result. Aix managed to retain its court of appeal and its university, founded in 1409. Even today these are factors which set the city apart, especially in terms of the faculty of law. Although the university belongs equally to Aix and Marseilles, most of the buildings are still located in Aix, some of them in the city center. The University of Aix-en-Provence also has a sizeable foreign student population.

Aix has emerged as a unique city, therefore, noted for a predominance of young people and its easy-going lifestyle. It has a picturesque old quarter, highly fashionable boulevards, important cultural institutions, and numerous festivals. Even though the place is popular with local and foreign tourists, they do not mar the overall picture. The Festival International d'Art Lyrique et de Musique, founded in 1948, attracts opera-and music-lovers every summer to performances which take place at historic sites. The downside of the attractions of the city and its new prosperity can be seen, above all, in the direction of Marseilles; the industrial zones in the suburbs of these two cities are threatening to fuse into a gigantic Mediterranean metropolis.

Cathedral of St-Sauveur

Only a few unspectacular city ruins remain from antiquity. Thus the importance attached to the excavations of the area of the cathedral in the last few years is that much greater. These reveal that the cathedral complex originated in the sixth century, and was built over the northern section of the Roman forum. To replace the Roman basilica at the south side of the forum square bordered by a row of Corinthian columns, the first cathedral building, the baptistery, which is still in existence, was built in the northwest corner of the square. The present-day nave was essentially built around 1100; the south side-aisle followed in the last quarter of the twelfth century, initially serving as the independent parish church of St-Maximin. Toward the end of the thirteenth century, the nave was extended by the High-Gothic choir (chancel), the apse, and the transept. The rounding of the hitherto unrounded nave was completed by the end of the fourteenth century. The belfry was also built during this period, and the west façade followed in the fifteenth century. The chapels on the north side originate from different Gothic periods, yet in 1697 they were extended to form one uniform nave (Notre-Dame-de-l'Espérance).

This complicated building history is reflected in the disparate features of the west front. On the south side, a typically neo-classical Romanesque portal leads into the twelfth-century side-aisle. The flamboyant portal, begun in 1504 by architect and master builder Pierre Soquet, in front of the central nave (see left) followed much later. The portal sculpture was removed during the Revolution, but the solid walnut door panels carved by Jean Guiramand in 1508-10, which show the prophets and sibyls, remain intact. Portrayed realistically on a small-scale, those who foretold the coming of Christ appear to be engaged in conversation with each other. Late-Gothic baldaquins, pinnacles, and other ornamentation frame this beautiful example of Renaissance sculpture. The tower on the north flank was begun in the 1320s, and was also built of giant Roman ashlar blocks.

On entering the cathedral, the first part of the church encountered is the well-preserved Romanesque part, the former parish church of Corpus Christi or St-Maximin. The effect is actually of an independent church building, which has been executed according to the traditional Romanesque style of Provence. The pointed barrel-vaulting is divided by twin-belted arches, resting on plates, which are flanked by columns in their upper areas. The baptistery on the south side is very reminiscent of the baptisteries of Riez and Fréjus. The Aix building had originally been built as a square central structure with an internal colonnade. In the third quarter of the eleventh century, the corners were filled in and provided with recesses,

which accounts for the present-day octagonal building. The cupola (see illustration above) was erected between 1577 and 1583. The tall columns made of Cipollino marble or granite were certainly acquired from a Roman building. They surround the octagonal font in the central area. The font itself was originally faced with marble and drew water from a channel to the northwest. Those being baptized would step into the font and there participate in the ceremony of the pouring over of water, or be submerged in the water.

The baptistery considerably limits the space available for the cloisters, which were built on in the late twelfth century to the east of it. They are therefore relatively small and simple, but are doubtless consistent with the type of cloisters that are also found occasionally in Arles, having piers with large figures set in relief. However, the artistic quality of the sculpture varies considerably, indicating that several workshops were involved. The St. Peter pier in the northeast corner, for example, is a simplified version of the Arles model. The creative diversity of the capitals may result from the fact that artistic elements from Languedoc, the Rhône valley, and northern Italy have also been worked in. Dramatic scenes appear on the capitals in the

west wing, including Balaam with the ass, and David and Goliath. Scenes from the life and Passion of Christ appear in the north wing. It is not possible to give a clear interpretation of the scenes in the east wing.

The Gothic cathedral, the central nave of the present-day structure, was integrated into the eleventh century cathedral-chapter church. When studying the south side of the first three bays, it is possible to appreciate how Gothic decoration was inserted into the ancient walls. Compared to the previous building, the church was extended eastward, and closed off with a polygonal, windowed choir (chancel) and apse. In actual fact, therefore, a single-naved church had been set next to the similarly single-naved Romanesque parish church at the south end. This type of Gothic building is consistent with the Maltese church of Aix, even in terms of its architectural elements, but this is one of the rare cases where narrow forms in terms of decoration and ribbing were applied. Obviously, the aim was to be associated with the development of High Gothic in northern France and Languedoc (as in the cathedrals of Narbonne, Toulouse, and Carcassonne). The same could be said to apply to the high tracery windows in the choir (chancel), which are extremely rare in Provence.

Aix-en-Provence
Cathedral of St-Sauveur.
Baptistery (4th or 5th century),
view of the cupola (above),
columns (below)

OPPOSITE:
Aix-en-Provence
Cathedral of St-Sauveur
South side: 16th century flamboyant gothic portico
leading to the main nave;
Ground plan of the cathedral
(below)

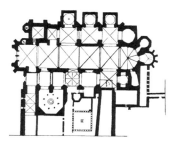

Late-Gothic painting

The jewel in terms of the collection of art treasures in the cathedral of Aix is the large triptych of The Burning Bush (see illustration on the left), which was donated by King René I and his wife Jeanne de Laval, whose portraits appear in the side-panels. The altarpiece was painted in 1475-76 by the artist Nicolas Froment (ca. 1435-84) for the Carmelite church of the city, where the heart of the king was allegedly buried. The panel painting is a major work in terms of fifteenth-century painting in France, and is simultaneously impressive evidence of the high esteem which was shown for new art in the Netherlands.

The painting focuses entirely on the Virgin Mary. Thus, strangely, it is the Madonna herself who is sitting in the burning bush, which can be interpreted as proof of her virgin state. The posture of the angel appearing to Moses is reminiscent of a depiction of the Annunciation. The altar depicting the legend of the holy miter is also attributed to the same painter, in the vertex chapel dedicated to St. Saviour above the sarcophagus of the saint.

Among the numerous other decorative items in the cathedral, mention should be made of the Burgundy-influenced stained-glass windows of the choir (chancel), which were made by Guillaume Dombet in 1444. Above the altar there are tapestries depicting the life of Christ, which date from 1511. In the outer west chapel there is the wall grave of Archbishop Olivier de Pennart (died in 1484) surrounded by lamenting figures, (*pleurants*) who are supposed to remind observers also to pray for the salvation of the soul of the deceased. A figure in a recumbent position has been replaced by a St. Martin from another tomb.

Another major work in terms of French painting in the late Middle-Ages hangs in the *Église de la Madeleine*, and is a monumental interpretation of the Annunciation, attributed to the Dutch painter Barthélémy d'Eyck, King René's court painter. The realistic and intricate anecdotal details of this true-to-life rendering of the subject matter is impressively combined with a monumental format for presenting the figures, which is entirely typical of the Middle Ages. The church edifices, painted in perspective, frame each of the figures. The inner rooms are consequently not systematically painted with any great attention to detail. Instead, each of the protagonists is allocated the space to which he or she is entitled. The Virgin Mary, who is represented by the church itself, occupies two naves simultaneously, illuminated from outside by the Holy Ghost, the Lux Nova. The Archangel Gabriel is allocated his own chapel like a baldaquin figure. Originally, the panel painting had side-panels depicting the prophets Jeremiah and Isaiah, which are now to be found in art collections in Brussels and Rotterdam.

OPPOSITE PAGE:
Nicolas Froment
The Burning Bush
Center panel of a tryptich, 1476
Painted on a wood panel, 13 ft 6 in (410 cm) high
Aix-en-Provence, St-Sauveur

BELOW:
Barthélémy d'Eyck(?)
The Annunciation
Center panel of a tryptich, ca. 1440
Painted on a wood panel, 5 ft 8 in (155 cm)
Aix-en-Provence, Ste-Madeleine

Aix-en-Provence
Place d'Albertas, 1742-46

Baroque secular buildings and squares

The large Archbishop's Palace complex, built between 1650 and 1730, stands behind the cathedral cloisters. Today, it houses an important tapestry museum, the Musée des Tapisseries (see page 199, top right). The highlights include tapestries from the workshops of Beauvais, a cycle of Don Quixote scenes, and a series of "Russian" (= rustic) games.

Traveling south in the direction of the wide boulevard known as the Cours Mirabeau, one passes numerous sixteenth and seventeenth-century Aix mansions (*hôtels privés*) in the Rue Gaston Saporta. Nowadays, the Musée du Vieil Aix is housed in the former Hôtel d'Estienne de St-Jean dating from 1660-80.

The Tour de l'Horloge, a clock tower, once a gate tower in the medieval fortress, is supported on blocks of antique stone. From the fourteenth century onward, the structure served as a clock tower for the local administration whose headquarters are right next door. Charles V's troops destroyed the medieval city hall in 1536. It was apparently re-built later, but no details are available. The present Hôtel de Ville (see illustration at bottom of page 199) was built by Pierre Pavillon from 1655-70. The street façade of this large three-story structure, arranged around a courtyard, was built in a classical style, and its individual elements are reminiscent of French-Baroque architecture. What is original in this respect, however, is the heavy framework of rustic buttress-like motifs on the edges of the building and the unusually clear emphasis on the central axis created by the addition of gables. Big cartouches above the windows break the horizontal lines, and on the top floor, porches over the windows create a frieze of festoons extending above the roofline. The old corn exchange (Halle aux Grains) was built in 1741 and stands facing the city hall, with its elegant Ionic columns (see p. 200) on the south side of the square.

On three sides of the beautiful Place d'Albertas (see above), which was built by Georges Vallon from 1742-46 on the initiative of Jean-Baptiste d'Albertas, a private individual, there are groups

FAR LEFT:
Aix-en-Provence
Hôtel Caumont, 1720
Detail of the façade

LEFT:
Aix-en-Provence
Musée des Tapisseries
1650-1730
Detail of entrance

BELOW:
Aix-en-Provence
Town hall, 1655-70
front entrance

Aix Baroque

Aix, more than any other city in Provence, is noted for its Baroque street plan and townhouses, because the Parlement de Provence turned the city into a prestigious residence for the French nobility. During the first phase in the third quarter of the 17th century, architects like Pierre Pavillon and Jean Claude Rambot in particular, remodeled Parisian designs to produce powerful, unconventional decorative effects. The basic style, however, remains Parisian. This is demonstrated by the street façades or the frequently observed arrangement of main building between courtyard and garden. During the second phase, from 1680 to 1725, Laurent Vallon and Thomas Veyrier introduced strong Italian elements, such as perspective effects and curved shapes. Sculptural decoration on the exterior of buildings decreased, but became more elegant. Soon, costly columns disappeared, and only the final upper frieze was retained and emphasized, while the windows were given curved frames and heavy embrasures topped with porches.

of Baroque façades, which form the backdrop for concerts in summer. A short distance away in the Rue Espariat there is the enormous towering Hôtel Boyer d'Eguilles, which has a U-shaped ground-plan. The massive pillars give this mansion its monumental character. The building now houses the Musée d'Histoire Naturelle, a Natural History Museum.

A little further to the east is the courthouse (Palais de Justice). The remains of a Roman city gate are contained within its walls. The building was extended during the Middle Ages to become the count's fortress, which in more recent times has served as the seat of the Parliament de Provence and other administration offices. In the late eighteenth century the entire neighborhood was rebuilt according to plans produced by Nicolas Ledoux, while the Palais was rebuilt as a cubic block with a large colonnade.

The Cours Mirabeau

The Cours Mirabeau is a mile-long avenue in Aix, one of the most famous baroque avenues in the South of France (see illustration on the right). Plane trees and fountains provide its cafés, pâtisseries, restaurants, and bookshops with refreshing coolness. This boulevard was built in 1649 to replace the medieval ramparts. The wide road was not intended as a kind of by-pass for horse-drawn carriages in a hurry, but as a route, closed off on the west side (until 1720), in which only high society was permitted to stroll and drive along in their carriages. Workshops were not allowed here. The first café opened, in the mid-eighteenth century. In 1778, the Cours became a proper street when the round tower which had been built at the western end formed a link to the country roads to Marseilles and Avignon. The Cours Mirabeau, named after the famous statesman from Aix in 1876, is lined with very beautiful façades of Baroque mansions, especially on the south side, while the wide sidewalk

on the opposite side of the street is occupied by restaurant terraces. At the eastern end there is a sculpture by David d'Angers, created in 1819-23; it depicts King René holding a bunch of Muscat grapes (see illustration on the left), a variety he is supposed to have introduced into Provence.

Even before the building of the Cours Mirabeau, the city was extended between 1646 and 1651 by adding a new district with parallel streets, south of the old city walls. This was initiated by Archbishop Michel Mazarin, a brother of the famous cardinal. Here, too, there are still numerous seventeenth and eighteenth-century baroque mansions. The intersection of the Rue du 4 Septembre and Rue Cardinale widens to become the Place des Quatres Dauphins, named after the fountain with four dolphins in the center (see illustration on page 192). The Musée Paul Arbaud is worth a visit (Rue du 4 Septembre); it contains a collection of Provençal faïence.

Aix-en-Provence
Cours Mirabeau (above)
Street market under plane trees

OPPOSITE:
Aix-en-Provence
The former 18th-century
Corn Exchange
Detail of the façade

Aix-en-Provence
Cours Mirabeau, King
René with scepter and bunch
of muscat grapes, 1819–23
Sculpture by David d'Angers

St-Jean-de-Malte

The Order of (the Hospital of) St. John of Jerusalem (since 1530 known as the Order of the Knights of St. John), which was founded in 1180 to defend the Jerusalem pilgrims, had an estate in Aix under its command. It was located outside the city gates, together with its church, on the road leading towards St-Maximin and continuing on to Italy. The Counts of Barcelona even elected to be buried here and Raymond-Bérenger V (1198-1245), the last of their lineage, donated money for the church to be rebuilt. This was done between 1272 and 1278, after which it also served as the tomb of Beatrix, the widow of Raymond Bérenger, and wife of the new ruler Charles I of Anjou.

The church building is one of the earliest Provençal examples of adopting the graphically refined High Gothic style that was developed in Paris from 1250 onward (illus. left). This can be seen in the extremely fine profiles and delicate tracery (eighteenth-century modifications were made on the west side). Nevertheless, both the church and the Cathedral of St-Sauveur with their single-nave ground-plans and narrow windows remained loyal to local traditions. The transept, the "horizontally-closed" choir (chancel) and the 218-ft (67 m) tower are worthy of attention. The façade was drastically altered in 1689 during the addition of the tower on the south side, incorporating an internal flight of steps. Of the gravestones destroyed during the Revolution in 1794, the only ones rebuilt in 1828 were those of Alfonso II, his son Raymond Bérenger IV, and his daughter Beatrix of Savoy in the north transept.

Musée des Beaux-Arts

The Musée des Beaux-Arts (Musée Granet) is housed in the former priory buildings of the Order of the Knights of St. John (illus. p. 203), and contains one of the most important art collections in France. It covers classical works and important remains of the city's medieval sculpture. Of particular interest are the large 3rd and 2nd-century BC Celto-Ligurian sculptures, which were found in the Oppidum d'Entremont. One represents a crouching warrior, and there are four busts of figures in armor. Paintings from the Dutch School, including works by Robert Campin, Dieric Bouts, and Jan Gossaert, and also numerous seventeenth-century Italian (Signorelli and Correggio) and Dutch works (schools of Rubens and Rembrandt) are also to be found here. The museum recently acquired paintings by the city's most famous son, Paul Cézanne.

The quality of the collection is due to a clever acquisition policy, particularly in the early nineteenth century. The museum owes its present name to its most important benefactor, François Granet (1775-1849), a collector and painter of the Napoleonic era, who bequeathed his estate to the city of his birth. The "modern" pictures by this painter, who came from a humble background, are among the most interesting exhibits.

OPPOSITE:
Aix-en-Provence
St-Jean-de-Malte, 1272-78
west façade

ABOVE:
Aix-en-Provence
Musée Granet (Musée des
Beaux-Arts), detail of the
façade; formerly headquarters
of the Knights of St. John
of Malta, 1671.

RIGHT:
Robert Campin
The Virgin in majesty between
St. Peter and St. Augustine,
gift from a religious
foundation, ca. 1430–35
Oil on wood,
22 x 40 in (55 x 104 cm)
Aix-en-Provence, Musée Granet

FAR RIGHT:
Egyptian relief figures
Musée Granet, entrance hall

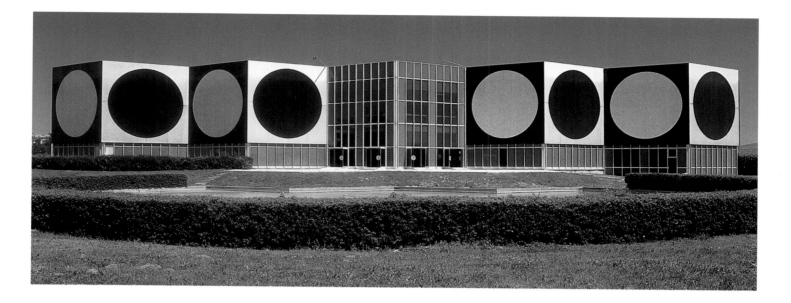

Pavillon Vendôme

A large garden on the Rue Van Loo looks very inviting. It surrounds the Pavillon Vendôme (see opposite page), originally a country mansion built by Pierre Pavillon in 1664-67 for Louis de Mercoeur, the Duc de Vendôme. An extra floor was added in the eighteenth century, and in 1730 the painter J.-B. van Loo moved in. The clear rectangular arrangement of the square block building's main façades is determined by the classical orders of the columns (Doric, Ionic, and Corinthian). Characteristic features of this prime example of Aix High Baroque are the huge sculptures in the form of gigantic vases in the narrow high recesses, and the statues of Atlas supporting the garden entrance. The interior has been renovated and furnished in the style of the time, providing the setting for exhibitions and events.

The route north to Oppidum Entremont leads past the curious Mausoleum of Joseph Sec at 6, Avenue Pasteur. It was built in 1792 in the shape of an L (for "Law") for the ardent supporters of the French Revolution, as a "Hymn in praise of the Law." There are 40 reliefs on the theme of Africa and the new Europe. A walk up the steep Avenue Paul Cézanne will take you to the artist's studio (see pp. 206-207).

Entremont

The origins of Aix can be traced at the Entremont archeological site (illus. right), located a few miles north of the city. The excavations began in 1946 and reveal the high state of development of the Ligurians who settled here from the third century BC. They include two fortified walls with square and round battlemented defense towers which protected the upper part of the city, and an extension to the city set out in front of it. In this part of the city there are foundation walls of small randomly-built dwellings. One of house still contains the lid of an oil-press.

The upper part of the city was arranged in a much more orderly fashion with straight lines of streets, a sewerage system along the city wall, and regular ground-plans of houses. The ground-plan of a large rectangular building has been excavated, which had apparently had a (colonnaded) portico front. What purpose this public building had remains unclear, however. The rich collection of remains from the Celtic city is exhibited at Musée Granet.

Fondation Vasarély

The Victor Vasarély Foundation is situated to the west of the city, in the corner between the A8 and A51 motorways (see illustration above). Built in 1975-76, the museum gives the impression of itself being a sculpture, since the façade consists of 16 black-and-white hexagons. The Foundation is not a museum in the strictest sense of the word, but displays the theories of color and pattern with which the Hungarian artist experimented.

Aix-en-Provence
Fondation Vasarély, 1975-76

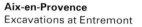

Aix-en-Provence
Excavations at Entremont

OPPOSITE:
Aix-en-Provence
Pavillon Vendôme, 1664-67
garden façade

Paul Cézanne
The life-story of the pioneer of modern painting (1838-1906) is closely linked with Provence. The crystal-clear light of the landscapes is the light of Provence. During the 1860s, Cézanne began to commute between Provence and Paris. Yet at that time his turbulent and dark-colored paintings were almost totally rejected by the critics. Despite a personal and stylistic connection with the Impressionists, his painting continued to be ridiculed and rejected by his contemporaries. In the late 1870s, Cézanne withdrew to Aix with his lifelong companion Hortense Fiquet. Here he produced work which was soon understood by the founders of modern art as a new way of treating chiaroscuro. Cézanne did repeated variations of specific subject-matter, such as still lifes, bathers, and Provençal landscapes. They became the models and subjects of formal experiments which then became the real focus of the picture. Concentration on the subtle nuances of color compositions made the imitation of spatial depth and perspective appear as a disturbing element, the contours of objects are broken up, and the art itself rather than what it depicts becomes the focus of the painting for the viewer. Cézanne added intellectual reflection to all this. The laws of nature are to be interpreted in the abstract, in the form of cylinders, spheres, and cones, and a painting should not be understood as an imitation of nature, but as a creation whose execution runs parallel to nature.

Cézanne's studio

In 1901, the painter purchased a small plot of land on the Traverse de Lauves and had a studio purpose-built to his own specifications (see illustration above and opposite). He died in 1906, and yet during those few years he produced that famous collection of late works in which landscapes and still lifes appear mirrored by non-material crystals. Cézanne had a view from the studio of Montagne Ste-Victoire, which from this perspective appears as a sharp "projection." The artist constantly painted this view from the studio on the Traverse de Lauves in many different variations. Although the studio was administered by the artist's descendants after his death, it was not open to the public until 1954, nearly half a century later. Of course, it is in the nature of a reconstruction, yet it gives a good impression of the atmosphere of a turn-of-the-century studio, when there was still a completely unobstructed view of Montagne Ste-Victoire. A signposted walking tour around the city follows in the footsteps of the painter.

ABOVE, LEFT AND OPPOSITE ABOVE:
Aix-en-Provence
Paul Cézanne's studio

OPPOSITE
BELOW LEFT:
Paul Cézanne
Still Life with Plate and Pears, 1895–1900
Oil on canvas, 15 x 18 in (38 x 46 cm)
Cologne, Wallraf-Richartz Museum

OPPOSITE
BELOW RIGHT:
Paul Cézanne
Still Life with Plate and Peaches, 1895–1900
Oil on canvas, 15 x 18 in (38 x 46 cm)
Zürich, private collection, on loan to the Kunsthaus Zürich

Aix-en-Provence, Montagne Ste-Victoire, Salon-de-Provence

"The idea of Provence lies dormant beneath the olive trees, the powerful landscape surrounds it, the scent of pine-trees radiates from it, the sun praises it ... yet one day, I became aware of this idea, which scattered the red earth, the rocks, the bright pine-trees, the plains, and the hills in a thousand places, when I looked at the paintings of Cézanne.
It sprang forth from them starkly and completely, and unique in a splendor which is simultaneously rustic and mystical, because it dominates in a magnificent and realistic way the entire work of this painter who was obsessed with clarity". (Joachim Gasquet, 1898)

OPPOSITE:
Montagne Ste-Victoire
View from the west (above)
Landscapes at the foot of the Montagne Ste-Victoire (below).

The surrounding area of Aix-en-Provence

Cézanne was irresistibly attracted to the towering white limestone mountain east of Aix, the 3370 ft (1011 m) high Montagne Ste-Victoire. However, he did not regard the mountain range merely as an impressive natural rock formation, its sunlight and shade produced an astonishing array of colors which could be captured on canvas. The many repeats of the subject-matter of the paintings render this insignificant.

On the other hand, the artist's colors gain intrinsically in importance, developing their own structure out of small, mostly square patches of color, whose contours are blurred. The background, the color of the canvas, plays an important role in the color composition, especially in some watercolor paintings of the Montagne Ste-Victoire, which are reduced to a few dabs of color.

The northern face of the mountain range is a sheer drop, but the southern slope is much much more gentle. In 1989, a forest fire destroyed large numbers of trees. There is a breathtaking view of the Mediterranean coastline from the summit at the Croix de Provence.

The road to the Val des Infernet passes the lake and dam of Bimont. The hilltop Château de Vauvenargues (illus. p. 211) was bought by Picasso in 1958. He spent a lot of time here at the end of his life and died here in 1973; he is buried on the terrace. The large sixteenth and seventeenth-century château is flanked by powerful round towers at each corner. Continuing in a westerly direction, you will reach the deeply carved ravines of Infernet.

The D17 road passes south of the mountain-range, through the village of Le Tholonet shortly before Aix. The people of Aix used to drive out here in around 1900 to walk around the foot of the mountain range. Cézanne also used to come to this place to paint. To the west of Aix on the D64, pass beneath the Aqueduc de Roquefavour (illus. p. 210, below) where the road meets the river Arc. This gigantic structure looks like a Roman aqueduct but was built in 1842-47 by the engineer Franz Mayor de Montricher, and carries the 56-mile (90 km) water pipe from the Durance over the valley to Marseilles. The 276-ft (83 m) high bridge construction is almost twice the height of the Pont du Gard.

Paul Cézanne
Mont Ste-Victoire, 1902–04
Oil on canvas, 28 x 36 in (70 x 89.5 cm)
Philadelphia, Philadelphia Museum of Art,
The George W. Elkins Collection

Montagne Ste-Victoire
Southern slopes

Aqueduc de Roquefavour
7½ miles (12 km) west of Aix
1842–47
Height 276 ft (83 m)
Length 1333 ft (400 m)

OPPOSITE:
Château de Vauvenargues
17th-century château where
Pablo Picassos spent his last
years and where he is buried.

Salon-de-Provence

The name of the city is probably attributed to a tribe of Celto-Ligurians, the Salliens or Salyens, who settled here, but also perhaps to the salt extraction at the Etang de Berre. The city was never on an important trade route, and did not become important until the Middle Ages. The archbishop of Arles had a hilltop retreat here in the tenth century, but the town that grew up around his residence did not come under the aegis of the counts of Provence, as it was ruled by the church.

When the kingdom of Provence became part of the Holy Roman Empire in 1032, Salon became subordinate directly to the emperor. The name of the château, Château de l'Empéri (from *empereur* and *imperator*) is a reminder of this. From the thirteenth century onward, Salon developed into a market town. It obtained local self-government, and was able to maintain this position when it fell to the House of Anjou, an offshoot of the French royal house, in 1246. In the sixteenth century, the privileges of the city fathers were repeatedly confirmed, and in 1655 the so-called consuls capitalized on their position by building a new city hall.

The cultivation of olive trees and olive-oil extraction have been an important economic activity here since the fifteenth century. In 1909, the region suffered a severe earthquake, which destroyed numerous buildings and cost the lives of 60 peoples. Today the city benefits from the military airfield located close by. In terms of interesting sights, Salon has important thirteenth and fourteenth-century buildings. A jazz festival is held here in summer at various locations around the city.

Salon-de-Provence
Château de l'Empéri
13th century
Gatehouse (left)
and inner courtyard (below)

Salon-de-Provence
St-Michel, ca. 1200
Detail of the tympanum on the
Byzantine western portico

The old district around St-Michel and the château has been extended and turned into a pedestrian area, surrounded by shady boulevards. Here, in the old city, the home of Nostradamus is still standing. The Musée Grévin de Provence, a waxworks, contains a series of 15 tableaux of lifelike waxwork figures depicting episodes from the legends and history of Provence.

The church of St-Michel, the only Romanesque church in the city, was built around 1200. The west portal is inserted as a block into the wall, flush with the latter and supported by two columns. Their capitals show the beginnings of Gothic foliated capitals. The curious twelfth-century tympanum (see illustration on left), like a fusion of different plates, has a fresco of St. Michael triumphing over a serpent. Beneath that is a lamb carrying a cross, signifying the sacrificial death of Christ. The provincial execution of the sculpted figure contrasts strangely with the mastery of the decorative work, as for example in St. Gabriel. The single-nave interior is swamped with rib-vaults, which may have been added at a later date. The apse vault, dates from the time the church was built, and represents an interesting example of an early rendition of the Gothic method of building in Provence.

The Château de l'Empéri

The Château de l'Empéri (illus. above and right) is one of the most interesting and largest medieval château complexes in Provence. The others are the château of Tarascon, the fortress of Aigues-Mortes, and the Palais des Papes (Popes' Palace) in Avignon. The archbishops of Arles built this massive medieval structure on a high rock that dominates the surrounding area. The present-day structure dates from the time of Archbishop Jean des Baux (1233-58) but was subsequently altered several times, though not basically re-built. It suits the rocky terrain and consists of a sequence of three interconnected courtyards. The gatehouse of the château complex was once separated from the main building by a moat. The latter towers over the entrance with a monumental frontage, in the southwest corner of which there is a gigantic tower, the Tour Pierre Cros, with battlements and machicolations erected 1374-88 with missile shafts. In the middle of the château wall there is a portal, framed by a pair of towers. This arrangement not only served as a defense, it was also a piece of ostentation which was probably modeled on the medieval Louvre (ca. 1200), of which a variation was the Archbishops' Palace in Narbonne or the Palais des Papes in Avignon. Around 1500, large windows were installed in the walls by Jean Ferrier, in order to cast more light in the rooms behind. The building's role as a *château fort* was no longer of prime importance.

The portal passageway (roofed with flat stone slabs) leads into the first inner courtyard. Here, too, the colonnades with their segmental arches and large windows are a legacy of the plan to make the château less gloomy, ca. 1500. The second courtyard contains the oldest parts of the château complex; note the strong walls of the twelfth-century fortress, especially in the western section of the north wing. In the southern section of the wing there is the château chapel, located at the museum entrance. The overall internal height was once 33 feet (10 m) and there is reinforced barrel-vaulting. In the thirteenth-century, intermediate

within the city boundaries until 1550. The foundation stone of the present building was laid in 1345, and at first the building work proceeded rapidly, but the west side was not completed until the end of the fifteenth century. Soon afterward, the church was elevated to the status of a collegiate church with a theological college for regulated canons. There are traces of a previous older building in the lower section of the west tower, otherwise the building is a fine example of fourteenth-century Provençal Gothic. Typical of this is the one-nave hall-type feature with side chapels, which developed from the middle of the thirteenth century onward and had its starting-point in Languedoc.

There are certain features which are typical of St-Laurent, including the wide supporting nave, the slightly retracted chancel, and the absence of capitals (see illustration on left). With these features, St-Laurent is directly related to the Avignon churches of St-Pierre and St-Didier which are the same age. The tower above the south portal is generously pierced with pointed-arch arcades, reveals a solution for the transition from square to octagonal, which is seldom seen in Provence, but frequently encountered in Northern France and Germany. Pinnacles are set in front of these angular sides and continue down the edges from floor to floor.

The northern surroundings of Salon

The Château de la Barben (illus. top of p. 215) stands in a unique position high on the rock. The building, which belonged to the Forbin family until 1963, has had a checkered history. In 1630, the people of Aix destroyed the medieval twelfth and fourteenth-century château, but they had to re-build it again soon upon the orders of the Parlement de Provence.

Salon-de-Provence
Former collegiate church of St-Laurent (14th-15th century), interior looking east (above)
Tomb of Nostradamus (right)

vaulting was installed, and a two-story double chapel emerged. On the north side, the inner courtyard is closed off by a powerful hall structure. All that remains of this building on the courtyard side is a ruin, but originally it had three ground-floor rooms covered with barrel-vaulting and above that, rib-vaulted rooms. An external tower incorporating an internal flight of steps built in the angle between the north and east wings collapsed during the earthquake of 1909. The château museum displays an extensive collection of military history, covering the periods from Louis XIV through World War I.

Collégiale St-Laurent

The former collegiate church of St-Laurent is located north of the old part of town. Some sources claim it is a former Dominican church, but in fact it was originally a parish church, which was for some reason was not included

In 1793, and again during the earthquake of 1909, the building was badly damaged. In addition, it was restored in the nineteenth century in an eclectic mix of medieval forms with Renaissance and Baroque elements. The large sloping driveways which lead up to this charming church are very impressive.

In the sixteenth century, Lambesc was regarded as the second capital of Provence, because in 1476 the city had been elevated to the status of a principality by King René I. A kind of council of cities met here every year. Numerous sixteenth-century houses still testify today to the town's prosperous past.

The parish church, a gigantic structure built according to plans by Laurent Vallon of Aix between 1700 and 1741, is a typical example of 17th-century "Aix Baroque." The three-nave basilica with the rounded terminations of the transept arms displays rich and heavy internal stucco decoration.

Vernègues

The impressive remains of a Roman temple podium stand in the middle of the Château Bas vineyard, in a semicircle built into the side of a hill. A nearby spring could have been the reason for building the temple here. In this case, it is a typical temple standing on a raised base, with frontal columns and large flight of steps. The six-step high *Krepidoma* (base) of the former portico with four columns are still standing. Above this on the northeast side, there is a massive wall and one of the front Corinthian columns (illus. pp. 216-217).

The capitals prove by their outstandingly worked individual shapes, that the temple was one of the earliest Roman monuments in Provence, built around 20-10 BC. The chapel of St-Césaire was built in the Middle Ages on the left side of the temple *cella*. Since the severe earthquake of 1909, nothing identifiable remains of the two châteaux in this area which were owned by the archbishops of Arles.

Château de la Barben
12th and 14th centuries.

Lambesc
Detail of the façade of the baroque parish church, 1700-41

Vernègues
Ruins of the Roman
Podium temple
ca. 20–10 BC

217

Pont Flavien
Roman bridge
near St-Chamas,
1st century

The southern surroundings of Salon

Lançon-Provence is a small city that nowadays almost seems to be part of Salon. It is built around a medieval château, which looks impressive even in its present state as a ruin. The round corner towers, the missile shafts on the coping, and the high arch apertures are reminiscent of the older section of the Palais des Papes in Avignon. The small Romanesque chapel of St-Cyr (illus. p. 219, below) stands in the cemetery.

St-Chamas has an interesting parish church (1660-69), which is consistent with Gothic traditions in Provence in terms of the ground-plan concept and the rib vaulting. A Roman bridge, the Pont Flavien (illus. above) still spans the Touloubre. Access to it is via a gateway in the style of a triumphal arch. Corinthian pilasters support a lintel covered with fine relief decoration but the whole structure has been heavily restored; of the four crowned lions, only one is classical, the others were restored in the eighteenth century.

A Caius Donnius is mentioned on the architrave of one of the two arches who, as a priest of Rome and Augustus, had the bridge constructed. The railroad viaduct for the Paris-Marseilles link built in 1847 is located nearby.

Etang de Berre

This brackish-water lake, which at 516 sq ft (155 sq. m) is the largest in the South of France, was for many centuries set in a sparsely populated landscape. However, the advantages of its protected position and easy access to the Mediterranean were recognized at an early stage. New Stone Age relics and especially Greek remains of colonies testify to this fact. This lake, which is 30 ft (9 m) deep at it deepest point, is surrounded by towering crags, and formerly provided an ideal environment for an abundance of fish in its warm, still waters. Numerous small fishing villages therefore emerged along its banks. Salt extraction was also an important economic factor. Since the mid-nineteenth

century, however, the Etang de Berre has
become a part of the port of Marseille. After
World War I, the lake was linked to it via the
Marseilles-Rhône canal which passes through
the subterranean Tunnel du Rove into the
Etang de Berre, and from there via Fos and
the Rhône Delta into the river. The calm
waters make for ideal seaplane landing conditions, and the lakeside airports of Istres and
Marignane are among the oldest in France. At
the same time, numerous oil and gas-process-
ing industries have sprung up around the
Etang. In 1968, a deepwater harbor was
opened in Fos as a petroleum trans-shipment
center. This enormous industrialization had a
deleterious effect on the animal and plant life
and, of course, on tourism. By 1957 there
was a ban on fishing in the Etang because of
water pollution, yet since the 1970s, there are
new institutions which ensure that environmental pollution is monitored and controlled.

Even though the Etang does not really
look inviting enough for an extended

ABOVE:
St-Chamas
General view, seen from above
the Etang de Berre

OPPOSITE:
Fos-sur-Mer
General view over the port (above)
Romanesque cemetery chapel of St.
Sauveur, 10th and 12th century
(below)

beach holiday, it is worth driving around, because the harbor and industrial area, like historical monuments, already belong to the Etang de Berre, and especially because it is possible to gain an insight into how the lake shore has been uninterruptedly colonized for centuries. The center of Istres is noted for its seventeenth and eighteenth-century houses, and the church, dating from 1560. The museum exhibits rich evidence of the classical past of the Etang de Berre and the region around Istres. The oppidum of Castellan (D 76 westward) is a settlement which was inhabited from 800 BC onward.

St-Blaise has a small Romanesque chapel and nearby extensive excavations are on view, which explain the prehistoric and Hellenistic history of the place. The walls of a Greek fortification are of particular interest, because in places some of the gigantic stones which would have already been produced by the pre-Greek population have been re-used. New Stone Age archeological finds have confirmed that there was an early settlement here. Large holes were found in the stones near a small portal in the Greek wall. These too are re-used stones which can be compared with the eroded Celtic stone lintels. The Greek defensive walls which were built in the year 200 surrounded the hill in the shape of a triangle. For this purpose, gigantic blocks of stone were hewn with extreme precision and positioned without the addition of mortar.

The Greek stonemasons' marks are still faintly discernible. The remains of the Greek wall were finally built over during the construction of a new fortification during the Teutonic invasions. However, in the thirteenth century, the city only occupied one-fifth of the space available, and one hundred years later it was totally destroyed, except for the chapel already mentioned.

The old Fos-sur-Mer, which is nowadays surrounded by a gigantic harbor complex, has a very well-preserved Romanesque cemetery chapel on view (illus. right).

Martigues was created by the merger of three fishing villages. It has a church built in 1625 and numerous seventeenth and eighteenth-century houses. It also has a recently opened museum, dedicated to Felix Ziem (1821-1911), the landscape painter and orientalist, which also exhibits paintings by other Provençal landscape painters.

Finally, in Marignane, on the outskirts of Marseille, there is a monumental château, which was extended in 1666 on the orders of the Marquis of Marignane, Jean-Baptiste II Covet. With its raised base, alternating gables, and powerful frieze of festoons, it is reminiscent of the palazzi of Bologna.

Santons—Christmas-nativity figures

Even in summer you can encounter Santons in Provence. They are colorfully painted pottery figures representing every conceivable traditional profession or activity, thereby conjuring up an image of the rich diversity of this enchanting province. Many of these figures are taken from country life, others from the *métiers de bouche*—anyone involved in making, preparing and serving food and drink. Thus there are the fishwife, the miller, the farmer's wife carrying a pumpkin, the hunter, the angler, the garlic-grower, goose-breeder, cheese-maker, baker, cook, truffle-hunter, olive-picker, wine merchant, chestnut-seller, and many more. If you take a close look you will spy a woman of Provence stirring the *aioli* (garlic sauce) and another holding the ingredients ready for the *Pompe*, the Christmas cake. All these figures are added to the crib at Christmas time. The Christ-child, the Virgin Mary, and the Blessed Joseph are still in their midst, of course.

Since the sixteenth century, it has been customary to erect a crib inside or outside churches at Yuletide. The emergence of Santons—from the Provençal word *Santoum*, meaning "little saint"—occurred at the time of the Revolution—when churches stayed closed, but families kept the tradition of the crib at home, just making smaller figures out of any material available,such as wood, plaster-of-Paris, clay, and bread-dough, then painted them or dressed them in clothes.

Jean-Louis Lagnel was the first to make plaster-of-Paris molds of the models, with which he was able to cast series of figures in clay. Other Santonniers continued dressing their figures. The first Santon mass took place in Marseilles in December 1803. The crib was given a special boost by the inclusion of the pastoral play "Maurel," which depicted how Jesus was born in a small village in Provence in the nineteenth century. In this way, the Provençal figures gained entry along with the biblical figures to the crib community, which reflected family life.

Each family member has a figure which represents him or her, whereas others recall relatives and friends. The whole family helps to furnish crib with moss, dried plants, pieces of wood, and beautiful stones, which they gather collectively in the countryside on the first Sunday in Advent. From the December 4 onward, the boxes in which the figures are stored are allowed to be opened, but the Christ-child is not added until December 24, before the big *souper*, and the Three Kings do not join the crib until Epiphany (January 6). Each year, the family crib is added to, so that it grows with each succeeding generation, and becomes absolutely vital for a Provençal Christmas. A proper crib presents a picture of the whole landscape with several houses, stalls, mills, and bridges.

You can enjoy this spectacle for just under two months, because the cribs are not dismantled until February 2, in celebration of Candlemas, when the figures are carefully packed away again and stored for the rest of the year in readiness for the following Christmas. However, there are a number of other festivals and events for which certain Santons have to be brought out of their summer hibernation, such as olive or wine-harvest festivals. Santons are also used as permanent decorations in many Provençal houses and gardens. There is a Santon fair in Aix-en-Provence in December.

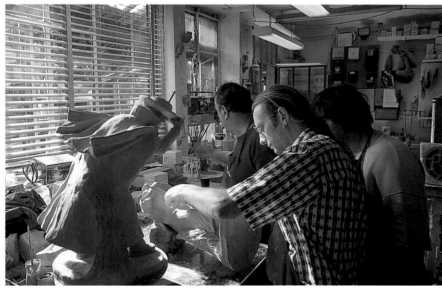

The Eternal Rebel

Marseilles and Eastward

1 Cathédrale de la Major
2 St-Laurent
3 La Vieille Charité
4 Musée des Docks Romains
5 Musée du Vieux Marseille
6 City hall
7 Les Carmes

8 St-Théodore
9 Arc de Triomphe
10 Museum d'Histoire
   de Marseille
11 St-Ferréol
12 Musée de la Marine
13 St-Vincent-de-Paul

Palais Longchamps with
14 Musée des Beaux-Arts
15 Musée Grobet-Labadié
16 St-Trinité
17 Calvaire
18 Notre-Dame-du-Mont
19 Préfecture

20 Musée Cantini
21 Opera house
22 Basilique St-Victor
23 Fort St-Nicolas
24 Fort St-Jean
25 Château
26 Lighthouse

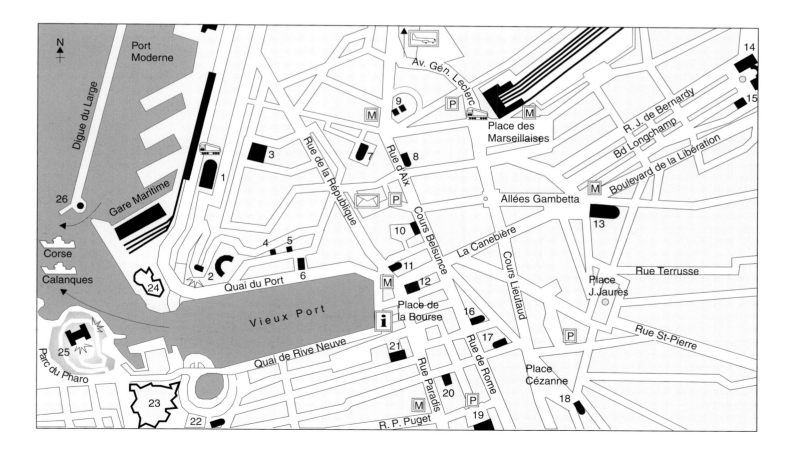

OPPOSITE:
Marseilles
The old port with a view of
the pilgrims' church of
Notre-Dame-de-la-Garde,
the symbol of the city

Marseilles
Yachts in the *vieux port*
(old port)

Marcel Pagnol, who was born in Aubagne in 1895 and died in Paris in 1974, filled his work with affectionate portrayals of life in Provence as being both humorous and folksy. His plays, though premièred in Paris, were mostly set in Provence, sometimes in Marseille or in the Provençal hinterland. The turbulent scenes tell of a people who are cantankerous yet forgiving, boastful yet reserved, simple yet cunning. As early as the 1930's, Pagnol also became involved in film-making, directing both his own material and, sometimes, that of his fellow Provençal, Jean Giono. Several of Pagnol's films and plays are set in Marseilles, whose old harbor he immortalized in "Fanny."

The History of Marseilles

The south's largest city with France's second largest population has been surrounded by negative clichés for a long time. The eternally rebellious city, the seedy dockside, the sinful city, the gateway to the Orient. Such annoyingly simplistic descriptions hardly do justice to the richness of the city's history which has been at the heart of Mediterranean culture for almost 3,000 years. One thing is sure: Marseilles has never been a city that had to rely on tourism.

Much has been done to attract tourists in the last few years. The city continuously uncovers more of its classical past and its rich collections are always presented in new and attractive ways. Marseille began as an important trading settlement called Massalia, founded by the Greek colony of Phocea in Asia Minor around 600 BC. The location was ideal, because the bay, today's Vieux Port, formed a naturally sheltered harbor. The settlement flourished quickly when the parent colony was destroyed by the Persians between 545-540 BC and many Phoceians emigrated to Massilia. From here the Greeks founded three more trading posts on the coast, Olbia (Hyères), Antibes, and Nice. From the third and second centuries, the city began to link itself to Rome to seek protection from the Saluvii who lived to the north in the settlement of Entremont near today's Aix-en-Provence.

When the Romans finally subdued the Ligurians and blocked the competing trading center of Carthage in 146, this greatly benefited the interests of the Greek trading settlement.

However, as soon as the Romans founded Aquae Sextiae, today's Aix, there was cause for dispute. Marsilia sided with Pompey against Caesar and after a long siege, the Greeks paid the price for favoring the losing side, with the forfeiture of their colonies. The huge area stretching as far as the Alpilles was handed over to Arles in 46 BC. Finally the Roman port cities of Fréjus and Narbonne became strong competitors. The Roman lifestyle, however, only gradually replaced the entrenched Greek traditions.

The Romans made the swamp area east of the city suitable for habitation and built a new city wall that stood until 1040. The harbor was expanded and a theater was built on the east slope of the Butte St-Laurent. The forum with a temple and other public administration buildings were located in the upper city.

In 314 at the latest, a Christian bishop resided in the city. With the construction of the Abbey of St-Victor in the fifth century, an important Christian center was created that played a decisive role in the conversion of Gaul to Christianity. Between the fifth and ninth centuries, Marseilles fell under various rulers, and was constantly threatened by Saracen, Norman, and pirate attacks. From this time onward, a tendency to autonomy is discernible. When, in 879, the Kingdom of Burgundy under Boso divided Provence into three counties (Avignon, Arles, and Apt) and several sub-counties, Marseilles' independence was recognized with a Vicomté (sub-county) to oversee the harbor area while the bishop was made lord of the upper city. At the end of the eleventh century, the two territories were separated from one another with a wall. In 1159, the cathedral chapter received its own district so that the city was divided into three sections. Marseilles was only granted the right to appoint a self-governing body, the consulate, at the end of the twelfth century arose, relatively late by local standards.

The deciding factor for such a move was that after the Crusades, Marseilles could expand its economic role as harbor and shipyard. Upon the death of the last Vicomte Roncelin (1215), only the resistance of the Abbey of St-Victor could hinder the commune from taking over the rights of the Vicomtes. The power-vacuum was filled by the Count of Provence. In 1245, the King of Naples, Charles I of Anjou, took over this function against the violent resistance of the commune in the lower city. In 1257, he also acquired the upper city. The Anjou dynasty resided in Aix and the requisitioned Marseilles fleet was destroyed in 1282 by the Sicilian Vesper. In the fourteenth century, a rapid decline took place, caused by an economic recession, pirates, and the consequences of the Hundred Years War, as well as a high taxation imposed by the House of Anjou to finance its military ventures. In 1423, Alfonso V of Aragon finally laid the city waste in a revenge attack. With the death of King René I of Anjou, Marseilles passed to the French crown in 1481.

In the thirteenth century, the city had spread to cover a territory that was bordered by today's Boulevard des Dames and the Cours Belsunce. The south side of the harbor was secured by its own wall which included the abbey-church of St-Victor in 1363.

The harbor entrance was guarded on both sides by fortifications built in the thirteenth (Tour St-Jean) and fourteenth (Tour St-Nicolas) centuries. In 1666, an extensive new design for the city was approved. The sprawling suburbs that had developed over the centuries were integrated into the new city area. The most important of the routes laid at this time was the famous Canebière. This new design preceded an economic upturn, beginning in the sixteenth century, because the kings built Marseilles into the most important French trade and military harbor in the Mediterranean, which finally became a free port. Despite an epidemic of the Plague which caused 100,000 deaths, Marseilles continued to prosper into the eighteenth century and its cultural life expanded.

Marseilles
St-Laurent, 12th and 18th century (tower and eastern aspect), in the vicinity of the Vieux Port.

The first opera house was built in the early seventeenth century, and in 1683 Jean-Batiste Lully established a music academy. The Académie de Marseilles, a part of the Académie Française, was founded in 1726, followed by an Academy of Art in 1753. The social differences between the nobility and the large working-class population turned Marseilles into a center of conflict during the French Revolution. The Reign of Terror hit Marseilles especially hard and numerous churches were destroyed.

The Marseillaise: the hymn of the French Rhine Army, composed by Rouget de L'Île, was first played on June 22, 1792 in the club of the *Fédérés* in Marseilles. The 600 volunteers from the harbor city whose purpose it was to support the revolutionary people of Paris, sang this song continuously during their long march to the capital. It also accompanied the revolt of August 10, 1792 which led to the abolition of the monarchy. In September, the song was accepted by the War Ministry as the official marching song, though Napoleon later banned it. The Marseillaise first became the national anthem of France under the Third Republic in 1878-1879, in recognition of the Republican ideal.

When the British implemented a naval blockade against France in order to curb Napoleon, Marseilles suffered greatly. It was not until the monarchy was restored did the city regain its status as a free port which sparked an unprecedented wave of prosperity. Trade with the French colonies, the railroad which arrived in 1844 and the opening of large factories (soapworks, shipyards, etc.) brought the city an economic power that was soon visibly translated into substantial urban improvements. The Palais de Longchamps, the Promenade du Prado, the stock exchange, the new cathedral, and Notre-Dame-de-la-Garde are only some of the magnificent, historical buildings that characterize the face of the city today.

The city's role as the "gateway to the Orient" made it into a melting-pot. Southern Italians, Armenians, Corsicans, and Spaniards lived side-by-side with the locals and French people from all the regions of France. The important connections with the Levant influenced the architecture, including the oriental styles in some places around the Canebière.

The city's murky reputation is founded especially on the political upheavals experienced between the wars. A corrupt city government and spectacular political murders rocked Marseilles. In 1934, King Alexander I of Yugoslavia and the French Foreign Minster, Louis Barthou, were both murdered on the Canebière; and the city was ruled by the state from 1939 to 1946.

World War II marks one of the most terrible chapters in the city's history. Many Jews and countless refugees from the Nazi regime lived in the city. Starting in 1942, over 40,000 people were deported and murdered. In 1943, the German occupiers, as a reprisal against the Resistance movement, destroyed the entire residential area north of the old harbor. In August of 1944 the Allies retook the city, but the Germans demolished the harbor facilities and the Pont Transbordeur that spanned the harbor entrance before capitulating.

The post-war period was difficult. Long neglected improvements in the infrastructure (medical services, traffic control, and especially refurbishment of housing) were sorely needed. The role of the harbor was also affected by the rapid decline of the colonies, changes in the Mediterranean trade, and a ship-building crisis. At the same time, Marseilles experienced a rapid population increase that lasted into the 1970s, from 600,000 to 1 million residents. An expansion and modernization of the harbor facilities to the north made way for a trans-shipment center for petroleum products that connected newly formed cities (Vitrolles) in the area around the Etang de Berre with the airport near Marignane which was renovated after World War II. Since then, the city has focused above all on leading research in the fields of technology and science. Last but not least, the city is becoming conscious of its rich archeological and architectural heritage from all periods, and has began to clean up a dilapidated quarter of the city between the railroad station and the old city. For the slums and the welfare high-rises in many of the outer quarters, such improvements remain a long way off, however.

LEFT:
Marseilles
New port with ferry to
Algeria (above)
Fort St-Nicolas (center)
Market scene (below)

ON PP. 228-29:
Marseilles
The old port
(vieux port)

OPPOSITE PAGE:
Marseilles
Old city hall, 1653-1672 (above)

Vieille Charité with domed
chapel (1704) inside the
courtyard (below)

Marseilles
View of the bay, the old port,
and the northern and southern
port districts.

Around the Old Port

Marseilles is a sprawling city that offers more than a few sights worth seeing, and their many aspects should be explored on foot and occasionally by bus or on the streetcar-subway. There is much to see in the old port area, including the ruins from antiquity, the abbey of St-Victor, and the beginning of the Canebière.

The classical city, the Hellenistic Marseilles, stretches from the rocky lands north of the old port to today's Fort St-Jean. The shoreline was way back from its current location. The ancient harbor installations can therefore be inspected in the middle of the city.

At the Centre Commercial de la Bourse, a part of the old city wall by the harbor can be seen in the so-called Jardin des Vestiges. The lower lying section of the wall in the stock exchange was once the outermost point of the harbor basin, next to which lay a rectangular freshwater basin and the remains of a dock. The city wall ran to the west from which two clearly recognizable towers formed a gateway, framing a street which was paved in Roman times. The remains of the city wall, which connected to another tower in the south, can still be seen on the sides of the towers. The masonry technique and the

Grecian mason's signs date the main part of this section to Hellenistic times, most likely the second century BC. In the Musée d'Histoire de Marseille set above an old part of the harbor basin, the excavation area continues (see below). The core of the collection is the 63 ft (19 m) long hull of a Roman trading ship that sank in the harbor between 160 and 220 AD. The remains were found in 1974 and painstakingly preserved on its original site. The museum also exhibits a large model of antique Marseilles, as well as other spectacular ship finds from the sixth century BC.

Marseilles
Excavations of the old city in
the Musée d'Histoire
de Marseille

The Roman city was surrounded by an outer wall that expanded the city area. South of the Rue Caisserie, large containers were found with diameters of up to 5ft 8 in (1.75 m), and 6ft 8 in (2 m) in height. These so-called *dolia* held wine, oil, and other supplies, and were a part of the Roman docks located here. In the Musée des Docks Romains the *dolia* are displayed, together with the remains of antique ships, anchors, etc., and the fragments of a third-century bath mosaic.

The museum stands in that part of the city that was destroyed by the Germans in 1943 whose significant reconstruction after the war can be largely attributed to Fernand Pouillon. The multistory houses are grouped on several monumental alignments that lead up to the hills with wide steps and broad avenues. The natural stone cladding applied to the austere shapes and numerous allegorical reliefs, clearly reflect the French neo-classical monumental architecture of the 1930s.

Of the older buildings, the old city hall built by Bernard Levieux in 1653-1672 is the most noteworthy. The arrangement of the façade is especially interesting (see right). In the middle section, the upper floors are slightly recessed; because a middle emphasis is missing, the front acts like a projection of a three-winged complex in a relief panel.

The Maison Diamantée is also of interest. Built between 1593 and 1620 by Nicola de Robbio, the palace, with its elegant diamond-shaped stonework, is based on the Palazzo dei Diamanti in Ferrara. The interior has mannerist decoration that includes traditional motifs of market life (cabbage leaves, crawfish, etc.). The Musée du Vieux Marseille, documenting the modern history of the city, now occupies the building. The harbor quarter is dominated in these parts by the Hôtel Dieu (started in 1684) with its overlapping rows of arcades.

The Quartier du Panier on the heights north of the old port with its stepped streets and narrow walkways is the last surviving part of old Marseilles, and is occupied at the present primarily by Arab and Asian immigrants. Having fallen into disrepair and neglected for some time, the quarter has been cleaned up in the last couple of years. Its focal point is the Vieille Charité (illus. right).

The Vieille Charité was originally built as a hospice for the poor by Pierre Puget in 1655, and was based on a similar institution in Lyon. In 1704, the church of the complex was finished, and received a portico in 1863. The entire complex, then as now, is a bulwark of concentration and inspiration due to the building's square construction, built around a gigantic inner courtyard and setting it apart from the surrounding quarter. Arcaded entrances on three floors overlook the courtyard; their

connecting passages lead to most of the rooms in the building, and due to their design they are always well lit and ventilated. The domed chapel which stands in the middle of the courtyard is a neo-classical building. The oval ground-plan of the entrance and altar area intersect the oval main area. In the transept, two spacious side-chapels are separated from the main area by a colonnade. All of the sections are connected via a narrow oval ambulatory. The original space-saving solution is copied in the Chapelle de l'Oratoire in Avignon. Since the early 1990s, the entire complex has been used as a museum and exhibition center, containing important collections of African, Far Eastern, Egyptian, Grecian, and medieval art. The Egyptian museum whose collection was mainly bequeathed by Dr. Clot-Bey (early nineteenth century) is the largest of its kind in France after the Louvre. The Celtic-Ligurian exhibits, especially those from Roquepertuse are of particular interest for the history of the Provence.

The Cathedral

The cathedral of Marseilles stands on a ledge below the Vieille Charité (see above), far from the center of the modern city. The splendidly colored building was designed by the architects Léon Vaudoyer, Henri Révoil and Henri Espérandieu. The building is over 466 ft (140 m) long and rises inside to a height of 200 ft (60 m). It is only too apparent from the dimensions and the combination of so many different architectural styles, that the prosperity of the city in the nineteenth century gave rise to the wish to build the "most beautiful post-medieval cathedral in France." The gallery choir was inspired by large, Franco-Roman buildings, the cupola by the Byzantine style, and the variegated stone by medieval Italian architecture.

Next to the cathedral, the old building of the episcopal church of Notre-Dame-de-la-Major stands humbly overshadowed by the new building, particularly since its nave had to give way to the ambitious new architecture. This church dates from ca. 1150 and is one of the most

OPPOSITE:
Marseilles
New cathedral, 1852-1893
(above)
To the right of it, part of the
original Cathedral of Notre-
Dame-de-la-Major (mid-12th
century) can be seen.
Interior of the New Cathedral
looking eastward (below)

inspiring examples of the Provençal Romanesque despite its fragmented condition. Stepped arcades support the raised nave of the basilica. A quadrilateral tower rises above a transverse rectangular bay that is not a transept in the true sense. In order to achieve a uniform quadrilateral foundation for the tower, a support had to be built over the inwardly stepped arches above the arcades. In the trompes in the corners there are statues of the Evangelists such as are found in other Provençal churches. The inside of the choir apse is also ornamented with blind arcades in the traditional way (see below).

The Lazarus altar in the northern transept was created in 1475-1479 by Francesco Laurana and Malvito da Como. The main altar stands to the left of the two double arcades topped with a pediment; to the right, the shrine containing a reliquary of the saints is housed under a pediment. There are statues of Lazarus between Martha and Mary Magdalene on the altar, of which the base depicts scenes from the life of Lazarus, beginning with his rising from the dead before he became a bishop and martyr in Provence. The Neapolitan sculptors were commissioned by King René I, and have produced here some of the greatest Renaissance sculptures on French soil.

The new harbor complex starts right by the cathedral and stretches several miles to the north. The Docks de la Joliette warehouses were built in 1858-1866 by the engineer Gustave Desplaces not far from the cathedral are of special interest. For reasons of fire resistance, the warehouses were built of stone, iron, and glass and are used today as exhibition and concert halls. This is also the place to find information about the Cosquer cave and its spectacular pre-historic paintings that were discovered in the Calanques in 1991.

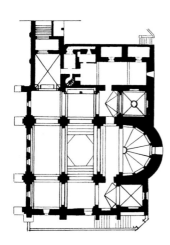

Marseilles
The Cathedral of
Notre-Dame-de-la-Major
ground plan (above)
View from the transept looking
to the northeast (right)
Group mourning the death of
Christ (far right)

Marseilles
New cathedral
Apse at the end of
the right-hand nave

remained preserved on the south side. When further construction took place in the thirteenth century, it was covered over and became part of the crypt. The present nave was part of the new building. Pope Urban V. (1362-70), the former abbot, enlarged the eastern part of the church and fortified it. After the French Revolution, significant sections of the abbey, such as the Romanesque cloister and the enclosure buildings were demolished. Now that these extensions have gone, the exterior looks rather plain and austere (see left). The defensive structures (battlements and missile shafts) strengthen this impression. The foundations of the Tour d'Isarn on the north side consisting of ashlar blocks survives from the eleventh century church. The church entrance consists of a portico within the tower. There is powerful band-ribbing under the strongly emphasized vault caps which are among the earliest examples of rib-vaulting. The interior of the thirteenth-century upper church consists of a three-aisled basilica of surprising plainness (see above). It is, however, a rare example of Provençal architecture between the great Romanesque tradition and the gothic building techniques. Romanesque features are retained in the pointed-barrel vaulting that covers the nave. The vaults do not seem to have been planned for originally, because the pilasters have pillars for the diagonal ribs of the ribbed-vaulting system, as in the side-aisles. The fourteenth-century eastern section clearly shows the intention to fortify the church. The walls are more than 10 ft (3 m) thick and have exceptionally small windows.

OPPOSITE:
Marseilles
St-Victor
View of the crypt.
View of the confessional (above and below left).
Detail of a late 4th-century wooden sarcophagus (above right).
Head of Lazarus carved on the wall by a capital (below right)

Marseilles
St-Victor (third quarter of the 14th century)
View to the Northeast (above)
Groundplan below)

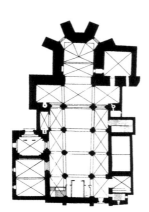

St-Victor

From the perspective of art history, the abbey of St-Victor, which stands on the heights south of the harbor basin, represents the most significant monument in the city. St. Victor, a Roman officer who converted to Christianity, is believed to have been martyred under Maximian in Marseilles and buried in a graveyard outside the city. The hermit Johannes Cassianus founded a monastery here at the beginning of the fifth century within whose precincts many Christians were buried. In the late tenth century, the monastery was reorganized on stricter lines. Placed under Benedictine rule in 977, and under the protection of the vicomtes in the eleventh century, the abbey became one of the most powerful in the western world and had a significant influence on the reform movement of this period. By the end of the century, the abbey had accumulated many estates around it. At the same time, a new church was built under the abbots Wifried (1005-20) and Isarn (1020-47). The early-Christian basilica of Notre-Dame,

Marseilles
St-Victor
In the transept looking east

The southern side-aisle contains a 5th-century sarcophagus, depicting the Giving of the Law, Abraham's Sacrifice, and the Healing of the Blind.

From the western end of the nave there are steps down to deep crypts which contain the oldest remains of the abbey complex. This part was altered so many times that the exact date of the foundation remains a mystery to some degree. It is significant to realize that this was first the site of an old stone quarry whose depths housed catacombs and tombs. In the thirteenth century this part was closed off from above with vaulting, and pilaster foundations were put in place in order to build the upper church. The central part is the Confessional, the three-aisled small structure under the southern side-aisle of the upper church. The so-called Chapelle Notre-Dame de Confession was built directly in front of a cliff face as a three-aisled building with an apse pointing to the north. The right-hand row of rectangular pilasters and the arcades with a patterned decoration of climbing vines and bunches of grapes date from this time. In the thirteenth century, the pilasters on the left side-aisle as well as the apse were removed, thereby creating a balde-quin visible on all sides. There are two third-century graves in this part of the church. Behind the Confessional, an irregular ambulatory leads into the cliffs; the relics of St. Victor are said to have been preserved here once. Later, Lazarus and Mary Magdalene were revered here. South of the Confessional, there was once an open atrium. In its original form, it extended from the structure of the small church.

The courtyard was surrounded by 20 ft (6 m) high rectangular pilasters, as is shown by the surviving upper cornice. Later, the atrium was raised and columns were placed in front of the old rectangular pilasters which are much too high for the small Confessional. Just exactly how the church is to be understood in its individual parts remains a mystery.

An additional part of the underchurch, a fifth-century memorial chapel lies beneath the northern entrance tower of the upper church. The frequently re-arranged apse in the eastern section consists of ashlar stone that is hard to date exactly, but was probably started in the first century. It may have been used to protect the clifftop graveyard which faces the sea. In the underchurch, there are several late fourth century sarcophagi featuring rows of arches and trees, distinguished by their powerful relief and lively narrative style. The sarcophagus which depicts the *traditio legis* (on the east wall of the crypt) displays a means of expression that was new in the fifth century and which is characterized by the shallowness of the reliefs, the serious expressions of the

Marseilles
The pilgrim church of Notre-Dame-de-la-Garde, 1853-70

figures, as well an emphasis on the pictorial symbolism. The gravestone of Abbé Isarn, who died in 1047, is near the stairs in the upper church and is one of the first figurative tombs of the Middle Ages. The recumbent figure of the deceased forms a relief covered in the middle by an inscription plate, so that only Isarn's head and feet can be seen. This figurative style that represents the presence of the deceased, accompanied by a written list of his accomplishments, is reminiscent of the illuminated manuscripts of the time.

Notre-Dame-de-la-Garde

From St-Victor, it is a 540-ft (162 m) climb up to the peak occupied by the pilgrim church of Notre-Dame-de-la-Garde (see above) that was built on the site of a medieval chapel. By the thirteenth century, at the latest, the church was integrated into the abbey of St-Victor, which could observe the sea from this position.

Since the late fourteenth century, a Madonna has been honored here, especially by seafarers, and asked for her protection. Henri Espérandieu, one of the cathedral masters, was the architect of the current church building.

The church of Notre-Dame-de-la-Garde has come to represent Marseille as one of its symbols. The church contains a lavish variety of materials and colors as well as a mixture of Byzantine and Italian styles. The tower is crowned by the highly visible statue of the Virgin which stands 30 ft (9 m) high. The interior is ornamented with mosaics and frescos. The crypts which run deep into the cliffs are full of votive offerings from seafarers and travelers asking for the Virgin's protection.

La Canebière and the Palais Longchamps

The famous Canebière connects the old harbor with the eastern parts of the city. Sailors and travelers embark and disembark here to and from all parts of the world. It is therefore an area of trade missions, hotels, and places of entertainment.

The Canebière began as the showpiece of a new town plan in 1666. At first, it was a cul-de-sac lying at a right-angle to the Cours Belsunce. In 1928, it was gradually extended to its final length and has been widened many times over the years. Today, one can guess how the city once appeared by some of the lower sections of seventeenth and eighteenth-century frontages. In 1860, the stock exchange building was placed, significantly, at the beginning of the street near the Quais (see below). The *bourse* was the first building in Marseilles to have an iron skeleton. The Museé de la Marine et de l'Economie de Marseille is housed on the ground floor. The opera house, built in 1924 in art déco style, is some way south of the stock exchange. The ionic colonnade remains from a previous building built in 1787.

The Cours Belsunce, badly damaged during World War II is closed off to the north by the Porte d'Aix, a city gate built in 1825-39 by Penchaud, and modeled on a monumental Roman arch. The Canebière leads to the east to the church of St-Vincent that was built in the middle of the nineteenth century in the high gothic style of northern France.

Progressing from the Canebière, the Boulevard Longchamps ends in the massive

OPPOSITE
Marseilles
Palais Longchamps, 1862-69
The waterfall in the center marks the end of a canal bringing the waters of the river Durance to Marseilles.

Marseille
Stock exchange, 1860
Detail of the façade

Marseilles and eastward

expanse of the Palais Longchamp (see opposite), created by Henri Espérandieu in 1862-69. This combination of a giant artificial waterfall, an art museum, and a nature museum serves also as the terminus of a canal that supplies the city with water from the river Durance, which makes its appearance in a neo-baroque well, enveloped by the allegory of the river, as well as wheat, wine, and a huge bull. Two facing stairways climb around the spot in a semicircle backed by colonnades. The corner building contains the Musée des Beaux-Arts and the Musée d'Histoire Naturelle. Behind the Palais, there is a good example of the kind of monumental architecture that was taught at the Parisian Ecole des Beaux-Arts. With all the means of a classical architectural language (columns, windows, niches) and its integrated sculptural effects, the street space is changed into a magnificent stage set which has only recently received the appreciation it truly deserves.

The art museum is one of France's most important "Provence museums," but it also contains paintings and drawings by Perugino, Rubens, Le Sueur, Rigaud, Greuze, Vernet, and Daumier. The Musée Grobet-Labadie stands opposite the Palais Longchamps. Its collection is typical of the bourgeois art collected in the nineteenth century.

Vallon des Auffes and the Château Borély

The sea is omnipresent in Marseille, especially on the waterside streets which run for a distance of 3 miles (5 km) to the south. The Château du Pharo dominates from the heights above the south side of the harbor. It was built by the architect Hector Martin Lefuel—better known for his extension of the Louvre—for Napoleon III. From the park, there is a great view of old Marseilles and the houses stretching into the distance. The Corniche Président J. F. Kennedy is the promenade which runs along the coast and is full of attractions, such as the picturesque fishing village of Vallon des Auffes (illus. opposite above left) which seems somewhat out of place in the middle of Marseilles.

The Château Borély (see above) lies far to the south. In the year 1767, Jean Borel, a rich local merchant, commissioned the architect Charles-Louis Clérisseau to design a country house. The first design was too reminiscent of an Italian country villa, so a typical French château plan with a clearly accentuated center raised section was finally produced. The interior decoration and layout and lovely grounds of the original are almost completely preserved. In the mid-nineteenth century, Alphan, a Parisian landscape architect, created a large garden that combines elements of both the English landscape garden and the French formal garden.

Marseilles
Château Borély, 1767-78
Garden frontage with gardens.

OPPOSITE:
Marseilles
Fishing village of Vallon des Auffes (above left)

Impressions of the fish market on the quayside of the upper harbor (above right and below)

Le Corbusier's Unité d'habitation

Somewhat further to the south, on the Boulevard Michelet, stands Le Corbusier's most important work. Built in 1947-52 under extreme protest, the Unité d'habitation is a synthesis of his concept of architecture and the resulting problems. The box-like high-rise, raised off the ground by curved stilts, was one of many commissions awarded for reconstruction in 1946.

The Unité d'habitation was supposed to form a self-sufficient subsection of the new city. The main idea of the Unité is the unification of private "cells" (i.e. more individual, planned for single families, with a shared public area for all residents) within an insulated, screen-patterned architectural structure. The block contains a total of 337 apartments with 23 different layouts (mostly duplexes) to house 1,600 people. The apartment units slide into the steel and concrete screen like bottles in a wine rack. Inside, the floors are divided by "street-like" corridors. In addition, there is also a shopping mall, a post office, and a small hotel. The roof terrace is equipped with a gymnasium, a daycare center, and a training circuit. The architecturally applied social utopia of a autonomous residential community has a monastic quality on the one hand and the look of an ocean liner on the other, the latter being clearly alluded to by the optical impression made by the roof construction. The closed system of the Unité has only been partially successful, because the apartment building has become something of a lived-in museum, with its concept known to all

of the residents. Le Corbusier created other Unités in Nantes, Firmigny, and Berlin that do not function nearly as effectively as this pampered example in Marseille.

Still further to the south on the Avenue d'Haifa is the Musée d'Art Contemporain—a complex consisting of uniform modules. It was opened in 1994 and is dedicated to modern French art, containing works by Daniel Buren, Arman, and Martial Raysse among others, with work by the local sculptor César (see below).

Marseilles
Thumb, Sculpture by César in
the Musée d'Art Contemporain

Marseilles
The Château d'If and a view of
the rocky neighboring island of
Ratonneau (right)

The rocky island made world
famous by Alexandre Dumas
in his novel *The Count of
Monte Christo* lies just off the
coast of Marseilles. King
François I converted the island
into a fortress in order to protect the city in 1524. The fort's
square design with its three
round towers—the most massive of which is a castle keep—
is based on medieval predecessors. The towers, however,
met the requirements of modern defensive techniques, in
that they are set off from the
main building and have terraces on the roofs on which-
canons could be placed. A single water-cistern and a chapel
shows that the complex was
fully self-sufficient. Since the
château was never actually
attacked, it was converted into
a prison and used for this purpose between the seventeenth
and nineteenth centuries.

The strange rocky outcrop that stretches between Marseilles and Cassis, the Massif de Calanques, is a spectacular sight. Steep rock needles of blinding white limestone plunge into the blue-green sea. These formations were caused by weathering when the sea rose and fell during the Ice Age, covering the land with ice or water. The last rise in sea-level, 10,000 years ago, flooded the caves which were then inhabited by prehistoric man.

One of these caves was discovered in 1991 by the diver and potholer, Henri Cosquer, near the peak of Cap Morgiou. Swimming through an underwater tunnel for 583 ft (175 m), he reached a large cave in which some former residents had painted and carved numerous images of animals some 27,000 to 19,000 years ago (see Marseilles, Docks de la Juliette, starting on p. 233).

The Calanques have a unique climate. They are fully exposed to the sun yet protected from the Mistral. It very rarely rains here, making for very hot and dry conditions. This unique microclimate has promoted the development of unusual fauna and flora. However, the Calanques are in constant danger from forest fires, the scourge of southern France. The history of the forest fire stretches from Caesar, who set fire to the trees in 49 BC, to the disastrous fire which swept the countryside in 1990. For this reason, driving or walking through the Calanque is strictly regulated. Only three routes are allowed. If coming from inland, there is the D 559 and various footpaths to the shore, or there is a road from the southern peak of Marseilles, or thirdly, a hiking trail from Cassis that follows the cliffs.

There is a fourth option, which is to see the magnificence of the Calanques from a boat (excursions are arranged from Marseilles or Cassis). Calanques is also a paradise for scuba-divers and snorkellers, due in no small part to the favorable climatic conditions. However, certain restrictions are in force, in order to prevent pollution.

ON PP. 244-45:
Cassis
Calanque de Port-Miou

LEFT:
Cassis
Town and harbor (above)

Cap Canaille
View of the coast between
Cassis and La Ciotat (below)

OPPOSITE:
Rocky bay near Cassis

Red Rocks and Blue Sea

The Côte d'Azur from Bandol to Antibes, via St-Tropez

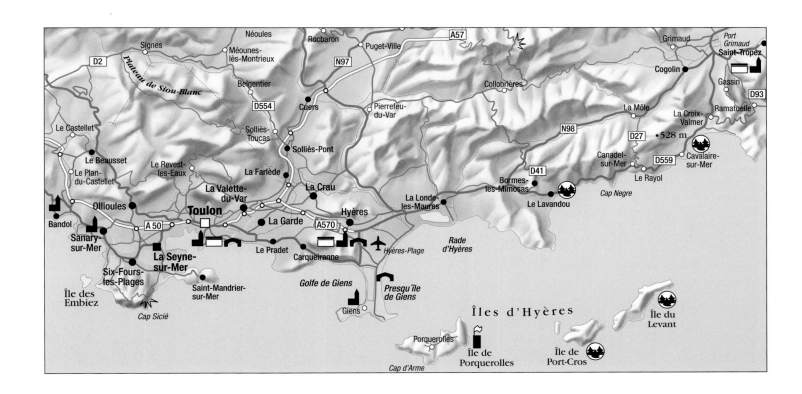

Sanary-sur-Mer
View of the harbor

Bandol
Bathing beach

The holiday resorts of Bandol
and Sanary-sur-Mer lie west of
Toulon, separated by the Cap
Sicié peninsula. From the early
20th century to the 1930s,
Sanary had a flourishing
colony of foreign artists.

OPPOSITE:
Toulon
General view of the city
showing the large harbors
and the St-Mandrier peninsula
in the distance.

Toulon

In Roman times, this was the site of the small settlement of Telo Martius, which specialized in purple dyeing. Although a bishop was in residence here from the fifth century onward, for a long while the town remained insignificant. It was only when Provence fell to France in 1481 that Toulon began to develop as a naval port, and this was to give the city its importance for the next five hundred years. When Louis XIV built his own fleet, he based it in Toulon, where he also opened extensive dockyards.

French colonization of Africa in the nineteenth century was organized mainly through this naval port. The price the town had to pay for its conspicuous military presence later proved to be a high one. In 1942, when Germans captured the unoccupied French so-called "free zone," the French military fleet sabotaged the port to prevent its use by Hitler's troops, scuttling 75 battleships in the harbor. After the war, it took

ten years to remove this barricade of ships. When the Allied Forces landed in France in August 1944, Toulon was one of the main positions to be taken after heavy fighting on August 19-26. During decolonization after the war, the city's crucial role in colonial times meant that thousands of French former colonists, particularly from Algeria, settled here. It was only recently, with the crisis in the shipbuilding industry, that the city discovered its tourist appeal.

Toulon's military past and the very hasty repairs to the extensive damage suffered during World War II mean Toulon is not exactly an attractive city. However, the panoramic views offered by the surrounding hills—particularly from Mont Faron to the north—over the vast bay, with the seaport located in the center (illustrations above and right), are impressive. The old quarters of the city alongside the Quai Cronstadt are also worth seeing, with the Cathédrale Ste-Marie-Majeure, which dates

back to the twelfth and thirteenth centuries. In the seventeenth century, the building was substantially extended toward the north, whilst largely retaining the medieval shape. The church of St-François-de-Paul (1744), with its curved frontage, is located almost at the edge of the harbor basin. To the west of the old town lies the Church of St-Louis, built in the austere neo-classical style by Sigaud in 1783-89. Tall Tuscan-style columns predominate, forming a colonnade in the nave with a coffered ceiling directly above, and without an upper gallery. The gateway to the Arsenal was built in 1738, in the form of a triumphal arch, decorated with allegories of Mars and Bellona (illustration left). To the north of this is the Place d'Armes, a large rectangular parade ground, built on the orders of Colbert in 1683. Toulon has created several museums to document its turbulent past, including the Musée de la Marine (at the Arsenal) and the Musée du Vieux Toulon (in the former episcopal palace).

The Tour Royale dominates the southern tip of the eastern access to the harbor. This

ABOVE:
Toulon
Old city hall, atlases by Pierre Puget, 1656-57

LEFT:
Toulon
The Arsenal, baroque façade with allegorical figures around the entrance, 1738

OPPOSITE:
Hyères
Rob Mallet-Stevens
Villa de Noailles, 1924. View of an interior and the cubist garden designed by G. Guévrékian

fortress was commissioned by Louis XII and built in 1514-24 by the Italian master fortress-builder Giovanni Antonio de la Porta. This imposing edifice is not blocked by bastions to keep the canon at a safe distance behind the lines, as was later to become a common practice.

Hyères

This sub-colony of Marseille, founded by the Greeks in around 350 BC, was given the name Olbia. The Romans built the settlement up into a fortress. In the Middle Ages, the city center shifted to the foot of the hillside. Under the Lords of Fos, the city resisted Charles I of Anjou until 1257 and later dominated the rival town of Toulon; from 1532, it was even the seat of a seneschal. However, in the seventeenth century, this office was transferred to Toulon and the fortifications had to be demolished. In the nineteenth century Hyères experienced a new wave of prosperity when it became one of the most popular and fashionable seaside resorts on the Riviera. Today, thanks to the excellent beaches on the Giens peninsula, it is a paradise for windsurfers in particular.

St-Louis, originally the church of the Franciscan convent outside the town, is thought to have been built in the thirteenth century. Outwardly unadorned, the interior with its three naves still features Romanesque barrel vaults. The central nave was ribbed at a later date. There are ruins of a large medieval château on the Colline du Castéou overlooking the city. Below this, on the edge of the Parc St. Bernard, stands one of the most important buildings in modern French architecture.

The Villa de Noailles

The Villa de Noailles was commissioned by the patrons Charles and Marie-Laure de Noailles in 1924 and designed by Rob Mallet-Stevens, on the principles of Le Corbusier the most important French architect of the "White Modernist Movement." In conjunction with other avant-garde artists, he created a tangible example of modern life. Gabriel Guévrékian designed a Cubist garden, Pierre Chareau and Marcel Breuer created the furniture, Jacques Lipschitz carved the garden sculpture. The architecture developed in the course of gradual extension of an initial villa project. The geometrical planes used in the shape of the building follow the reliefs of the hillside and create a striking pattern of light and shade in the harsh light of the Mediterranean sun. The boundaries between interior and exterior have been deliberately eliminated; a walled garden is furnished like a room, complete with windows. Of particular importance was a fitness room with a swimming pool and swings. In 1929, Man Ray made one of the early architecture films in the villa entitled *Les mystères du Château au dé* (The Mysteries of the Dice Castle).

Hyères
Flowery decoration on an entrance to a private house

Porquerolles island
Botanical Park

The Giens Peninsula and the Iles d'Hyères

Olbia, several remains of whose checkerboard ground plan are still visible on the beach of Almanarre, opposite the N 559, was a Roman settlement. Part of the eastern city wall of huge stone blocks still stands, as does the gateway which led to the ancient harbor, now the site of the airport. To the south lies the Giens peninsula, an unusual natural phenomenon. The rocky plateau of Giens is linked to the mainland by two parallel sandbars. The western one is very narrow and the wind erodes the dunes, so that sea water constantly flows into a lagoon between the two sandbars, providing the ideal habitat for seabirds, particularly flamingoes. Salt is extracted from the northern part of the lagoon. The constant, powerful west wind and the long, uniformly flat beach on the western sandbar provide ideal conditions for windsurfers. There is a ferry across from La Tour Fondue at the southern tip of the peninsula to the Iles d'Hyères.

Rising to a height of almost 666 ft (200 m), the thickly wooded islands off the coast between Hyères and Le Lavandou are some of the finest natural attractions of Provence. Both Greeks and Romans had settlements here to enable them to control shipping. However, from the fifth through the sixteenth century, the islands served as a base for pirates and all attempts to drive them out failed. At the close of the sixteenth century, anyone who went to live there was offered exemption from taxes, but this did not work either, as fear of the pirates was a powerful deterrent. Then criminals were incarcerated on the island in the hope that they would keep the pirates at bay, but they themselves soon took over the pirates' trade. It was only under Cardinal Richelieu that control was gained over the undesirable inhabitants and fortresses were built. The islands served a military purpose for the last time during World War II, when the Germans set up bunkers and heavy artillery here. This meant that during the Allied landings in August 1944, the German defenses had to first be destroyed.

In the nineteenth century, the islands were sold as individual country estates. The main island, the Île de Porquerolles, benefited from this in a most unusual way. From 1911 through 1971, it was owned by a Belgian engineer who had made his fortune in Mexico. He transformed the island into an exotic garden. Fort Ste-Agathe, beneath whose walls one lands on the island, was built in 1532. The massive corner tower of the trapezium-shaped structure is still evidence of this. Until well into the nineteenth century, when it was abandoned, it was constantly adapted to suit changing military requirements.

The whole of the Île de Port-Cros is a nature reserve where Mediterranean flora and fauna

Porquerolles-Insel
Plage d'Argent

can grow wild. On the southern side of the island, the cliffs rise to a height of 650 ft (195m). On the northern side of the island, even inexperienced divers have the opportunity to explore the underwater world.

The Île du Levant, of which only a small area to the west of the island is accessible (the rest is a military zone), has been a nudist colony since the beginning of the twentieth century. It was founded here in 1931 as the expression of a healthy lifestyle by a Dr. Durville, and given the name of Héliopolis (Sun City).

The Massif des Maures

Like the Massif de l'Esterel, the Massif des Maures is a special geological feature, because it does not consist of limestone, like the rest of the Côte d'Azur, but of bedrock (in particular gneiss and slate). The three mountain chains of Hyères that stretch across to St-Raphaël, are fairly-flat topped, sometimes resembling an elevated plain.

Pines and conifers are the natural vegetation only along the coast, inland it is chestnut and oak trees that predominate. Cork- oaks were planted here particularly in the nineteenth century for use in the production of bottle corks. In recent decades cork production has again increased in importance, which is why oak trees can be seen everywhere with half their bark removed.

A veritable tree museum containing over 500 different species of tree has been created in the Gratteloup arboretum (on the N 98). Other sights worth visiting are the Chapel of Notre-Dame-des-Anges high on the hillside and the village of Gonfaron with its small museum about the manufacture of corks. Nearby, on the D 75, is the "Tortoise village," where attempts are being made to re-establish the European tortoise (*Testudo graeca*), previously common in the Massif des Maures but now largely extinct.

The Chartreuse de la Verne (illus. page 259) top) is located amid impressive scenery, close

to a spring but in complete isolation. The Carthusian monastery was founded in 1170, but the buildings visible today were built mainly in the seventeenth an eighteenth century.

Grimaud (illus. left) is the ancestral home of the Grimaldi family. In the tenth century, Gibelin de Grimaldi was given the site to protect it from the Saracens. The castle, which still dominates the village and its narrow lanes, was built in the eleventh century.

The area is otherwise only sparsely populated; in late antiquity, it served as a refuge from the Saracens, who themselves seem to have maintained a kind of fortified castle close to where La Garde Freinet is located today. Otherwise, activities focused on the coast and the sea, although even here along the Corniche des Maures there were only small fishing villages. The hinterland remained virtually unpopulated. Recent decades have seen a further population increase along the coastal strip with its attractive beaches and bays.

Massif des Maures
Cork-oaks

LEFT:
Grimaud
Village with
11th-century château

Massif des Maures
Cork-oaks (opposite)

Charterhouse of la Verne and
surrounding forests (right)

St. Tropez

According to legend, St. Tropez was where the boat came ashore in which St. Tropes, a Roman soldier condemned to death in the year 68 under Nero, had been cast adrift; he was subsequently buried here. St. Tropez, which probably grew out of a Greek settlement called Athenopolis Massiliensum, was a small fishing village until the fifteenth century. In 1470, the harbor was extended on the orders of King René I. At the same time, 60 families moved here from Genoa.

The economic upturn which led to St. Tropez becoming a fashionable seaside resort began in the second half of the nineteenth century, when first the Impressionists (see also Paul Signac), then the French avant-garde (Cocteau, Colette, etc.), and finally film and show-business stars such as Brigitte Bardot, discovered the idyllic location, which nowadays can hardly cope with the influx of visitors.

The old town has nevertheless remained rural and picturesque. A market is still held in the large Place Carnot, surrounded by shady plane trees. The museum in the Chapelle de l'Annonciade in the harbor, contains many paintings by the great exponents of French modern art—Bonnard, Vuillard, Braque, Matisse, etc.— and is well worth a visit. The citadel above the city was begun in 1583. The regular hexagonal building, flanked by towers, offers an outstanding panorama. On leaving the city on the N 98A, one finds the Hôtel Latitude 43 (where the road forks), built by the architect Georges Pinguisson in 1932 as a huge artists' colony (illus. bottom left). The long continuous balconies, round windows, and bow-like curves of the white building make it look like an ocean liner, and lends the whole structure an air of the modern and fashionable.

At the centre of the St. Tropez peninsula is the ancient wine-making village of Ramatuelle, certified in 1056 as the property of St-Victor in Marseille. Modern buildings hardly intrude on the small village, located on its virtually circular site. A patchwork of crooked lanes and narrow steps crisscrosses the concentric rows of houses. A footpath begins at St. Tropez and encircles the peninsula, mostly hugging the coastline. This path was laid in the nineteenth century for the use of customs officers whose job it was to ensure that no contraband reached the shore. Nowadays the path, which is over 12 miles (20 km) in length, leads over rocks and sandy beaches to the beach of Cigaro on the south side of the peninsula, where there is a botanical garden.

St. Tropez
View of the harbor and of the bay at dusk (above and opposite)
Hôtel Latitude 43, 1932 (left)

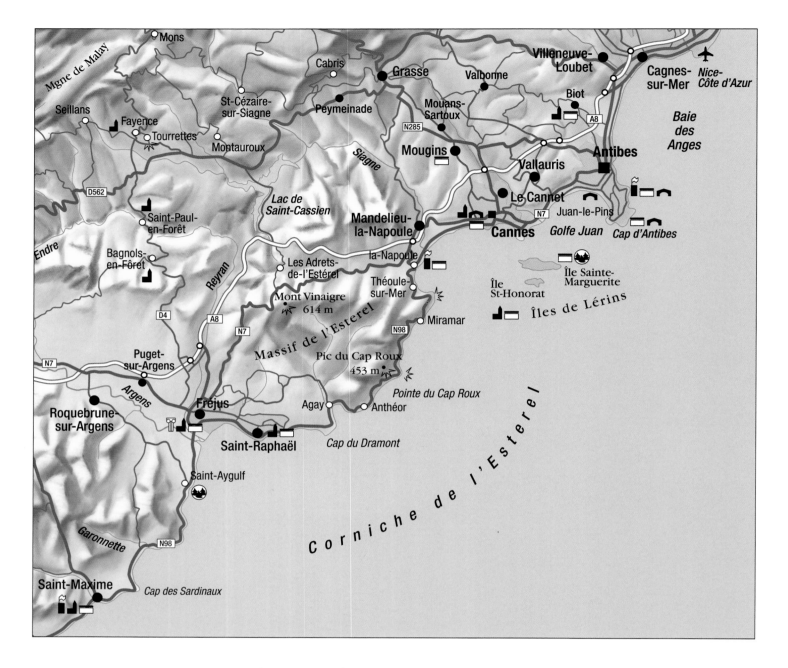

Fréjus, the Pompei of Provence

By 49 BC, Caesar had founded the Forum Julii, presumably a military base on the road over the Massif de l'Esterel. The city soon had a harbor, because Octavian, later Emperor Augustus, had large docks built and Cleopatra's warships, captured in the sea battle of Actium, were brought back here. Shortly afterward, the city was handed over to the veterans of the Eighth Legion and subsequently enjoyed a golden age as a military port and the seat of a prefect. From around 374 AD it became a bishopric. The following centuries, however, saw a substantial fall in the population and the destruction of the city by the Saracens operating out of St. Tropez. Urban life only revived in the eleventh century, as testified to by the building of new ramparts round the city, albeit encompassing a much smaller area than in Roman times. At that point, only the area around the cathedral

was fortified. However, sea trade—particularly with Genoa—soon enabled the city to prosper again and it gradually spread beyond its walls. In the sixteenth century, a larger wall was built to enclose the new neighborhoods, which had grown toward the Porte des Gaules. However, the area of the city at that time still barely covered a quarter of the ancient site. The harbor began to silt up, becoming unusable by the seventeenth century, and the resulting marshland became a breeding ground for epidemics. Only in the early nineteenth century, when the old harbor basin was filled in, could the area be used for agricultural purposes.

In the early 20th century, Fréjus was the scene of a milestone in aviation history, when in 1911 an airfield was built for seaplanes, and in 1913 when Roland Garros took off from here on the air crossing of the Mediterranean (Fréjus-Bizerta). In 1959, Fréjus suffered one of

France's worst environmental disasters. Over 400 people lost their lives when the Malpasset dam (illus. right) burst. Today, in addition to the regional distribution of agricultural produce (especially flowers), summer tourism constitutes the city's main source of income.

There are still many sites where the extensive old city with its harbor can be seen, but compared with Arles, the remains are less spectacular. The harbor, which covered an area of about 55 acres (22 ha), was triangular in shape. The eastern side was the harbor exit, which was marked by the Lanterne d'August, still visible today. Its pyramid-shaped top appears to have been added during the Middle Ages. The quay wall is also still very visible. A channel led from here out to the open sea. The actual harbor basin formed the other side of the triangle. The western side of the triangle is still marked by the Butte St. Antoine, the Porte d'Orée, and the Avenue Aristide Briand. The Butte St. Antoine was a sort of platform, built to safeguard the harbor and parts of its foundation walls still exist. To the south, the counterpart to this was the so-called *Plate-Forme*, with the docks directly beneath it. In the *Plate-Forme*, underground sections of the Roman city can still be viewed today. These include the remains of the city fortifications, a peristyle courtyard, plus remnants of the small thermal baths and a water cistern. The *Plate-Forme* marks the eastern tip of an ancient city built in the shape of an irregular rectangle. Not far from here, on the N 7 towards Cannes, there are the impressive ruins of the aqueduct which brought water to the city from the Siagnole spring 25 miles (40 km) away.

At the most westerly point of the Roman city stood the amphitheater, the best preserved historical building in Fréjus (illus. right). Going by its slightly irregular stonework, it must have already been built in the early part of the first century. It measures only 376 ft (113 m) in length and 273 ft (82 m) in width, so it was considerably smaller than the amphitheaters of Nîmes and Arles, which were built somewhat later, although the arena, at about 6 ft 8 in (2 m) depth and paved with stone, is almost the same size as its counterparts in the other two cities. The 16 rows of seats in Fréjus were able to accommodate around 12,000 spectators. Along the upper edge, a colonnaded hall with a wooden roof truss led around the structure, a feature which was lacking on similar later buildings. Since the amphitheater in Fréjus was generally simpler in design and smaller, the complicated passageway and corridor system could be dispensed with in the outer supporting structures. The *cavea* also follows to a certain extent the slope of the hillside. Of the stone façade, virtually nothing remains, because this material was used in the Middle Ages to build new fortifications.

The burst dam of Malpasset
In 1856, plans were made to master the problem of water shortage in Fréjus by damming the Reyran near Malpasset a few miles inland. The idea was, however, only put into practice after World War II, creating an artificial lake with 166 million cu ft (50 million cu m) capacity by 1954.
On December 2, 1959, torrential rainfall caused the water level of the lake to rise steadily, with emergency discharge facilities unable to release sufficient water. At 9.10 pm, the dam finally burst and within 20 minutes a 183 ft (55 m) high wave surged down to Fréjus, sweeping hundreds of people, animals, and monuments along in its path. The remains of the dam, which was never rebuilt, are not far from the motorway (D 37 from Fréjus, parking below the motorway, then take the footpath).

LEFT
AND BELOW LEFT:
Fréjus
Amphitheater, first half of 1st century interior and exterior.

The cathedral complex of Fréjus

The cathedral area, with its baptistery, cloister, and bishop's palace, constitutes the focal point of Fréjus. Today, it has been largely cleared of annexes and is surrounded by attractive squares with cafés. The oldest standing parts of a bishop's church, especially the baptistery, are thought to date from the time of Bishop Leontius who held office in the year 433. Once Count Guillaume de Provence had driven out the Saracens in 975, he handed over half of the city, including the harbor, to Bishop Riculfe in 990, who thus became the first episcopal lord of the manor in Provence. Going by its stonework, the current cathedral (illus. left) must date back to the second half of the twelfth century. The cloister followed in the thirteenth century.

The entrance to the complex is via a portal built in 1530 and featuring fine carvings which, like those at the entrance to the cathedral in Aix, combine Late Gothic and Renaissance elements. To the west of the adjacent porch is the octagonal baptistery (illus. page 265, top left). The sides of the lower floor feature alternating flat and semi-circular niches, separated by pillars almost 13 ft (4 m) high. These originate from a Roman building, as do six of the eight Corinthian capitals. On the upper floor, the octagon becomes sixteen-sided. Unlike other early Christian baptisteries, the small building in Fréjus contains no separate gallery around the central octagonal baptismal font, which was originally lined with marble. In its basic form the building is similar to the early Christian baptisteries in Aix, Marseille, and Riez. However, it shows the greatest resemblance to the baptistery in Albenga on the Ligurian coast which, thanks to its mosaics, can be dated back to the fifth century. The baptistery in Fréjus would therefore seem to have been built at around the same time.

On the north side of the baptistery, the chapter-house, built around 1200 and referred to as the *Capitou*, looks like a mediaeval palace. The twin naves of this cathedral, which has no transept, perhaps retaining the memory of an early Christian church group, were built at the same time. Work on the current building began toward the end of the twelfth century, the narrower northern nave being given a pointed barrel vault. When it came to vaulting the main nave, a different solution was chosen, because ribbed vaulting was later installed mounted across three square crossbeams (illus. page 265, far right). This meant that every second pillar already built had to be reinforced, although the supports between them could be removed. Of the cathedral furnishings, especially the choir stalls carved by Flameng de Toulon in 1441, are worthy of note (illus. page 265 bottom left).

Fréjus
Cathedral and Baptistery,
Exterior view (opposite page)

5th-century baptistery,
Interior (above right)

Wood carving on the Cathedral
door, 1530 (center right)

Choir-stalls in the Cathedral,
1441 (below right)

Cathedral, interior
(extreme right)

The Côte d'Azur from Bandol to Antibes

LEFT:
Fréjus
Cathedral, north side of the side-nave
Altar painting of St. Margaret by Jacques Durandi, second half of 15th century.

OPPOSITE PAGE:
Fréjus
The cathedral cloister
Wooden balcony support (above)
Interior courtyard of cloister with fountain (below left)
Colonnade in the cloister (below right)

The small cloister was originally meant to contain a ribbed vault, but instead was covered with a flat timber ceiling. The squares between the beams contain some astonishingly well-preserved paintings depicting amusing scenes. Today, the cloister contains the city archeological museum, which contains, among other things, a completely preserved Roman mosaic.

The Massif de l'Esterel

The Massif de l'Esterel is the mountain range stretching from Fréjus to Cannes (illus. pp. 269-71). Like the Massif des Maures, it is not the limestone rock generally found in the foothills of the Alps, but is a jagged block of bright red and sometimes blueish porphyry. This creates a unique blend of color, particularly on the coast around the Bay of Agay and Cap Roux, where the red of the rocks contrasts with the blue-green of the water and the deep blue of the sky. The mountains also rise sheer along the coast, the highest point being the Mont Vinaigre at 2060 ft (618 m).

Today the massif is only sparsely wooded and mainly covered with low, stunted vegetation. This was not always the case, because like the Massif des Maures, live oaks and chestnuts should grow naturally in this region. However, countless forest fires have decimated the woodland here. The forestry authorities are now trying to encourage a mixed forest, which is not only less susceptible to the risk of fire, but also meets the natural requirements of the region and fits in with the wealth of fauna, which is why in addition to cork and sessile oaks the land has been planted with fruit trees, cypresses, acacias, and many other species. As late as the early twentieth century, the Esterel was still virtually inaccessible, hence its long notoriety for the robber bands which had retreated here. Much of it is the stuff of legend. The highwayman Mandrin, who committed his crimes mainly in Savoy in the eighteenth century, is unlikely ever to have seen the Mediterranean coast. Gaspard de Besse and his gang, on the other hand, lay in wait for travelers close to Mont Vinaigre, and ambushed them. In 1780, the highwaymen were caught and executed. The Via Aurelia and the roads which later followed this same route have been used by travelers since Roman times to cross the mountains, and the N 7 still follows basically the same path today. There are various hilltops along the coastal road which allow a view of the coast from the Massif de l'Esterel, including the Sémaphore du Dramont, the Pointe de l'Observatoire, and the Pointe de l'Esquillon.

There is a curiosity just off the coast at Dramont called the Île d'Or. In 1897, this tiny rocky island was acquired by the Parisian doctor Auguste Lutand, who built a fortified tower in the mediaeval tradition and declared the rock to be an independent kingdom. The eccentric King Auguste I died in 1925, having become one of the best-known figures in the fashionable society of the Côte d'Azur.

The highest peaks in the range are the Pic du Cap Roux 1506 ft (452 m) and the Pic de l'Ours 1640 ft (492 m). A climb to them gives a view from almost 1666 ft (500 m) above sea level. The Mal Infernet with the Lac de l'Ecureuil have a delightful microclimate, because here it is always cool and pleasant even in mid-summer.

The Environs of Fréjus

The immediate environs of Fréjus offer a number of remarkable sights. Situated to the west, in the direction of Le Muy, there is the picturesque city of Roquebrune-sur-Argens with its sixteenth-century church and a museum dedicated to the prehistoric and ancient history of the region. Further west is a small jagged massif, the Rocher de Roquebrune, which forms the foothills of the Massif des Maures.

The D 4 north from Fréjus leads to the Missiri Mosque (illus. above), which was built for West African soldiers stationed in Fréjus. This is a replica of the Missiri de Djenné Mosque in Mali. To the east of Fréjus, along the N 7, is the Hong Hien Pagoda, built in 1917 for Vietnamese soldiers in French military service (illus. center and left).

LEFT:

Near Fréjus
Missiri Mosque, 1920s (above)
Hong Hien Pagoda, 1917 (center and below)

OPPOSITE:

Massif and Corniche de l'Esterel
Mont Vinaigre (above left)
Coastline near Agay (above right and below)

PP. 270-71
Corniche de l'Esterel
Cap Roux and the
Pic du Cap Roux

Cannes

Cannes was for a long time an insignificant fishing port, whose early history took place mainly on the islands lying offshore, the Îles de Lérins. According to the writers of antiquity, the largest of these islands, Ste-Marguerite contained a Roman settlement and a harbor. This is confirmed by discoveries of ancient walls, mosaics, and ceramics dating back to the period between the third century BC and the first century AD. In 405, St. Honoratus, who was destined to become bishop of Arles in 429, adopted the way of life of the hermit monks (anchorites) who had lived throughout the eastern Mediterranean since the third century and moved to Lerina, the smaller island now named for him. The colony of monks which grew up here set up its own order. Lérins is therefore one of the earliest orders founded in Gaul, alongside the one set up by St. Martin of Tours, near Poitiers, and the order of St-Victor in Marseille established by St. Jean Cassianus. In the fifth century, the hermit movement was still spreading to other places in Provence, such as Vence and Cimiez, and throughout the rest of Gaul. In 660, the Benedictine Order was established in the monastery. Countless priories, particularly in Provence as well as in Northern Spain and Italy, testify to the wealth of the cloister. To protect themselves from the Saracens, the monks also founded a colony on the mainland opposite the islands, the nucleus of what Cannes is today. The small port remained a dependency of the monastery until it was dissolved in 1788.

The city's transformation into a luxury vacation destination began in the nineteenth century. In 1834, the English aristocrat Lord Brougham found Cannes a pleasant place in which to escape England's winter fog. Many of his compatriots followed his example, with the French and particularly the Russians doing the same, and a boom rapidly set in. Prosper Mérimée, Guy de Montpassant, and Stéphen Liégeard frequented Cannes. Liégeard, a nineteenth-century novelist, is virtually unknown nowadays, but it was he who, in a novel published in 1887, christened France's highly colorful Alpine coast the Côte d'Azur. From the 1930s, Cannes became a fashionable summer seaside resort, concentrating on the upper-class tourist trade. Virtually nowhere else are there so many luxury hotels and restaurants, with gastronomy playing such a major part of the local economy. In addition, Cannes is also immensely active as a congress and festival city. The famous international film festival is just one of many events held here each year; others are dedicated for example to the music business, television programs, etc.

Cannes is dominated by its large residential complexes and hotels, many of which—especially along the Boulevard de la Croisette—still display the splendid, luxurious façades of the Belle Epoque. The famous boulevard itself was already laid out in 1868 with palms added several years later. In the harsh winter of 1985,

Initiated by Jean Zay, the Minister for Culture in the Popular Front government, the Cannes International Film Festival was due to be inaugurated on September 1, 1939, but the outbreak of War prevented it. It was not until 1946 that the idea of the festival could be revived. The films were shown in the city 's casino, with Michèle Morgan and Ray Milland being awarded the first prizes for acting. The Palme d'Or went to *La Bataille du Rail* by René Clément, the Grand Prix de la Critique to *Brief Encounter* by David Lean. By 1947 a festival hall had been built especially for the event, which was to be held regularly in May of each year. The Festival has become a focal point for producers, directors, actors, film distributors, and journalists. The public are only allowed in to see a selection of films. Accompanied by extremely lively mass media participation, Cannes delivers verdicts on new films which have to meet strict selection criteria. The films must have been produced in the 12 months preceding the festival and must not have been shown at any other competition. The festival in Cannes has established itself as one of the world's leading film festivals, alongside Venice and Berlin.

many of them died. The sandy beach below the Boulevard, so inviting to bathers, was not there originally; in 1963, 415,000 cu ft (125,000 cu. m) of sand were deposited here, with breakwaters to prevent it being washed away. The current festival building is the second one to be built, the first, opened in 1947, was a little to the east of the boulevard and was demolished in 1990.

When the new Palais des Congrès, designed by Pierre Braslawsky, François Druet, and Hubert Bennet, opened in 1982, there was an instant storm of protest. The huge block, with rooms which could not be fully utilized, was immediately labeled "the bunker" and had to be remodeled at once. A large glass panel on the north side now alleviates some of the heaviness and the flight of steps leading up to the building has been re-designed, as have many of the rooms inside. To the left of the flight of steps, concrete slabs have been laid in which famous film stars have left handprints.

Cannes
Boulevard de la Croisette (above)
Carlton Hotel with the Boulevard de la Croisette (left)

The Suquet, the former monastic district at the heart of Cannes, is set back from the sea on a hill. It contains the church of Ste-Anne, a single-nave chapel begun in the twelfth century which has undergone substantial changes, particularly in the upper sections. Ste-Anne was the parish church until the sixteenth century. Notre-Dame de l'Espérance was the new parish church built between 1521 and 1648. The Suquet Tower was built in 1070 as an observation tower and modified in 1385.

The Îles de Lérins

The Îles de Lérins—St-Honorat and Ste-Marguerite—are now idyllic islands. The decline of the isolated hermitage of St-Honorat had begun in the Middle Ages, when it was repeatedly plagued and plundered by pirates. The virtually abandoned complex was however only officially dissolved in 1787 and sold to a private individual. In 1870, the Cistercians returned, restored the buildings, and replaced the church with a new structure. The monastery now owns the whole island and has turned it into a park-like landscape of pine trees. The ruined main church of St-Honorat was replaced in 1876 by a new neo-Romanesque building. The previous structure, which had a triple-nave and no transept, had been built in the last thirty years of the twelfth century. The small museum and the abbey garden contain the remains of the abbey. The individual chapels scattered across the island are relics of the erstwhile solitary lifestyle and from the twelfth century onward were places of pilgrimage. The best preserved of the seven remaining chapels are the Chapelle St-Sauveur in the northwest of the island and the Chapelle Ste-Trinité (illus. page 275 bottom left) in the southeast. The former is built to a central octagonal plan and would appear to date back to the early eleventh century. The Chapelle Ste-Trinité, built at around the same time, follows the trefoil plan typical of cemetery chapels in Provence (cf. Montmajour). The Château St-Honorat at the western tip (illus. page 275, above) is the most impressive building on the island. The fortified monastery seems to have been built initially in the late eleventh century, although the parts of the building visible today mainly date back to the 13th century. The castle features all the facilities necessary for a cloister, in a close configuration: at first, it would seem, only a large residential and escape tower was planned - this can still be seen on the north and west side. Inside the monks' castle there is a cloister on two levels, with two chapels, a refectory, dormitories etc. leading off from this. From the roof gallery there is a wonderful view of the island and the Mediterranean.

The larger of the two islands, Ste-Marguerite, is now a botanical garden crisscrossed with footpaths. The inhabitants of Cannes had already started felling trees on the island in the

The Côte d'Azur from Bandol to Antibes

Vallauris
Exhibition of pottery art from
the Madoura workshop at the
*Biennale Internationale de la
Céramique d'Art*

fifteenth century to clear it for agriculture and at the end of the sixteenth century the Abbot of Lérins officially sold them the right to do so. In 1617, the Abbey also handed over the title to the land to the Governor of Provence, who had the fort built in 1624-27. Richelieu captured the island and in 1712 the master fortress builder Vauban further extended the fort. From 1685 until the twentieth century, it was also used as a state prison; the cells are now sometimes used by youth groups vacationing on the island. The fort has a small aquarium and, more important-ly, a museum housing impressive archaeologic-al finds, including the hull of a Roman ship, amphorae, Roman ceramics, etc. Since the nine-teenth century, the city of Cannes has taken pains to ensure that the island remains a tran-quil paradise. A few restaurants on the quayside are the only concession to the bodily needs of hikers and ramblers.

Vallauris

Vallauris, the mecca of artistic ceramic ware, is a few miles north of Cannes. In the thirteenth century the ancient settlement of Vallis Aurea became part of the priory of Lérins, and in the sixteenth century the city was completely rebuilt on a grid pattern. Potters, mainly from Genoa, predominated among the new

inhabitants. The craft continued to be practiced until well into the twentieth century and no less a figure than Picasso used the craft potters to produce his ceramics from the 1950s onward. Today, this particular craft continues to domi-nate the small town, which is also why it holds the Biennale Internationale de la Céramique d'Art. The former convent chapel, which is probably thirteenth century, now contains a museum dedicated to Pablo Picasso. The crypt is hung with a huge painting produced in1952-54 and entitled *"War and Peace."* The Musée Magnelli and the Musée de la Poterie contain further examples of ceramic manufacture, as practiced by numerous other studios.

Antibes

Antibes is a city whose powerful fortifications have prevented the old center from being dis-figured by modern tourism. It has neither a beach promenade nor large, majestic hotels. The city of *Antipolis* was founded back in the fifth or fourth century BC as a trading post for the Greeks of Massilia. Under the Romans Antipolis remained an important strategic base and it soon had its own bishop. The bishopric was moved to Grasse in 1244, however, after repeated attacks on the city through the cen-turies had made it unsafe. Work on extending

Antibes
Church of the Immaculate
Conception (17th century) and
lane in the old town (above)

The late 16th-century
Fort Carré (below)

the fortifications began only under King François I and lasted into the eighteenth century. In the twentieth century, Antibes became famous primarily for its cultivation of roses. The Château Grimaldi, which lies right by the sea, stands in the center of the old city. The Grimaldi family resided here from the four-teenth through the early seventeenth century. Most of the complex was built in the sixteenth century around a rectangular keep dating back to the twelfth century. In 1928, the local history museum moved into the fortress and in 1946 the city allowed Picasso, who had earlier set-tled on the Côte d'Azur, the use of several rooms. The lack of raw materials at the time forced the artist to paint his large formats on fibro-cement slabs. Using this technique, he produced huge mural-like paintings depicting subjects from ancient mythology (the centaur triptych), still lifes, and the life of fishermen. A few years later, the artist donated some of these works, together with numerous ceramic pieces, to the city of Antibes; these form the core of the Picasso Museum, which now occupies most of the fortress. Other important works by twentieth-century French century artists can also be seen here, particularly those of the abstract painter Nicolas de Staël, who spent the last years of his life in Antibes before commit-ting suicide in 1955 at the age of 41. The muse-um also contains earlier works of interest, such as the altar panel depicting the Deposition from the Cross by Antoine Aundi (1539), which has been erected in the former chapel.

The seventeenth-century parish church is immediately adjacent to the Château (illus. page

PAGES 278-79:
Cap d'Antibes

Antibes
Sculpture of a woman's head by Picasso in the Picasso Museum of the Château Grimaldi

LEFT:
Antibes/Cap d'Antibes
Jardin Thuret

OPPOSITE:
Biot
Musée National Fernand Léger,
1960
Façade showing the large ce-
ramic mosaic (above)
Detail of the mosaic
Bird on a yellow background
from the eastern façade
(below)

277, above) though the old Romanesque apses can still be identified on the eastern side. In the south transept, there is a large panel entitled *Our Lady of the Rosary* by Louis Bréa, dated 1515. The Fort Carré (p. 277, below) on the other side of the yacht harbor is a star-shaped fortress set on a spit of rock jutting out into the sea, which may have been designed by the master fortress builder Vauban. The regular complex is grouped around a circular inner court from which the pointed bulwarks project on all four sides.

The many exhibits on display in the archeological museum to the south of the castle complex trace the 3,000-year-old history of the city. The collection consists mainly of artefacts found underwater, including shipwrecks and their cargoes.

Further south still is the Cap d'Antibes. From the top of the hill called the Colline de la Garoupe, there is a panoramic view as far as the Alps, the coast, and the sea. The Jardin Thuret, near the hill, is a fine botanical garden (see p. 280).

St-Pierre, near Biot, is where the painter Fernand Léger spent the last years of his life. A spacious museum designed by André Svetchine was opened here in 1960, which exhibits works from all the creative phases of the painter's life. Dominating the façade is an enormous mosaic executed according to the artists's designs and measuring 150 ft (45 m) in width and 30 ft (9 m) in height. This work was originally planned to be installed at the Stadium in Hanover, Germany. Thus, the museum is not merely a neutral setting for the painter's works, his large-scale creations—the colored stained glass windows, for example—form an integral part of the whole. In 1987, a side-wing was added to the main building.

Jewels of the High Middle Ages

St-Maximin-la-Ste-Baume, Brignoles, and Le Thoronet

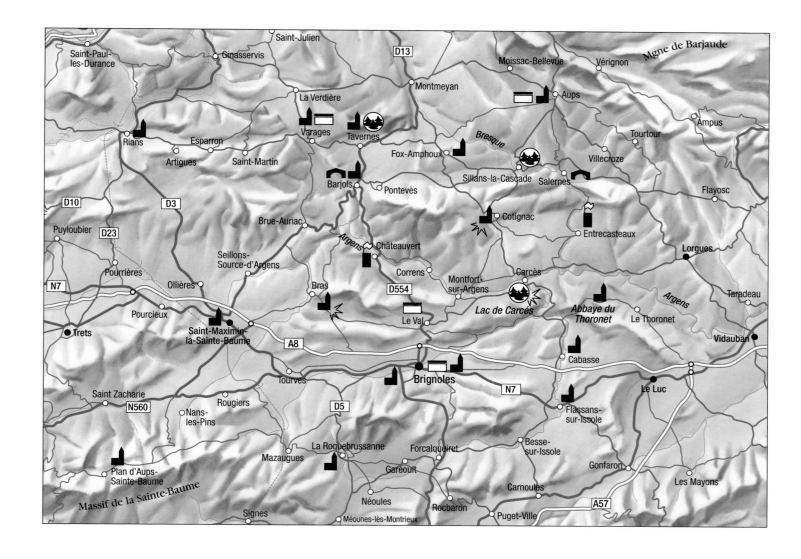

OPPOSITE:
Le Thoronet, 1160-80
Cloister

St-Maximin-la-Ste-Baume
View of the monastery with the church of Ste-Madeleine (late 13th to 16th century) from the southwest

St-Maximin-la-Ste-Baume

St-Maximin-la-Ste-Baume occupies a vital place in the history both of Provence and of France. The monastery is visible from far away, its huge church building standing out in the landscape like a vast, strange ship. It is said that St. Mary Magdalene is buried here together with her companions Maximin and Sidonius, as well as her servant Marcella. The story was that Mary Magdalene, having come with her followers to Provence from the Holy Land on a boat with no helmsman, did her 30-year penance in the Grotto of the mountains of Ste-Baume. The legend arose in Provence back in the eleventh century, but for a long time it competed with a different version confirmed in the thirteenth century, according to which, the mortal remains of the *apostola apostolorum* are said to be located in the Burgundian town of Vézelay. In order to settle the matter and to secure the presence of one of the most esteemed saints in Christendom, decisive action was taken by Charles I of Anjou, who had become Duke of Provence in 1246. Indeed, such action was

necessary, for as son of King Louis IX, known as St Louis, his policies had to be directed at legitimizing his controversial assumption of power in Provence and his new centralized politics even from the spiritual point of view. Accordingly, in 1279, he had his son Charles II carry out excavations in a church which, at the time, belonged to the Monastery of St-Victor in Marseilles. The findings left no doubt as to the authenticity of the remains; the legend was confirmed by four sarcophagi from late antiquity standing in a sepulcher. Moreover, the panels on the sarcophagi appeared to show scenes from the lives of the saints. The Monastery was given to the Dominicans, and in addition plans were laid to establish both a university and the burial place of the Anjou line here. Eventually, in 1295, Pope Boniface VIII confirmed the new legend and the authenticity of the relics.

Work began immediately on the construction of a huge edifice which was to become the main church of the Dominicans in Provence. By 1337, however, only the eastern sections and three of the chapels along the north aisle had been

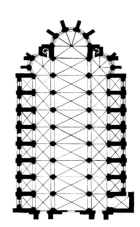

St-Maximin-la-Ste-Baume
Ste-Madeleine, interior looking east (opposite) and ground plan (below)

completed. Only very slowly—for the Anjous had in the meantime become increasingly focused on their second main residence in Naples—were further chapels added (to the south side by the beginning of the fifteenth century), and on the east side the nave was vaulted. Not until the beginning of the fifteenth century—and up until 1550—was work on the church progressed with more speed, although the western façade remained an unfinished shell.

The Dominican friars were driven out of the monastery during the French Revolution, but they returned in 1858. In the twentieth century, the monastery acquired notoriety when it became a place of refuge for extreme right-wing Catholics fighting for the reintroduction of the monarchy. This was partly why the Dominicans left the monastery in 1957, and in 1966 it was purchased by a private consortium.

The town plan alone shows how the Monastery was the center and starting point of development for the surrounding locality. The building consists of three aisles, with a longitudinal section staggered in basilica form, and ending in the east in a three-apse unit without a transept (illus. p. 285). While the main choir has the usual five or seven-sided polygon shape, it is unusual that the side-choirs are also made into diagonal chapels. The nave contains side-chapels which are lower than the side-aisles, so that they have an unusual row of windows of their own. All the windows are relatively narrow double-faced lancets. Thus, there are compact wall surfaces everywhere, and this is true also of the columns, which are walls left standing in the foundations, their edges beveled and with strikingly large round shafts. This design, of astounding simplicity and unity, was also retained for the three somewhat lower west bays in the sixteenth century. The first architect thus did not wish to create an edifice displaying the elegant Gothic forms of the time, as can be seen,

St-Maximin-la-Ste-Baume
Ste-Madeleine from the southeast (top)
14th-century cloister (above)
Decorative medaillons from the wooden choir-stalls (right)

for instance, in Aix Cathedral. Overwhelming scale with maximum simplicity and economy: this was the vision which the sponsor of the work, Duke of Provence and King of Naples, wished to achieve.

The crypt which, curiously, is situated in the middle of the nave, is still basically just as it was in 1279, despite some minor alterations. Directly after it was discovered, it was preserved almost as if it were an archeological site. The ancient, barrel-vaulted sepulcher holds the four sarcophagi (illustrations above). Mary Magdalene's sarcophagus (probably dating from the third quarter of the fourth century) is decorated with five arches showing the Anastasis Cross and the keepers of the grave, as well as the miracles of Christ. At the center of Maximin's sarcophagus (second half of the fourth century), there is a representation of Peter receiving the holy laws.

The impressive choir in the upper church was completed at the end of the seventeenth century. The wooden choir-stalls, with 94 seats, are decorated with wooden panels showing the saints in 22 medallions (illus. p. 286, below). The sumptuous concave ceiling of the chancel, dating from 1756, depicts the raptures of Mary Magdalene. The north side apse contains the holy altar by the Venetian Antoine Ronzen, dating from 1520. In the third but last chapel on the south side, contains the choir robe of St. Louis of Toulouse. The saint died in 1297 in nearby Brignoles, shortly after a visit to St-Maximin. The large cloisters (illustration in center of page 286) belongs to the first construction phase of the church. Like the church, the cloisters too exhibit a simple, almost earthy form. Large sections of the western end of the monastery buildings were substantially altered in the seventeenth century.

The Massif de la Ste-Baume

The mountain range known as the Massif de la Ste-Baume, which runs some distance south of the town, has a direct relationship with the site of the shrine of St. Mary Magdalene in St-Maximin. *Baoumo* means "cave" in Provençal, and it is here that Mary Magdalene is said to have withdrawn into a grotto and lived in penance for 30 years. The mountain ridge, which is 7½ miles (12 km) long and 3,820 ft (1,146 m) high also presents unique geological and botanical features. In their east-west dimension, the mountains are similar to Mont Ventoux, but in the case of the Massif de la Ste-Baume, the south side rises quite evenly, while the north edge ends abruptly in a 1,000 ft (300 m) high cliff. At the foot of the north side there is a high plateau, the Plateau du Plan-d'Aups, upon which a large but sparse forest has become established, a botanical rarity in this climate zone. The sheltering mountain range creates a relatively cool microclimate, which allows evergreen oaks, elms, poplars, and the like to flourish amid the limestone rocks. Nonetheless, it is nothing short of a miracle that the forest has endured for centuries. It was the sanctity of Mary Magdalene's place of retreat which for centuries led rulers to prohibit any kind of forest-clearing in the area. This continues to be the case, and thus, the foot of the Massif de la Ste-Baume is a tranquil botanist's paradise, ideal for extended walks and mountain hikes.

The ascent to the Holy Grotto at 2,953 ft (886 m), the ascent commences at the Carrefour des Trois Chênes or from the nearby hostel and takes about 30 minutes. The destination is a monastery built on the steep rocky cliffs, with the place of penance on a small ledge. The marble statue of the saints of Ch. Fossaty (late seventeenth century) is, in reality, one of four mourners which the Duke of Valbelle had made for his grave in the Carthusian Monastery of Montrieux. The Grotto itself contains an eighteenth-century statue of Mary Magdalene. In the past it was usual to climb up to Mary Magdalene's Grotto at Christmas carrying lanterns and even today, many pilgrims visit the site at that time of year. Veneration of the Grotto dates back to the fifth century, when monks from St-Cassien settled here. The sacred aura is also reflected in the legend of St. Mary Magdalene, who was also ordained in the tradition of the hermits. Pilgrimages to the Grotto likewise date back further than discovery of Mary Magdalene's grave, having begun in the twelfth century. Indeed, St. Louis himself, the king, visited the Holy Grotto in 1254. It was this tradition of veneration which was enhanced still further through discovery of Mary Magdalene's grave in 1279.

From the Grotto, it is possible to climb up to the summit of St-Pilon, from where there is a splendid view of the coast and its hinterland.

Massif de la Ste-Baume
"L'Hôtellerie" hostel near Plan-d'Aups-Ste-Baume, at the foot of the north face of the massif (above)
Steps to the grotto of St. Mary Magdalene (below)
There are 150 steps in the flight, representing the 150 *Ave Marias* in the rosary.

OPPOSITE:
Massif de la Ste-Baume
Tête de Roussargue

Brignoles

Brignoles, a picturesque market town, appears in written records from the sixth century onward. In the Middle Ages, the Dukes of Provence established a summer residence here. The town's principal activity continued to be that of trade in the agricultural produce of the region, particularly wine and the famous Brignoles plums. There were also important tanneries and dye works in the town. A reddish-brown-to-purple marble was extracted from the quarries of Candelon in the south. In the nineteenth century, Brignoles became the capital (préfecture) of the département of Var, and thanks to various administrative reforms, it is still a sous-préfecture.

The tranquil town has almost entirely retained its old oval shape with its narrow streets. At its center is the fifteenth-century parish church of St-Sauveur, a typical broad, transeptless Provençal church with side-chapels. Today, the Musée du Pays Brignolais is accommodated in the former thirteenth-century Ducal Palace. It is famous the world over for containing the oldest Christian monument in Gaul, the sarcophagus from La Gayole

(see illus. above). The third-century tomb, of outstanding quality, was probably imported from Italy and displayed in the small sanctuary of Notre-Dame de la Gayole in La Celle (west of Brignoles). The front, with its harmonious frieze, has been preserved. On the left, there is a personification of the sun in the form of a bust, and beside it a fisherman at work. Rams surround a tree containing birds and then there is an anchor. A woman raises her hands in prayer, accompanied by a lamb. By way of counterpart to the left side, the right-hand side also depicts a tree. The middle scene, with a profile of a seated figure, has been severely damaged. Beside the damaged part on the right-hand side we see a Good Shepherd and an additional figure. On the far right, a man sits on a rock raising his hand in greeting. Some of the symbols—fisherman, anchor, figure at prayer, Good Shepherd—represent Christian symbols, but these appear among pagan symbols, such as the sun. On a Merovingian Cippus, an unidentifiable individual folds its hands over its stomach; the stone panel was later revered as a symbol of fertility (see right).

Barjols and the area to the east

The picturesque town of Barjols is at an altitude of 833 ft (250 m), having developed around a now ruined château and a collegiate church, founded in 1060 by Archbishop Raimbaud of Arles, with renovation of the choir area in around 1300. The nave was renewed in the 16th century. For the Marcellus Altar in the left side aisle, it is clear that the Romanesque tympanum was again used as an antependium. Two angels are wearing a mandorla in which Christ appears on His throne, accompanied by the symbols of the Evangelists. From out of the clouds comes the hand of God. Traces of pigment serve as a reminder that Romanesque sculpture was once finished in color. The date of the relief remains uncertain, but possibly it is a piece made before the large tympanum reliefs in Arles or St-Gilles, which would situate it at the beginning of the 12th century.

To the east of Barjols are several beautiful villages in the midst of a splendid landscape, where only few tourists find their way; amongst them, the tiny village of Fox-Amphoux, lying at over 500 m, rises up on a wooded slope. A walk along the edge of the forest near the small town of Sillans-la-Cascade takes you to a hidden waterfall; in a 150 ft (45 m) cascade, a river plunges into turquoise water surrounded by rocks and tall trees. The wine-growing locality of Cotignac (illustration page 294-295), somewhat further down the valley, is protected by a high rock wall riddled with caves, crowned by a Medieval château ruin. Here, too, somewhat to the south, are waterfalls.

Barjols
Town view (top right)
and 2 of the 30
Old-Barjols fountains (right)

LEFT:
Landscape near Barjols

OPPOSITE:
Sunset at Fox-Amphoux

PP. 294-95:
**Cotignac
The 266 ft (80 m) volcanic,
tufa rock is pitted with hollows
and caves**

From St-Maximin-la-Ste-Baume to Le Thoronet

Le Thoronet

Raymond de St-Gilles, Duke of Toulouse, founded the Monastery of Notre-Dame-de-Florièges in 1136, near Tourtour in the diocese of Fréjus. In 1160 it was moved about 10 miles (15 km) further south to its present location. A small stream flows from here, from which water would have been taken. The forest which today surrounds the abbey serves as a reminder that in the twelfth century, this was a remote area only brought into agricultural use by the monks. Richly endowed by foundations and gifts, the Cistercian monastery saw rapid development, so that by around 1200, all the monastery buildings and the church had been completed. But with the general decline in the economic significance of the Cistercians in the south of France from the thirteenth century onwards, Le Thoronet fell even further into decline. Nevertheless, a new refectory was built in the fifteenth century, and at the beginning of the eighteenth century, the church was decorated in Baroque stucco style. The monastery was closed and sold off during the Revolution, and in 1854 the monastery was purchased by the state. The restoration work, which began in 1873, radically removed all the modern alterations, with the result that the present optical impression of sobriety and rigor immediately evokes the asceticism of the life led by the monks. In fact, the Cistercian building regulations forbade any decorative representation of figures on the basis that it distracted the senses, and ambitious and costly elements, especially tall church towers, were also prohibited. Nevertheless, the building of churches such as that at Le Thoronet always spared no expense. Not least, this is evidenced still today by the precisely chiseled ashlar and the massive vaults, which would have involved much painstaking work.

The church, dedicated to the Virgin Mary like all Cistercian churches, is likely to have been built in the years 1160-80. The structure of the nave, staggered in basilica-like fashion,

and the conspicuously extending transept, create a clear external form devoid of all decorative elements such as arch friezes. The round interior transept chapels are set into an externally straight wall structure protected by a sloping roof. Inside, an important element is now missing, namely the choir-screen in the nave, which separated the monks' area from a comparatively small area in the west to which the lay brothers were allowed access.

The columns of the nave, with its three bays, are of interest; together with the arcade wall, they form one level and are thus very similar in construction to a Roman aqueduct. The transept is lower and narrower than the nave. There is thus no actual crossing, since the barrel-vaulting of the nave is continued up to the wall of the choir.

Le Thoronet
Modern decoration of the monastery church: Romanesque Madonna

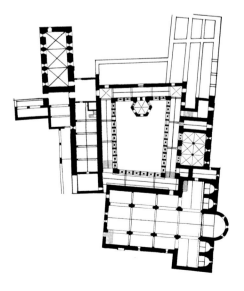

Le Thoronet
Monastery church, 1160-80. looking east (opposite)
Ground plan of the monastery complex (right)

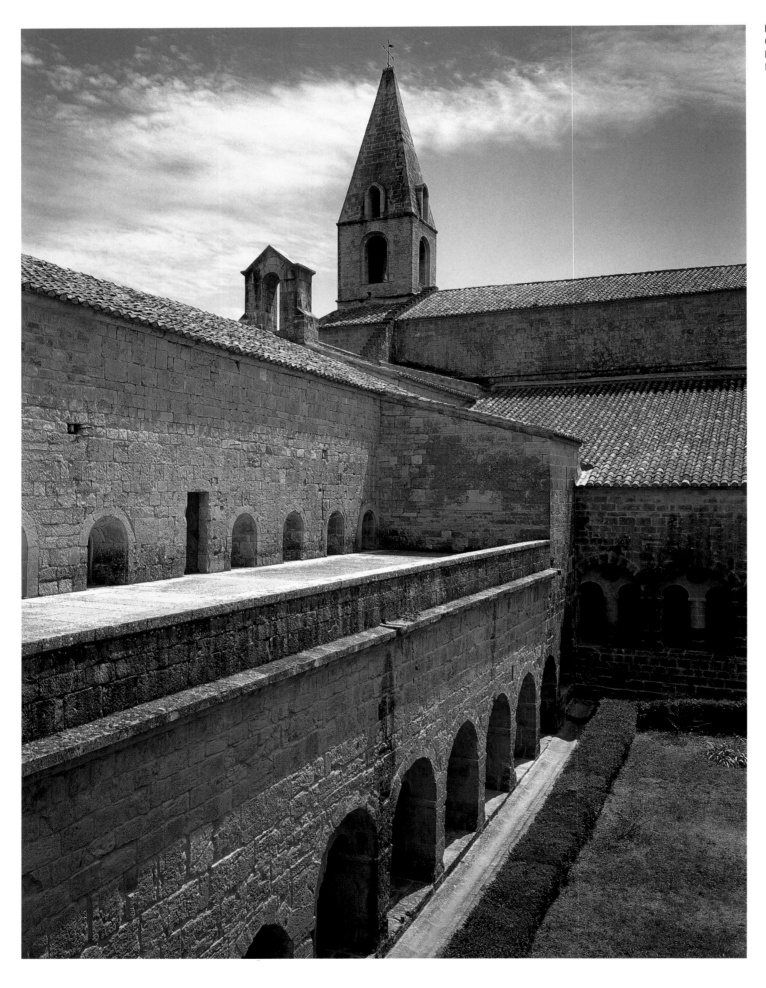

One of the most famous abbots of Le Thoronet was Foulques de Marseille. The son of a Genoese merchant, he initially became a famous troubadour. Even Dante praises his ability as a poet. Foulques sang in Aix, at the court of King Alfonso II of Aragon, Duke of Provence, and at the court of Raymond VI, Duke of Toulouse. The courtly homage rendered by a knight to his lady and the liberation of the Holy Land were the most common themes of his songs. In 1196, Foulques entered the Cistercian order, and in 1201 he was appointed abbot of Le Thoronet. When, five years later, he was appointed Bishop of Toulouse, a position which he held until his death in 1231, Foulques took on the huge task of taking action against the heretical movements which were widespread in Languedoc, the Cathars and the Waldensians, as well as reforming the whole of religious life in his large diocese. Amongst other things, he initiated construction on a new and elaborate cathedral including a huge ribbed vault. The new style of building, which Foulques had experienced at close hand in his Cistercian abbey in Provence, was then copied in other regions of southern France.

OPPOSITE:
Le Thoronet
The Chapterhouse

BELOW:
Le Thoronet
Dormitory

The cloisters also have smooth, unadorned walls and vaulting. The south wing, with its round barrel-vaulting, was probably built at the same time as the church. The east, north and west wings have fan vaulting. The vast vaulted arches rest on block consoles. In the northeast and northwest corners, massive ribbed vaulting has been used. The ends of the ribs have been set into the wall in the form of elaborately carved stonework. All this points to these three wings of the cloisters having been built as late as 1200. The cloister arcades do not display the rhythmical forms created by large, prominent arches that are otherwise typical of the Romanesque cloister formation of Provence, but the arrangement of the monastery buildings follows a common design, with the library linked to the transept. The monks read manuscripts on the stone steps which are still to be seen in the south wing, while in winter they would sit in the chapterhouse. The scribes worked in the furnace room. At the entrance, above the triangular lintel supported on a pillar, there is a small niche for holding a lamp. The chapterhouse is somewhat lower than the cloisters. Two sturdy pillars with double rows of leaf capitals support the grand rib-vaulting. The lowest rib stones have been hewn out of a single block using a labor-intensive technique. In addition to the capital sculpture, the rib vaulting is the most important means used to reveal the status of this room, ranking second-highest after the church itself.

This is where the abbot was elected, novices were accepted, and where the rules of the order were elucidated. The adjacent parlatorium serves as a throughway into the garden. This leads to the steps leading to the dormitory. The last gateway led into a room now no longer in existence, laid out in a northerly direction. The hexagonal pump room is in the north wing of the cloisters. In the north wall, the doors leading to the refectory, kitchen, and furnace-room can still be seen. The dormitory was on the upper floor of the east wing; from here the monks could directly access the transept in the church via the stairs. In the southeast corner of the fan vaulted area, a room was later walled off which served as an archive and treasure chamber. Above that, a small room with a small window overlooking the interior of the church was set up for the sacristan. From here, the mass could be followed and the bells sounded at the right moment. The storage room, to the west of the cloisters, was presumably built in around 1200. The large press and two supply containers preserved here serve as a reminder of the immensely important role played by the Cistercian monasteries in the economic life of the region.

The lay brothers' room is line with the west wall of the storage room, which also contains the entrance lobby. The refectory, on the lower floor, is a three-windowed room. The ribs, set somewhat clumsily on consoles, were deliberately intended to be technically simpler than the rib-vaulting in the cloister area, reflecting the proportionately lower status of the lay brother's area. The lay brother's refectory is on the upper floor. In the north wall is a door leading to the latrines, directly across the adjacent stream.

Château Entrecasteaux
View of the château and garden

Château Entrecasteaux

The château of Entrecasteaux overlooks the Bresque valley, dominating the old houses and narrow streets of the village. From the fourteenth century, the locality was a fiefdom of the dukes of Provence, while in the sixteenth century it passed into the hands of the Grignans, which is why Madame de Sevigné (see p. 22) occasionally lived here. Finally, in the eighteenth century, manorial control fell to Bruni d'Entrecasteaux, who in 1791 was commissioned to undertake an expedition to Peru from which he never returned.

What remains of the château today originates largely from the sixteenth and seventeenth centuries. A beautiful French garden at the foot of the rock was designed by Le Nôtre. It is thanks solely to Scottish painter Jan McGarvie-Munn that the château did not fall into total disrepair many years ago, for the painter initiated restoration work which was completed in 1982.

The rooms on the ground floor, displaying works by McGarvie-Munn, are open to the public, as is the old kitchen and annex to the château. The painter's heirs are striving to turn Entrecasteaux into a cultural center through concerts and exhibitions.

The Eternal Luster of the Belle Epoque

The Côte d'Azur from Nice to Menton, via Monaco

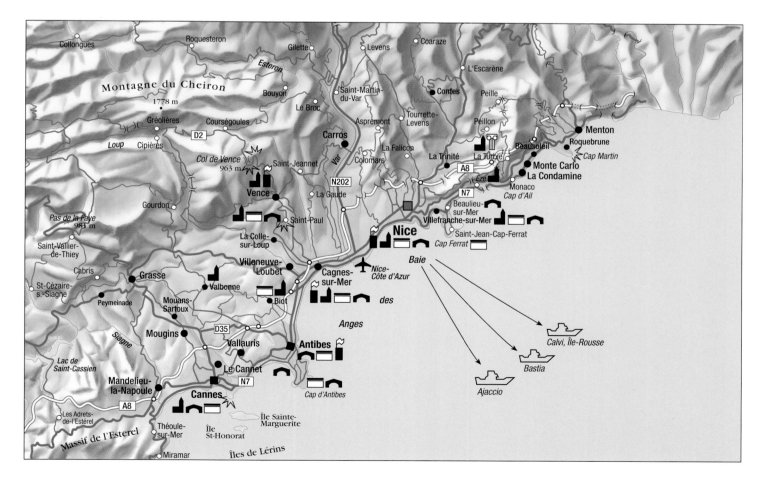

Collongues
Roquesteron
Gilette
Levens
Coaraze
Esteron
L'Escarène
Montagne du Cheiron
Saint-Martin-du-Var
Contes
Peille
1778 m
Bouyon
Le Broc
Tourrette-Levens
Péillon
Menton
Gréolières
Coursegoules
Aspremont
Roquebrune
D2
Carros
La Falicon
La Trinité
La Turbie
Beausoleil
Cap Martin
Loup
Cipières
Col de Vence
Saint-Jeannet
Colomars
A8
Monte Carlo
963 m
Var
Éze
La Condamine
N202
Gourdon
Vence
La Gaude
Monaco
Cap d'Ail
Pas de la Paye
N7
Beaulieu-sur-Mer
983 m
Saint-Paul
Villefranche-sur-Mer
Saint-Vallier-de-Thiey
La Colle-sur-Loup
Saint-Jean-Cap-Ferrat
Cabris
Villeneuve-Loubet
Cap Ferrat
St-Cézaire-s.-Siagne
Grasse
Nice
Baie
Peymeinade
Valbonne
Cagnes-sur-Mer
Nice-Côte d'Azur
Mouans-Sartoux
Biot
des
Siagne
Mougins
D35
Anges
Lac de Saint-Cassien
Vallauris
Calvi, Île-Rousse
Antibes
Mandelieu-la-Napoule
Le Cannet
N7
Bastia
Cannes
Les Adrets-de-l'Estérel
A8
Cap d'Antibes
Ajaccio
Théoule-sur-Mer
Île Sainte-Marguerite
Massif de l'Estérel
Île St-Honorat
Miramar
Îles de Lérins

OPPOSITE:
Nice
Coast road and part of the harbor

305

1 City hall   2 St-François-de-
Paule   3 Opera house
4 Galerie-Musée Raoul Dufy
5 Chapelle de la Miséricorde
6 Palais Grimaldi   7 St-Suaire
8 St-Jacques   9 Ste-Réparate
10 Tour de l'Horloge   11 Palais
Lascaris   12 St-Martin-St-
Augustin   13 Theater
14 Musée d'Art moderne et
d'Art contemporain   15 Place
Garibaldi   16 Cemetery
17 Château
18 Directional panel
19 Elevator 20 Musée des
Beaux-Arts   21 Musée
Masséna   22 Casino Ruhl
23 Musée d'Histoire Naturelle
24 Palais des Arts du Tourisme
et de Congrés Acropolis
25 Musée Chagall

A Convent of Notre-Dame
B Musée Matisse (Villa
des Arènes)
C Musée Archéologique

Nice and the Alpes Maritimes

Nice, the "Queen of the Riviera," is undoubtedly the main center of population on the Côte d'Azur, and this has been the case for 2,500 years. In fact, some evidence of Stone Age settlements over 400,000 years old has been found to the east of the present-day harbor. Around 600 BC, there were two Celto-Ligurian *oppida*, one in Cimiez to the north, another on the steep hill by the coast. In the sixth century BC, Greeks from Marseille founded a trading post, known as Nikaia, here. In 154 BC, the Romans defeated the Celtic Ligurians, whose attacks had repeatedly threatened the Greek colony. The Romans settled in what is now Cimiez, developing Cemenelum as a garrison and administrative center. Since then, a Greek and a Roman city have existed in close proximity.

In early Christian times, both Nice and Cimiez were bishoprics. In the case of Nice, a bishop was appointed in the year 314. In 465, the two dioceses were combined, with Nice confirmed as the episcopal see. From the end of the tenth century, the city belonged to the comté of Provence, control over the city being shared between the bishop and the abbot of the Benedictine Abbey of St-Pons on the eastern slope of Mount Cimiez. Nice emerged as a maritime trading post in the early twelfth century, and gained a measure of autonomy by the formation of an independent city council, the Consulate, which lasted until 1230. At this time, Count Raymond-Bérenger V ruled the city, but in 1246 all his land passed to the House of Anjou.

Encouraged by wrangling within the House of Anjou, Savoy annexed Nice in 1388, and it remained under Savoyard control, despite many French sieges, becoming an independent province in 1526. During the French Revolution, the city became part of France, but soon afterward, at the Congress of Vienna in 1814, it passed to the Kingdom of Sardinia. In the 1860 plebiscite, held after the

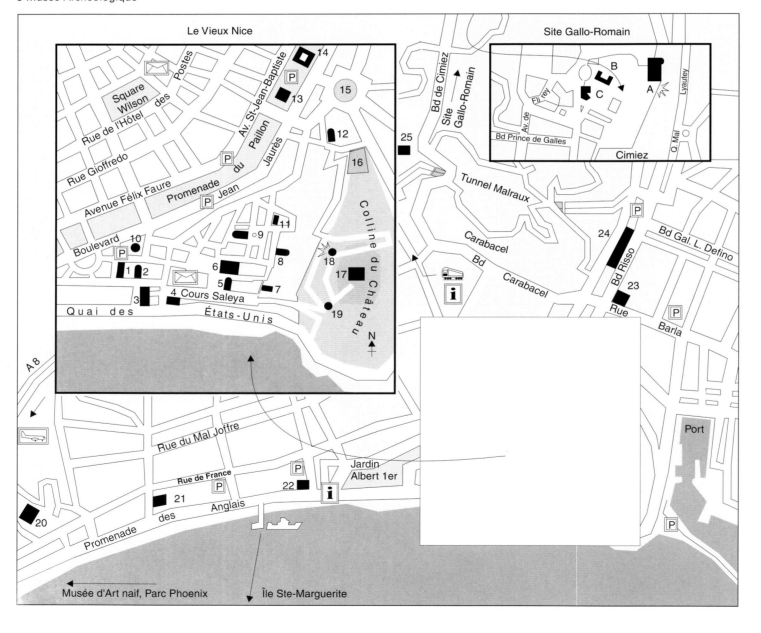

Franco-Austrian war of 1859, Savoy and Nice were finally ceded to France.

In the eighteenth century, the English in particular favored the city as a winter resort. In the nineteenth century, tourism and culture became Nice's mainstays. Wide avenues, theaters, a casino, magnificent hotels, multi-story apartments, and extravagant villas came to dominate the central beachfront area. At around this time, Nice also developed rail links with the Italian Alps and Paris. Today Nice is the undisputed cultural capital of the Côte d'Azur with a university, a music academy, and an art college, as well as a flourishing artistic community. It is also has one of France's busiest airports.

Nice is a huge city whose tourist sights and attractions are widely scattered. There are always new and fascinating discoveries to make. Between the coast and the station, for example, there are many Art Déco residences as well as public buildings and churches dating from the first half of the twentieth century. Incidentally, this part of the city was not developed until quite late. It actually lies some distance from the old district, which is in the east.

The same is true of the famous Promenade des Anglais. The spacious coast road, which is now so popular with walkers, bathers, skateboarders, idlers, and people-watchers, was originally lined with some very old buildings, but these have gradually been redeveloped. In order to put a stop to the widespread practice of begging, in 1820 Lewis Way collected money to pay the poor to build a narrow coast road. Twenty years later, the city council took over the scheme, extending the road as far as Baumettes and renaming the "Camin dai

Nice
Hôtel Negresco on the-
Promenade des Anglais

Anglès" or "Promenade des Anglais." The road has been repeatedly altered. In 1930, it was doubled in width and lined with lawns, gardens, and palm trees. In 1965, the boulevard was extended as far as the airport. The hotels and houses that were built in the east during the nineteenth century are still quite simple, the wall reliefs restrained. The more elaborate buildings are to be found to the west.

One particularly striking example, the Hôtel Negresco (see above), was built in 1912, next to the Musée Masséna by the leading architect of the Belle Époque, Edouard Niermans. The Musée Masséna—a villa built in the Italianate style of the First Empire (Napoleon I)—was designed in 1901 as the winter residence for Victor Masséna, the Duke of Rivoli. It now houses a collection of Napoleonic memorabilia and many fifteenth and sixteenth-century works by painters of Louis Bréa's École de Nice. The equally interesting Musée Jules Chéret is further to the west and somewhat set back from the coast. It is housed in a large, Italian Renaissance palazzo built in 1875 for the Russian prince, Leo Kotchubey. The paintings on display there date from between the seventeenth and twentieth centuries and are mainly from the French, Dutch and Italian schools (Carle van Loo, Fragonard, Dufy, etc.). However, works by the painter, Jules Chéret (1836–1932), provide the focal point for the collection. He produced paintings of many buildings along the Côte d'Azur before and around 1900 and the restrained elegance and unfamiliar colors of his artistic language also found expression in posters, an art form which he played an important part in developing.

On the initiative of Tsarina Maria Feodorovna, the St. Petersburg architect, M.T. Preobrayenski built a Russian Orthodox Church for the Russian community in Nice, which was completed in 1912. The colorful domed structure (see p. 309, above left) is in the style of sixteenth and seventeenth-century Russian church architecture, principally St. Basil's Cathedral. The iconostasis and the numerous icons inside are typical of Russian churches of the period.

Nice
Russian Orthodox cathedral of St. Nicholas, 1912, detail of cupola.

Nice's main station was completed in 1865. Its steel construction which allows plenty of light to stream in is still used as the concourse. The new city spreads out from here in a fan-shape toward the Promenade des Anglais, the Promenade du Paillon, and Place Masséna. This square and the adjoining Jardin Albert Ier were laid out by Joseph Vernier between 1836 and 1850 beside the Paillon river, which separates the Old City from the new city. The spacious square is surrounded by arcades modeled on the squares of Turin. Between 1879 and 1882, a broad boulevard was constructed, which spanned the river. It had two carriageways some distance apart and the casino stood between them, on what is now the Espace Masséna. This casino was demolished in 1979 to make way for a staggered complex of hanging gardens.

Continuing to the north, the boulevard leads to the Musée d'Art moderne et d'Art contemporain and to the new theater (see page 307 below). Both complexes are raised on a platform and were designed by Yves Bayard and Henri Vidal. They opened during 1989. The theater is an abstract octagonal block, whose form is repeated in reverse in the courtyard of the museum complex. The courtyard itself consists of four large cubes, positioned on the diagonal sides of the octagon. The important collection consists mainly of American and French contemporary art (post-1960), which at the same time underlines Nice's role as one of the leading French centers of 1960s art, in particular the art of the Nouveaux Réalistes. While Nice-born Yves Klein was creating his famous blue canvases,

Arman, another native of Nice, was putting together his jumbled collection of everyday *objets trouvés*.

On the other side of the Paillon lies the famous Old City. Its colorful houses and church façades demonstrate clearly that the city of Nice has for a long time had closer links with Italian rather than French culture. The Old City is still dominated by Renaissance and Baroque styles, partly because the population only gradually moved down from the rocky plateau and settled around the base of the rock, partly because in the nineteenth century the city expanded mainly along the shoreline and to the west.

Nice
Musée d'Art moderne et d'Art contemporain

Nice
Theater (opened in 1989) and Museum (architects: Yves Bayard and Henri Vidal)

Nice
Sculpture in the Jardin Albert I

Nice's Baroque churches

During the sixteenth century the cathedral was moved from the rocky outcrop to the St-Réparate church (illustration opposite above and below right) in what is now the Old City. In 1649, the architect Jean-André Guibert presented a plan for a completely new church, which was finally consecrated in 1699. The present façade, was only added between 1825 and 1830, however. The ground plan—triple-naved and barrel vaulted with a triconch east side and crowning dome—is based on Roman models. The extensive stucco decorations with a color scheme of white, blue, and gold are particularly striking. Other examples of the lavish forms and richly ornamented polychromes of Nice Baroque can be seen in St-Jacques (see illus. right), St-François-de-Paul (see illus. below left) and the Chapelle de l'Anonciation.

The Chapelle de la Miséricorde is right beside the long and attractive Flower Market (see illus. opposite above left), which dates from 1736. The first impression given by the convex façade continues in the richly-modulated interior. A lengthy oval, extended by the porch and the chancel, is accompanied laterally by side-chapels which are also oval. The model for this complicated ground plan with its curving arches and geometric intersections was unmistakably the work of the principal exponent of Baroque architecture of Piedmont, Guarino Guarini. The sacristy not only contains an altar by Louis Bréa's École de Nice, but also the *Vierge de la Miséricorde*, a Madonna with a protecting cloak, created between 1430 and 1440 by Jean Marailhet, a painter from Montpellier. The Madonna is flanked by saints Cosmas and Damian, Sebastian, and Gregor, with Christ above them as the Man of Sorrows. Directly behind the chapel stands the Palais de la Préfecture, built in the mid-seventeenth century for the King of Sardinia.

An overview of Nice

From what is known as the *Château*, a hill 306 ft (92m) high, Nice has a natural outlook, a panorama that takes in the red-tiled rooftops of the Old City, the even curve of the shoreline which sweeps round as far as the airport, and the hustle and bustle around the harbor to the east of the hill. In the public park laid out here, man-made waterfalls send wind-blown spray in all directions, but the cooling effect is often very welcome. At the summit, some parts of the old city have been excavated. In the twelfth century, a triple-naved cathedral was built above the Greek and Roman ruins which include a raised temple. The same site was then used for the palace of the Count (later Duke) of Savoy. An elevator on the coastal side of the rocky slope makes the journey up and down a lot easier, and is also a good place to view the surroundings. The Musée de la Marine with its interesting collection of model ships is easily reached from here.

The Côte d'Azur from Nice to Menton

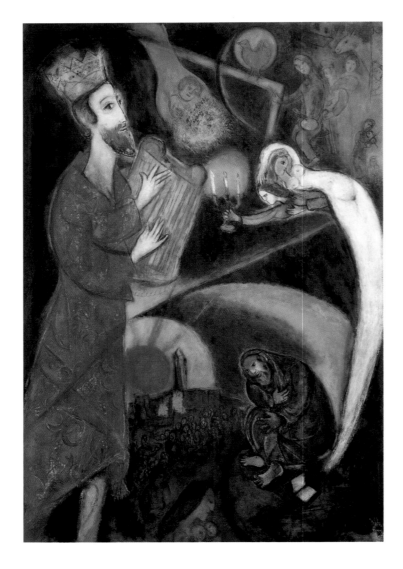

Marc Chagall
King David, 1950–51
Oil on canvas, 77 x 53 in
(194 x 133 cm)
Nice, Musée National Message
Biblique Marc Chagall

Close to the city freeway, beside the Boulevard de Cimiez which leads up the hillside, lies the Musée Marc Chagall, whose exhibits include 17 huge pictures that form the artist's famous Biblical Message (1955–58, see illus. above). In 1966, Chagall bequeathed part of his work to the French government, which in 1972 commissioned the architect, André Hermant, to design a gallery for it. Other important works with religious content created in the latter part of his life are grouped around the core exhibits. Several superb residences dating from around 1900 can be seen in the area around the museum and along the boulevard (nos. 35,39, and 46).

The site of Cimiez

Cimiez on Mont Gros (see illus. right and p. 317) clearly demonstrates Nice's Roman origins and the transition to Christianity. From 13 BC the Via Julia linked the city of Cemenelum with the Italian mother country. At this time, the city was the capital of the Maritime Alps military region. However, it remained a *municipium*, in other words the inhabitants did not have the citizens' rights usually granted to a *colonia*. The

first phase of intensive building work took place in the second half of the first century. By the end of the second and during the third century, the city was completely restructured and large public buildings were built, many of which can still be seen today. As part of an administrative reform, the provincial capital was moved to Embrun, so the importance of Cimiez waned rapidly. It remained the seat of a bishop, but in 466 the diocese merged with that of Nice.

The relatively small area of which the ancient city consisted can be identified more clearly by the necropolis which lies just outside the city's confines. During the third century, the city measured about 2000 ft (600 m) along its north-south axis and was mainly occupied by large public buildings. It is possible to make out the paving for two east-west streets (Decumanus I and II; parallel to the Avenue Monte Croce or in line with the Musée Matisse). The best-preserved remains are the north baths dating from the early third century and located to the north of Decumanus I. In the first room there is a swimming-pool which was once surrounded by colonnaded gallery. At the north-east corner there were latrines with outflow channels. A rectangular colonnade to the north of the swimming-pool forms the entrance to the complex. Adjoining this to the west is the cold bath or frigidarium. The building was used for many years as a farmhouse, and the walls have survived as far as the base of the vaulting. Part of the arch shoulders are easy to identify; slabs lodged in between formed the barrel-vaulting. The walls, made from ashlar interspersed with layers of bricks, were originally clad with marble slabs. On the northern, narrow side there was another cold water pool; a statue of Antonia Minor (now in the museum) once stood in the center of it. Further west lies the narrow, rectangular warm room (tepidarium), with a circular steam bath that was added later. In a

LEFT AND OPPOSITE: :
Nice-Cimiez
Gallo-Roman excavations
North baths, summer bath (left)
Frigidarium of the north baths
(above right and below left)
Amphitheater (below right)

few places, the hypocaust can still be identified. This blew hot air into the hollow bricks of the side-walls from beneath the floor, itself supported on short brick pillars. During the second half of the third century, the east baths were built on the other side of Decumanus I. The size and layout of the rooms roughly match those of the northern baths.

Decumanus II was lined with residences, which on the street side housed studios and shops. Another baths complex was built as an annex to the west of the east baths, which was probably reserved for women. Of particular interest here is the evidence for the conversion of the baths complex into a cathedral church during the fifth century. The frigidarium was altered to form the east apse and its walls and bench are easy to discern. All that remains of the altar is the base-plate with four indentations for the table's supporting columns. The hypocaust system was filled in and the walls between the bath-rooms adjoining the apse were demolished so that the longitudinal hall could be built. The old boiler room to the north was converted into a baptistery. Within the trapezoid room an octagonal, colonnaded structure surrounded the font. To the east of the baptistery there was a room for foot-washing and a cloakroom for the benefit of those undergoing baptism. The cathedral complex displays characteristics similar to those of other early Christian church sites in Provence, but it was only used as an episcopal church for a few years, because, as mentioned earlier, the episcopal see was moved to Nice in the mid-fifth century.

The many finds from the excavation work are exhibited in the site museum, together with several prehistoric and ancient artifacts from the region. Of special note here are a Hellenistic Silenus bronze mask, the statue of a dancing satyr (first century), and a statue of Antonia Minor, the wife of Drusus and the niece of Augustus (38 BC- 37AD), that collapsed into the swimming pool.

Outside the fenced-off excavation site lies the amphitheater (see far right). It was situated on the northwest corner of the ancient city and was not aligned with the city's road network but with the Roman road from Nice into the Alps. The amphitheater's peripheral position helped to keep the densely-packed city center free from throngs of visitors, fighters, animals, and tradesmen.

The site is actually unusually small (223 x 186 ft (67 x 56 m)). An initial building, assembled from quarried stones, had three tiers of seating and could only accommodate about 500 people. It is possible that wooden staging increased its meager capacity. The amphitheater in Cimiez is actually a rather simple, very early version of its type, befitting a city that was only classed as a municipium. Nine additional tiers were added in the third century , thus increasing capacity to 4,000 spectators.

Nice-Cimiez
Musée Matisse/Villa
des Arènes, 1670

Musée Matisse and Franciscan Monastery

Near the amphitheater, a large, slightly curving staircase leads down into a courtyard which forms the new entrance to Nice's Musée Matisse (see illustration above). The new, underground wing was designed by Jean-François Bodin and opened in 1993. With this successful extension, the architect has skillfully avoided any obstruction to the original museum, a beautiful, gleaming red palace that the Genoese consul to Nice built in 1670.

Henri Matisse lived in Nice from 1917 to 1954, and bequeathed many important pieces of his work to the city. The museum's exhibits trace the various stages of his career through many examples of his work, and special exhibitions are often organized here.

At the other end of the park which surrounds the Musée Matisse and the excavation site there is a Franciscan monastery, which is itself situated within an attractive garden. In 1543, after the monastery had been destroyed during a siege, mendicant monks took it over. It had previously been inhabited by Benedictine monks from St-Pons. The core of the church is late Romanesque, but it was ribvaulted in the thirteenth century. With the arrival of the Franciscan monks, the monastery was given Renaissance features. The imaginative neo-Gothic west façade was added around 1850 (see illus. opposite). Inside there are three important works by Louis Bréa, the main exponent of the Nice School: a pietà, a Crucifixion, and a Descent from the Cross, commissioned by the Franciscans between 1475 and 1512. Certain elements in the last two paintings, such as the depiction of the landscape, the expressive gestures, and the subtlety of the composition, show clearly the effectiveness of the new pictorial medium of the Italian Renaissance.

Near the summit of Mont Gros, high above Nice, stands the gleaming white Observatoire. Raphael Bischoffsheim, a passionate astronomer, had this fine structure built between 1880 and 1887, by none other than Charles Garnier and Gustave Eiffel. The telescope, 60 ft (18m) in length and 30 in (76 cm) in diameter, was the most powerful of its kind at the time. Above the entrance to this temple-like structure, stands a large bronze of the sun god Apollo leaving the constellation. Bischoffsheim originally endowed the conservatory to the University of Paris, but in 1972 it was handed over to the University of Nice.

OPPOSITE:
Nice-Cimiez
Franciscan monastery,
neo-Gothic façade (1850)

Villefranche-sur-Mer
Chapelle de St-Pierre,
Façade (above)
Bay of Villefranche (right)

Villefranche-sur-Mer

Charles II of Anjou founded this little town in a sheltered bay in 1295 when he resettled the inhabitants of nearby Montolivo on the site of the old Roman harbor of Olivula. The Dukes of Savoy built a maritime fortress here in 1557. Just prior to that, the Turks had attempted a landing in the bay—Villefranche remains a naval base to this day. The main point of interest here is the small Romanesque fishermen's chapel of St-Pierre (see illustration above), which was decorated by Jean Cocteau in 1957. Elegant curving lines inspired by pottery painting cover all the walls with scenes from the life of St. Peter. The interwoven frescoes of varying scale create a surreal but lyrical setting.

LEFT
AND OPPOSITE:
Cap Ferrat
Villa Ephrussi de Rothschild
(Villa Île-de-France), 1905
Garden façade of the Villa and
views of the garden

Cap Ferrat and Beaulieu-sur-Mer

Cap Ferrat, a narrow peninsula which extends
far out to sea, boasts numerous attractions all
within a fairly small area. There is, for example,
a small zoo and a circular footpath which follows the peninsula's coastline. One spectacular
sight is the Villa Ephrussi de Rothschild, which
was built by Baroness Béatrice Ephrussi de
Rothschild in 1905. Although the most famous
architects from that period were willing to play
a part in the project, the eccentric Baroness herself repeatedly intervened in its design. What
followed was a model of eclecticism. A four-
winged complex surrounds a large arcaded
courtyard which from the outside is typical of
the Italian early Renaissance, but which also
has Gothic gabled arches. The interior contains
a carefully assembled collection of French
Rococo furnishings, in some places concealing
modern sanitary fittings, as in the bathroom.
The main section contains a huge collection of
art objects and paintings from all periods,
though eighteenth-century porcelain and art
predominate. The fairy-tale palace complex is
supplemented by a range of garden styles.
Grouped around the French garden on one side
of the villa (see illustration on page 323, above)
there is an Italian Renaissance garden, a collection of Provençal and exotic vegetation, a
Spanish garden, and a Japanese garden.

Beaulieu-sur-Mer
Villa Kerylos, 1902
Inner courtyard (above) and
living-room (right)

Within sight of the Villa Ephrussi, there is an alternative approach to stylish living which makes interesting viewing. The archeologist, Théodore Reinach, and the architect, Emmanuel Pontremoli, worked together in 1902 on the Villa Kérylos in Beaulieu-sur-Mer with the aim of reviving Greek antiquity (see illustration above and right).

While Ephrussi de Rothschild sought to intermingle various styles, Reinach used his archeological knowledge to build, with meticulous attention to detail, a modern version of Greek life around the fifth century BC. An inner courtyard surrounded by Doric column is set directly above the water, suffusing light and air. Grouped around it at a lower level are the study, dining room, the lounge, and communal baths. The bedrooms are on the upper floor. The complex makes a particularly impressive whole, as all the internal furnishings have been preserved. The designers sought to faithfully recreate Greek furniture so that it would be possible to live according to the lifestyle of the ancient Greeks. In the dining-room, for example, meals were taken on recliners. But at the same time modern hygiene was acknowledged. To one side of the peristyle courtyard there is a marble-clad communal bath, while on the first floor there is a modern shower, which also has a Greek design.

Èze

The Petite Corniche coast road runs from Nice to Monaco via the Cap d'Ail. Èze was originally a small coastal village for La Turbie but in 1879, Baron de Pauville laid the foundations for a winter resort here; it was soon to be a key location in opening up the coast for tourism. A footpath (to the right of the railroad station) allows visitors to view the strange coastal formation at close quarters.

Èze stands on a rocky outcrop at 1423 ft (427 m) above sea level by a steep mountain slope on the Moyenne Corniche (see illus. left). It is a village whose origins date back to Celto-Ligurian times. Frederick Nietzsche was a regular visitor to this picturesque, but now very popular spot and the German philosopher wrote the third part of his masterpiece *Thus Spake Zarathrustra* here. A footpath dedicated to him leads down to the sea. In the church there is a Spanish crucifix which dates from 1258. The beautiful, exotic garden, which was laid out on the site of the fortifications, has a fine collection of succulents and cacti.

Monaco

The rock which drops steeply into the sea on three sides of the bay was much appreciated by the Phoenicians, Greeks, and Romans as a defensible, natural harbor. Yet no large settlement developed here for many hundreds of years. In 1162, the Genoese were granted rights over the whole of the coastal area from Nice to Ventimiglia on the present Franco-Italian border by Emperor Frederick Barbarossa. In the struggle for power in Genoa—as in many other Italian cities—the aristocratic families supporting the Emperor (Ghibelline) and those supporting the Pope (Guelfic) were at loggerheads. In 1291, one of the largest Guelfic families, the Grimaldis, decided to withdraw to Monaco. Genoa had been weakened by the struggle with Venice and this boosted the autonomy of the Grimaldi family, who by the late fourteeth and early fifteenth centuries were the undisputed masters of Monaco. During the sixteenth century, the Spanish Habsburg dynasty became protectors of the small principality. However, in 1641, the Grimaldis allied themselves with France. In 1792, the citizens of Monaco proclaimed their city-state a republic, and a year later it was united with France. At the Vienna Congress, however, Monaco was, like Nice, ceded to Sardinia. It was 1860 before most of the region was handed back to France, but Monaco was excluded, preferring to remain an independent principality though under the protection of France. The tiny enclave could only survive with the aid of massive amounts of imported wealth. It was for this reason that Prince Charles III, owner of the Société des Bains de Mer, a company which had become famous for its casino, waived the usual restrictions on gambling. For the many very rich

OPPOSITE:
Monaco
Courthouse, early 20th century (above)
Institut oceanographique, 1889-1910 (below)

Monaco
Royal palace
East wing, 17th century

residents of the Côte d'Azur, Monaco with its casino now became a magnet where they could indulge their passion for gambling without restriction. Reports about wealthy aristocrats who committed suicide after gambling away all their worldly possessions in one night were certainly not the product of journalists' imaginations alone.

Albert I (1889–1922) played a part in transforming Monaco into a center of music, drama, maritime research, and sport. Diaghilev's *Ballets Russes* gave their first performances in Monte Carlo at the beginning of the twentieth century, the underwater explorer, Jacques Cousteau, became director of the Musée Océanographique, and the famous Monte Carlo Rally was held for the first time in 1911. Relieving the residents of Monaco from the obligation to pay tax has turned the city-state into a tax-free haven, which attracts wealthy private individuals and corporations. The result of Monaco's special status can be seen in the high-rise architecture. Many of the tower blocks built in the post-war years and now dominating the skyline are over 30 stories high. To ease traffic congestion, the railroad station and railroad line were moved underground. However, since the 1980s, a new strategy has been adopted and this has had less impact on the city's appearance.

Storage areas, cellars, and parking lots, have been hidden away in giant caverns excavated out of the rocks. The Old City is now subject to very strict planning regulations.

The royal palace (see illustration above) started out in the thirteenth century as a Genoese fortress and has been extended many times since. Much of its present impressive façade dates from the 1520s. From the

Monaco
Luxury seaside villas

forecourt, three towers with dovetail merlons—renovated features from the medieval site—can be seen on the right. The wings, which have enclosed a square courtyard since the sixteenth century, have been preserved in a simple form. The east wing, however, was built in 1632 by Honorius Grimaldi II in lavish style. Inside the courtyard, a ceremonial white marble staircase leads up to a loggia, whose ceilings are decorated with murals depicting the feats of Hercules by the Genoese Orazio Ferrari (1605–1657). The restored external frescoes on the opposite side of the court are said to be the work of Luca Cambiaso (1527–1585). Until the French Revolution the rooms were richly ornamented in Baroque style, but in 1865 Prince Charles III had much of the furnishings replaced by older pieces.

The architect, Charles Lenormand, built the Cathedral between 1875 and 1884 after Monaco had become a bishopric. His choice of architectural style is actually more reminiscent of Burgundian than Provençal Romanesque. This was the best way to simultaneously express religious devotion and architectural splendor. The St. Nicholas altar in the south transept was carved in Louis Bréa's workshop around 1500.

The Musée océanographique is almost certainly the most spectacular museum in the city. Between 1899 and 1910, the classical-style building by architect Delafortrie, was extended to house the vast collection that Albert I had amassed on his numerous scientific expeditions. The museum complex has always been more than simply a display of exhibits, it is also renowned as an important center for maritime research. Nevertheless, the collection is certainly impressive. Of the many tanks, the largest—and also one of the oldest— has a capacity of 10, 000 gallons (40,000 l). Visitors to the museum can see thousands of different fish species and other sea creatures. The zoological collection of whale skeletons, giant crabs, turtles, etc. is just as interesting. One section of the museum is devoted to the history of underwater exploration. Exhibits include the first submarine and a reconstruction of the Titanic disaster.

Above the Palais du Prince there is a large botanical garden, the Jardin Exotique, which boasts a wide selection of tropical plants including several huge cacti that thrive in the extremely mild climate of Monaco. One way out of the garden leads to a cavern, the Grotte de l'Observatoire, where archeologists have found evidence of human habitation dating from 200,000 years ago. The Musée d'Anthropologie Préhistorique in the Jardin Exotique illustrates clearly the prehistoric wildlife population and also sheds some light on the early human settlement along the Côte d'Azur. Elephants and mammoths once lived in these parts. The museum also displays finds which depict the evolution of *Homo sapiens*.

Monte Carlo

In architectural terms, the magnificent gambling casino (see illustration left) symbolizes the aspirations of the upper middle classes and the aristocracy at the end of the nineteenth century. Casino and opera are housed in one building and linked by a shared foyer. The building was designed by Charles Garnier, who also planned the Opera in Paris, and built between 1861 and 1875.

In 1863, François Blanc opened the first casino on the Plateau des Spélugues. This soon proved to be very successful and it was not long before it was nationalized under Charles III. A new building dating from 1868 in the style of a Palladian villa was soon found to be too small and so in 1878 the famous architect, who had been responsible for the Paris Opera House, was commissioned to design new premises. They opened one year later. Everything here, from color and surface appeal to sculptural opulence, is intended to create a suitably grand setting for the high-ranking clientele. For example, the auditorium in the opera house is laid out in a rectangular shape, rather like a banqueting hall, with the stage having the effect of a striking wall decoration. The casino hall is covered with grand ceiling paintings and bows outward at the sides in much the same way as the opera house auditorium in Paris. Allegorical figures dance or relax amid large-scale, richly-colored, and very varied decorations of which the huge occuli are typical. The roulette players and opera guests played a full part in this theatrical manifestation of oriental splendor. Above all, the women in their stylish gowns and glittering jewelry blended perfectly with the splendor of the casino, whose purpose was to display wealth in every possible visual way.

A Japanese garden laid out on very strict Shintoist guidelines is located on the Menton side of Monte Carlo. A Japanese bridge and a Zen garden are part of a complex symbolic whole.

Roquebrune-Cap-Martin

Roquebrune-Cap-Martin was an important staging post in the life of Le Corbusier, whom many regard as the greatest architect of the twentieth century. Not far from the spot where he suffered a heart attack while bathing in the sea in 1965, the celebrated designer had built a vacation home—an ironic footnote among the array of elegant villas here. The *Cabanon* ("little hut") is only 12 ft x 12 ft (3.66 x 3.66 m) square and is constructed simply from wooden planks. For the architect, however, the building represented a primitive unit of habitation for easy and comfortable living and the interior furnishings were multi-functional. Everything was measured against the *Modulor*, a system of proportion based on the Golden Rule. Corbusier's Cabanon can be reached via a footpath along the beach, starting from the Cap-Martin railroad station.

Roquebrune-Cap-Martin
View of Old Roquebrune
(above)
Promenade Le Corbusier (right)

OPPOSITE:
Monte Carlo
Casino façade, 1878 (above)
Detail of the left side of the
frontage (below)

High above Cap-Martin lies the historic heart of Roquebrune (see illustration page 333, top). From 1355 through 1861 it belonged to the Grimaldi family, who used and extended an existing fortress here. The lower sections of the large keep are all that remain of this remarkable building. In the twelfth century, an additional keep was added, but the site was finally rebuilt in the fifteenth century. A small tour of the château, particularly the prison, armory, turrets, and battlements, gives some idea of its military function. The kitchen and a communal hall are right in the center. Sound simulations and shadowy figures help to create the atmosphere that would have existed in such a medieval fortress.

La Turbie

In 7- 6 BC , the Roman Senate ordered the building of a victory monument on the border with Roman Gaul, in honor of Augustus (see illus. left). An inscription on the *Alpium Tropaea* refers to the conquest of the 45 Alpine tribes. Opponents of the Roman occupation under Augustus were defeated, paving the way for the merging of Gaul, conquered earlier by Julius Caesar, with Roman Italy. It was for this reason that in 12 BC work began on the construction of the Via Julia Augusta between Ventimiglia and Cimiez through the Maritime Alps. During the twelfth century, the monument was converted into a fortified château. La Turbie was later used as a keep and a watchtower. It was then left to decay, the process being accelerated by an attempt to blow it up in 1705. Excavation work began in 1905, but between 1929 and 1933, Jules Formigé undertook extensive restoration funded mainly by the American, Edward Tuck.

It is a huge structure which should be viewed from all sides. The substructure consists of a rectangular, slender-based and corniced podium with precise, large-scale ashlar stonework. Some of the original 24 columns for the surmounting circular temple have been reconstructed. The smooth columns bear Tuscan order capitals. These were clearly intended to be viewed from afar, because when inspected at close-quarters, it is evident that the detailed work was not very carefully executed. An 11-stepped pyramidal roof, thought to have been topped with a statue of Augustus together with two prisoners, surmounted an attic story.

A small museum is located next to the monument. It houses other remains and documents the restoration work. As the monument was very badly damaged, it is unlikely that Formigé's restoration work is true to the original. The restoration team seem to have been heavily influenced by the conventions of twentieth-century classical architecture.

Menton
Old town and port

Menton

The attractive old town quarter of Menton with its narrow alleys and tightly-packed houses retains a charm which recalls the city's many centuries of links with northern Italy. Like Roquebrune, Menton belonged to the Grimaldi family until 1860. Nowadays Menton is not just a popular beach resort and vacation destination, it is also an important center for the arts. The museum on the main road out of city to the west contains many important works, such as a Madonna by a thir-teenth-century master of the Order of Magdalene and an altarpiece by Louis Bréa (c. 1500). Every August, a chamber music festival with open-air concerts is staged on the squares around the city. The platform-like square at the heart of the Old City offers a fine view over the beach and out to sea. It is framed on the west and south sides by two church façades. The church of St-Michel (1619–1675) can be identified by its three portals, the upper story recessed above the volutes, and the strongly-dimensioned towers, while the inside is a triple-naved, barrel-vaulted basilica of extrava-gant splendor. The Church of the Immaculate Conception (1687) stands at right angles to it but about 30 steps higher up and overlooks the square (see illus. above).

Menton
Church of St-Michel, 1619-1675 (left side) with the Church of the Immaculate Conception, 1687 (above)
View of the beach from the old town (left)
Stepped street in the old town (below)

The Côte d'Azur hinterland

One of the most impressive journeys undertaken during a stay on the French Riviera is an excursion into the Alps, whose limestone slopes descend steeply from the ranges behind Monaco and Roquebrune straight down to the coastline. In the nineteenth century, the valleys were opened up by railway engineers. One such line connects Nice with Digne and still serves as an excellent alternative route for those wishing to travel to the Mediterranean coast by rail. This single-track line runs mainly through unspoiled countryside, small villages, and old railroad stations. The *Train des Pignes* (Pine Cone Line) was completed in 1911, having taken 25 years to build. The track is more than 94 miles (151 km) long, and the train has to negotiates a difference in altitude of almost 3,330 ft (1,000 m)! Such inclines required the construction of many hairpin bends and these forced trains to travel at such low speeds that the firemen could gather pine cones from the passing trees! These were then added to the boiler to boost the steam pressure for the steep climb ahead. In World War II, the line assumed great importance as it was used to keep the Côte d'Azur supplied during the bombardment of the coastal region. The private company which now runs the line uses modern rolling stock, and the journey from Nice to Digne-les-Bains takes just three hours.

Trains leave Nice from their own railroad station to the north of the main SNCF (French railroads) station. The old station building is in danger of decaying still further, despite having been recently modernized. Initially, the railroad track runs along the Var valley. If exploring by automobile, it is worth turning off at Plan-du-Var into the Gorges de la Vésubie valley. After a few miles, the road climbs steeply up to the small city of Utelle (see illustration right). Even today, the remoteness of this hilltop village serves to remind visitors that Nice's hinterland has very little in common with the coastal strip. These little villages way up in the mountains were almost completely self-sufficient. Some recycled Romanesque capitals are built into Utelle's beautiful, sixteenth-century triple-naved church. The church is clad with Mannerist stucco. An ever-narrowing road extends beyond Utelle as far as the shrine of the Madonna of Utelle, a place of pilgrimage which apparently owes its existence to Spanish sailors who claimed a light on this hilltop delivered them from a storm in 850. The view from here, at an altitude of 3913 ft (1,174m), not just of Nice, but also towards the seemingly endless array of snow-covered Alpine summits, is beyond compare.

Another monument to the railroad age, which also provides an opportunity to appreciate the full scenic beauty of the area, is the section of line from Nice to Cuneo, on the other side of the Italian border. Even before Nice was annexed by France, there were plans for such a

line over the Alps. Initially, a small section starting from Cuneo, was completed in 1864, but for strategic reasons the French hesitated about proceeding with this route and initially only the track from Nice to Sospel was built. In 1909 the economic benefits of such an undertaking were finally recognized and work began on closing the gap. The line was eventually opened in 1928 and within a few years it had been electrified. There was now an uninterrupted railway line through the western Alps. This route reduced by a third the 562 mile (900 km) long detour via Geneva, Lyons and Marseilles. However, the line was almost completely destroyed during World War II. It took until 1979 to make good the damage but the line is now back in regular use. Many bridges and tunnels were necessary to deal with the often dramatic contours. There

RIGHT:
Breil-sur-Roya (above)
Utelle, general view (center)
Detail of the pilgrim church of Utelle (below)

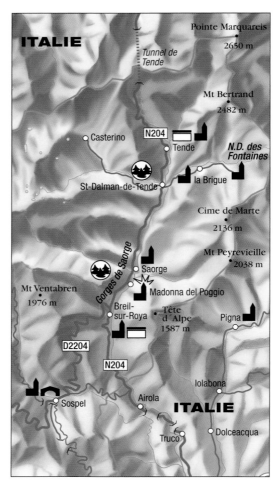

are 50 on the French side of the border and these account for more than half of the whole line. Some of them have actually been cut through the rock in a spiral, so that trains wind upward underground.

The attractive towns along the line are of interest not merely because of their picturesque railroad stations. Sospel, for example, occupies a beautiful position straddling the Bévera. From the outside, the St-Michel cathedral is an austere structure, but inside it radiates with lavish seventeenth-century decorations. Two reredos (ca. 1500), both produced by the École de Nice artists, hang on the walls.

Saorge was once a fortress which controlled the pass from Tende. In addition to old houses, some of which date from the fifteenth century, the city also boasts La Madone del Poggio chapel (see illustration above left), a building which originated in the eleventh century. Fragments of murals from the studio of Jean Baleison can still be seen in the apse.

Before World War II, St-Dalmas-de-Tende was the border town between France and Italy. It has a huge palatial station building, now a relic bearing witness to the city's earlier historical importance.

The church in the Alpine village of La Brigue looks as if it is of Romanesque origin even though work did not start on it until the late

LEFT:
Saorge
Chapelle de la Madone del Poggio, 11th century (above)

Tende
Mountain village on the Riba de Bernou cliff (below)

OPPOSITE:
Near La Brigue
Pilgrim church of Notre-Dame-des-Fontaines
Late 15th-century wall painting

PP 342-43:
Saorge

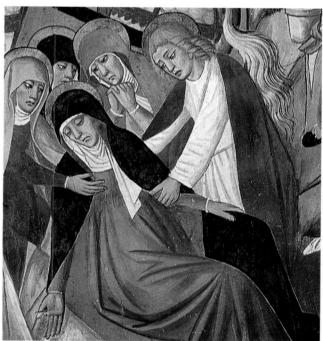

fifteenth century. Inside, the Crucifixion and Nativity altarpieces (ca. 1510) represent two important works from Louis Bréa's École de Nice.

A few miles outside La Brigue, there is the pilgrimage chapel of Notre-Dame-des-Fontaines, to which pilgrimages have been made since the fourteenth century. According to legend, seven springs near the chapel dried up, but after an appeal to the Mother of God, they began to flow again. On one occasion while the church was being built, the water is said to have turned to wine. The well-preserved paintings which cover the walls in the large chapel (see illustration above and right) are a spectacular sight. An inscription on the north wall attributes the work to the cleric, Jean Canavesio. This Piedmontese artist is mentioned in several other places in Liguria toward the end of the fifteenth century. The paintings are not frescoes, painted on wet plaster, they are painted in tempera, colors in which oil is replaced by egg yolk. They have remained in such superb condition because for centuries

they were covered by a layer of plaster which was not removed until the twentieth century.

The works illustrate three themes. The front wall depicts the life of Mary and the childhood of Christ, the side-walls depict the Passion of Christ, and the west wall the Last Judgment. Jean Baleison almost certainly painted the scenes from the life of Mary in the chancel (ca. 1480). The figures here are in large format and display a certain elegant stylization. The paintings in the nave display all types of graphic narration. The facial expressions and gestures have the effect of presenting the Passion as a popular drama. For this purpose, the painter made use of some tension-enhancing effects. Many of the protagonists and their deeds can be followed through the various pictures. Thus, for example, the soldier who nails Jesus to the cross can be identified repeatedly by the hammer that he is carrying. On the north wall a large-format portrayal of a hanging Judas, his entrails spewing out, serves as a dire warning to the beholder.

The Fragrances of Provence

Grasse, Vence, and Draguignan

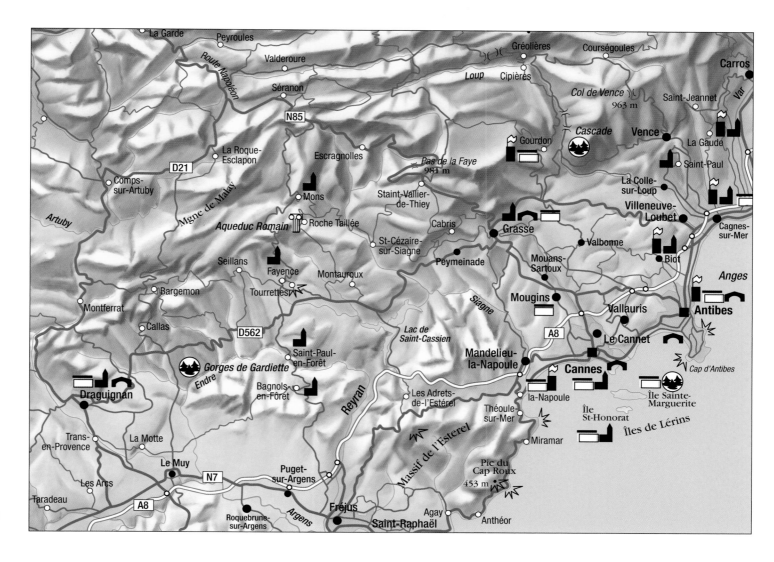

OPPOSITE:
Tourettes
Village near Fayence (between Grasse and Draguignan)

Cagnes-sur-Mer
Musée Renoir

Cagnes-sur-Mer

Cagnes, the attractive center of what is today a somewhat overdeveloped area, was founded in the fifth century when the monks of Lérins founded a branch of their Order here. In the fourteenth century, it became the seat of the Grimaldi family, who constructed a substantial château which has occupied its present site since 1620. It contains amongst others a famous painting *La Chute de Phaëton* by Carlone and a museum about olive cultivation, once Cagnes' main source of income, as well as an exhibition of contemporary art. The château and the adjacent St-Pierre Church are a part of the almost complete thirteenth-century fortification wall which encircles the old town and is about 333 ft (100 m) in diameter.

Tucked away, at Les Collettes, stands the house used by the painter Auguste Renoir (1841–1919) in his last years from 1907. In 1900, Renoir went to the Grasse area with his family. Though confined to a wheelchair, while in Cagnes the artist devoted himself to sculpture, producing for example, with the help of Richard Guino, the famous *Venus Victrix*, a bronze of which is in the Museum garden.

Renoir-Guino
Vénus Vitrix (detail, 1915–16)
Cagnes-sur-Mer.
Height of the Sculpture:
72 in (180 cm). Length: 44 in (110 cm).
Cagnes-sur-Mer, Musée Renoir.
When Renoir was an old man, the dealer Ambroise Vollard encouraged him to try his hand at sculpture. Inspired by the naturalism of classical works, especially Grecian sculpture (such as the Venus of Arles in the Musée de l'Arles Antique) he produced this Venus.

OPPOSITE:
St-Paul-de-Vence

St-Paul-de-Vence
Fondation Maeght
Sculpture garden
Mobile by Alexander Calder

St-Paul-de-Vence

St-Paul-de-Vence is one of a number of small towns consisting almost completely of buildings from the Middle Ages or slightly later. It was fortified by François I who built walls around the hill on which the town stood. The church at the highest point has its origins in the twelfth and thirteenth century. It originally had a single aisle, but in 1300 it was extended with two side-aisles to provide a wide and spacious nave. Buttresses and rib-vaulting were added for strength. In 1740, the nave received its present ridge roof.

Near St-Paul on the hill of La Gardette, set among pine trees, is the famous Maeght Foundation. Aimé Maeght, a former lithographer working on modern art, created an impressive museum of modern art here, which features an exquisite collection of works by Joan Miró, Giacometti, Alexander Calder, Julio Gonzalez, Pierre Bonnard, and others, and stages impressive special exhibitions. The museum building, designed by the Catalan architect Josep Lluis Sert, was opened in 1964. The relatively low, but wide, spacious structure with its series of courtyards creates an inspired combination with the large organic forms of the numerous works of art particularly those of the 1960s.

Red brickwork, glass walls, and concrete floors are produced as independent elements, as are the works of art placed in the surrounding parkland. The roof shape is particularly striking, consisting as it does of open, upward-curving, half- cylinders of concrete. The architect here demonstrates in a grand gesture the interaction of the building with the heavens, appearing at the same time to be open rather than just enclosing the interior. However, the roof construction actually has a practical function because it guides the incoming light downward through the openings thus providing almost constant natural light for the exhibition rooms. In this way, the architect Sert has provided individual lighting for each gallery, the Chagall Gallery being somewhat more "mysterious" than that of the brightly-lit Miró Gallery.

The grounds of the Museum contain of one of Joan Miró's Labyrinths. Numerous large primitive sculptures are on permanent display and form part of the structure, playing the role of gargoyles, fountain figures, or woodland creatures. The chapel on the site, dedicated to Maeght's son who died young, is partly built of medieval stonework, another example of the harmonious blend of old and new in this exciting and unique structure.

OPPOSITE:
St-Paul-de-Vence
Fondation Maeght
Museum building (1964) by
Josep Lluis Sert and the Giacometti courtyard (above)
Sculpture garden (below)

Vence
Street in the old town (above)
Cathedral: choir-stalls, mid-15
the century, carved by Jacques
Bellot (above right)

Vence
Town hall façade

Vence

Vence and St-Paul-de-Vence are among the most popular vacation destinations in Provence. This is because both places are within easy reach of the coast and were once quiet little towns in the foothills of the Alps. The plan oval layout of the old town can still be recognized. Walking through what was once the fortress—perhaps through the Porte de Peyra (ca. 1200) on the west side—the houses in the narrow streets appear to lean toward each other. These lanes open up from time to time into concealed, irregular squares.

Vence has an ancient history. The Roman *Civitas Vintium* had its own bishop from the fourth century. This was the smallest diocese in France until it was abolished during the French Revolution. From the eleventh century, the bishop shared the town administration with the local nobles. From 1231 to the Revolution the local lords were the Villeneuve family, the counts of Provence. After the revolution, Vence's fortunes declined, while those of Grasse rose, since it is more conveniently located for transport.

The cathedral stands in the center of the town and blends in with the surrounding buildings. It is almost certainly an eleventh-century structure, and is one of the older churches in Provence. The building is of massive construction, both inside and out. On the west side, the flat stonework of the original building is still visible. Panels carved with reliefs and a braided strip were also used here, as can be clearly seen from the remains of the Carolingian altar-rail from the earlier building. The interior of the three-aisle, transeptless building (originally with three apses) was completely distorted when it was restored in 1824. A new main arch was introduced, the medieval semi-circular cladding removed and the wall surfaces covered with a uniform layer of plaster. In the

side-aisles, the corners of capitals together with transverse arches can still be discerned, though these were merely ripped out and discarded. Relief panels with braided strip ornamentation still exist in the chancel area, the south side-aisle, and the tower chapel. In the fifteenth century, Jacques Bellot of Grasse carved almost all the beautiful choir-stalls on the west gallery (see above).

On the other side of the valley there stands the Dominican nunnery whose chapel was designed, fitted out, and painted by the painter Henri Matisse in gratitude to the sisters who nursed him. The Chapelle du Rosaire (see above), its architecture, decoration, the stained glass windows, and fitments were consecrated in 1951. The building is laid out on an angular plot of land. The nuns have therefore been able to reserve for themselves an area from which they can attend Mass without being seen by others. The artistic decoration has the religious content so spread out in pictorial representation that it almost appears to consist of hieroglyphics.

The wall decoration in the nave, consisting of black brush marks on white ceramic is particularly fascinating in this context. The lettering *Ave* is used as a graphic, almost short-hand, representation of the Madonna. The Stations of the Cross on the opposite side consist of crude, oversimplified sketches, and only the indication of the station number makes it possible to reconstruct the pictorial theme presented. Overall, the designs illustrate the Passion using a complex language of interpretation. Clearly, Matisse developed the pictorial representation of religious subject-matter into a form that became hardly recognizable. The painter went so far with the generally known presentation forms—the Madonna, the Stations of the Cross—that he did not merely "abstract" them, he changed them into a picture-text without preconditions.

OPPOSITE:
Vence
Chapelle du Rosaire or
Chapelle Matisse (1947-51)
in the Dominican convent
of Vence

"Despite of all its imperfections, I consider it to be my masterwork — the result of a lifetime's search for truth".
HENRI MATISSE

Grasse, the Capital of Perfumery

Ever since the tenth century a town has occupied these steep rocks at the intersection of roads leading either to the Alps or their foothills. The power vacuum in the region enabled the town to enjoy extensive autonomy. It was protected by Genoa and in 1227 first became the capital of Provence. However, the town became French in 1481. The sixteenth century was an age of terror. In 1536, Grasse was sacked by the troops of Emperor Charles V and was destroyed again in 1589 during the Wars of Religion. Because cattle could be raised in the rocky landscape around Grasse it developed from the Middle Ages onward into a tanning and glove-making center.

This was to be the destiny of the town. With the growth of the fashion for perfumed gloves in the seventeenth century, the town flourished, as it was particularly well supplied with the raw materials necessary for their manufacture. In addition to the leather, the essences of roses, lavender, jasmine, oranges, and other fruits and flowers grew easily in the soil and climate of the Provence. Perfumery developed from that time into the most important business of the town. With the beginning of the nineteenth century, the perfumeries of Paris stepped up their production, Grasse reacted by concentrating on the manufacture of fragrances which are still exported all over the world for further processing and refinement. Previously, the local perfumeries concentrated on extraction of essences through distillation, now they are extracted from the flower with the use of solvents.

The flourishing town has expanded into the surrounding countryside, so that the old medieval town has been left behind. However, the old houses and narrow lanes have been lovingly preserved. For some years appreciation of this area has grown, and parts of the old town are now restricted to pedestrians.

OPPOSITE:
Grasse
Molinard Perfumery (above)
Fragonard Perfumery
Display of perfume bottles
(below)

Grasse
Cathedral of Notre-Dame
(1244) with the old town and
bishop's palace

OPPOSITE:
Grasse
Cathedral of Notre-Dame
Interior looking west,
ground plan (below)

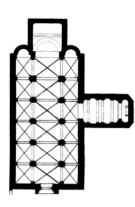

Grasse
Cathedral of Notre-Dame,
Chapel of the Sacrament, *The
Washing of the Feet of Peter* by
Fragonard

Peter Paul Rubens
*The Crowning of Christ with
Thorns,* 1601
(one of three Rubens paintings
in the Grasse cathedral)

The cathedral was built from brilliant white limestone on a rocky outcrop in 1244 with the transfer of the episcopal see from Antibes to Grasse. The interior, a three-aisle basilica without a transept, typical of local construction, is surprising because of an extreme lack of adornment which emphasizes the clear traces of a devastating fire during the Revolution on the round pillars. The cathedral is vaulted with strong ribbed bands and therefore has similarities with the episcopal church in Frejus. The rectangular choir was built in the early eighteenth century. The most spectacular feature of the church is a painting of the Washing of the Feet of Peter, an early work of the Grasse-born Rococo painter Jean-Honoré Fragonard, and there are also three paintings by Peter Paul Rubens on the south side of the aisle.

The paintings *Christ's Crowning with Thorns, St. Helena* and the *Crucifixion* were commissioned by Archduke Albert for the Helena chapel of S. Croce in Gerusalemme in Rome and were painted in 1601-02. Within a few years, the paintings were so badly damaged by the damp in the chapel, that they had to be restored in 1614-15. A copy was produced of the *Crucifixion.* In the early nineteenth century the copy and the two original paintings were sold to a citizen of Grasse, M. Pérolle, who bequeathed them to the local Hospice. The pictures have hung in the cathedral since 1972. This cycle of pictures is nothing less than Ruben's first public commission. His Italian experience can be clearly recognized, above all in the *Crowning of Thorns* and it can be seen how Rubens further developed the chiaroscuro effects and emulated the composition and placing of figures used by Titian.

The former bishop's palace is next to the cathedral and is now used as the city hall. The fabric of the building is essentially medieval with the bishop's chapel serving today as the place where civil marriages are performed.

Visitors are able to see how perfumes are manufactured in Grasse. The Musée International de la Parfumerie traces the fascinating 3,000-year-old history of the production of scents and the major and famous perfumery companies—Fragonard, Molinard, and Galimard—allow visits to their workshops. The Villa-Musée Fragonard is an impressive late-seventeenth-century mansion. Alexandre Maubert, the cousin of the painter Jean-Honoré Fragonard, acquired it in the eighteenth century. Today it exhibits original works or copies of works by the famous artist and his family, such as the cycle "*Progress of the Love in the Heart of a Young Girl*").

La Route Napoléon

Grasse is an important stage on the route to Paris which Napoleon took in 1815 on his return from exile on Elba, the so-called "hundred days." The route is indicated with numerous commemorative plaques and road signs identified by the Napoleonic eagle. So carefully and meticulously has the route been laid out, one might imagine the Emperor himself had been responsible for it! In fact, the route was signposted in 1932 from the Golfe-Juan, through Grasse, Sisteron, and Grenoble as a memorial to the Emperor. Following Napoleon's defeat in 1813 and the subsequent internal political crises in France, the Emperor was removed from office in 1814 and he himself resigned on April 6. He was exiled to the Isle of Elba over which he ruled as its sovereign. Less than a year later, he again took power. On March 1, 1815, he landed at Golfe-Juan and took his troops to Paris, sometimes through fields to avoid being caught. He overcame the military resistance sent out against him on the Rhône road. During the march, he quickly won popular support and in Grenoble was enthusiastically received by the populace.

Upon reaching Paris, he once again took office but Napoleon's reign was brought to a rapid end by his final defeat by the British at the Battle of Waterloo (June 18, 1815). Napoleon was exiled to the Island of St. Helena, in the distant South Atlantic, where he died in 1821.

Gorges du Loup
Waterfall of Courmes

In the northeast, the Grasse hinterland is precipitous and craggy. There are many interesting places to visit in this area, including Cabris, St-Vallier-de-Thiey, and Caussols. The D 6 road through the Gorges des Loup passes the Courmes waterfall and the higher D 3 runs through the town of Gourdon on the edge of the cliffs, where a huge château was built in 1600. In Bar-sur-Loup, the church of St-Jacques contains a fifteenth-century wood panel featuring St. James from the painting school of Nice and a *Dance Macabre*, showing dancing couples being struck from all sides by the Arrows of Death. The inscriptions explaining the paintings are in Provençal.

The village of Gréolières is divided into two parts. The older part is early medieval, dating mostly from the eleventh and twelfth centuries. There is an old fortress, built in the year 1400, on the hilltop in the district known as Gréolières Haute. A new fortress was erected in Gréolières Basse, lower down the hill, which was rebuilt in the seventeenth and eighteenth century.

The Romanesque church is rather massive in design, with a squat tower but contains a lovely reredos with a representation of St. Stephen, St. John the Baptist, and St. Anthony. Gréolières-les-Neiges is reached via the D 2 and the D 802.

Gorges du Loup
Gorge in the mountainous Grasse hinterland

LEFT:

Valbonne
Town square with inn, the
Auberge provençale (above)

Fayence
Lanes in the old district of this
vacation destination between
Grasse and Draguignan. The
area now contains many arts
and crafts workshops (below)

OPPOSITE:

Mons
Ancient village on a rocky spur
in the mountainous area west
of Grasse (above)

Roche Taillée
Section of a Roman aqueduct
system near Mons (below)

Valbonne

Monks from the Congregation of Chalais, a
small order based on the Cistercian rule, settled
here in 1199 and built a monastery. During the
fourteenth century, the monastery was abandoned and acquired by the Abbey of Lérins. In
the sixteenth century, the Abbey required the
monastery and its outbuildings to be reoccupied.
It was therefore redesigned as a town on the grid
pattern, including central arcaded squares which
still exist today. The cloistered church, dating
from around 1200, is similar in style to the austere Cistercian churches. The single-aisled nave
with pointed vaults is closed off with a transept
from which a flat, closed chancel leads off.

From Grasse to Draguignan

The road from Grasse to Draguignan passes the
Lac de St-Cassien, which offers many opportunities for relaxation and indulging in water-
sports for which facilities are available. This
artificial lake was created in 1964-67 in order
to improve the drinking water supply and to
serve as a reservoir for fighting the all-too-
frequent forest fires in the area, as well as sup-
plying hydro-electricity.

Not far away, on the edge of the Préalpes, the foothills of the Alps, there are some lovely Provençal villages, among them Montauroux, Callian, Fayence, Seillans, and Bargemon. Although these villages have many visitors, mainly in high summer and in winter, and some of the houses have been turned into second homes for wealthy Parisians, the old charm of the places remains intact. In the little town of Tourettes directly opposite Fayence—with which it has engaged in constant rivalry for centuries—a huge château was built in 1840, by an engineer named Alexandre Fabre. Fabre had worked as an engineer in Russia for twenty-five years where he made his fortune building roads. His retirement home dominates the whole valley.

North of here in the direction of Mons, there is an interesting Roman industrial monument, the *Roche Taillée* (there is an information panel about the site on the D 37 before it crosses the river Fil). This is part of an aqueduct system which brought water to Frejus. In order to guide the water along the steep cliffs, some arched bridges were constructed. At other points, the Roman engineers simply hollowed out the rock over 166 ft (50 m) sections to create deep cuttings up to 33 ft (10 m) deep and 12 ft (3.6 m) wide into which water could be channeled (see right).

The small town of Mons (see above) is one of the few places in the Provence which appears to have been untouched by modern life. It covers a rocky ridge from which there is an excellent view of the surrounding country, especially from the Place St-Sébastien. The town, which existed in the eleventh century, was abandoned in 1348, but in 1468 it was resettled by a colony of Genoese immigrants. A long wall of broken stone was erected for protection, which gave the residents the nickname "Les Chinois de Var" (the Chinese of the Var). The local dialect, *Figour*, is still spoken by some residents.

The painter Max Ernst spent the last years of his life in the pretty little town of Seillans. Romans lived here from the second century. In the Middle Ages, Seillans belonged to St-Victor in Marseille. In the nineteenth century, the town supplied Grasse with flowers as the raw material for perfumes. The thirteenth-century chapel of Notre-Dame-de-l'Ormeau, a jewel of Romanesque architecture, stands east of the town.

Gorges de Pennafort

The Pennafort Gorges are not as well-known as other similar rock formations in the area. They can be seen east of Draguigan along the D 25 (footpath to the south from the point at which the road crosses the stream). Though they are not as spectacular as the Gorges du Verdon, they are full of rocky outcrops, sparkling, rushing streams, and many waterfalls. Geologically, the gorge is of interest because it is created from a variety of different types of rock and minerals, most of them volcanic, including gneiss and granite, diorite and porphyry. Their reddish tones also offer the visitor a wonderful display of colors.

To the south near to Le Muy (on the D 54), there is another waterfall, the Saut du Capelan, on the river Naturby. There is a 116 ft (35 m) drop over which the water rushes, only to disappear through a cleft in the rocks and reappear some 333 ft (100 m) further away, this time at ground level.

Draguignan

In the sixteenth century, under the reign of François I, Draguignan was an important seat of government. The town improved its position during the Revolution, when it became the capital of the newly created *département* of Var. This function was only transferred to Toulon in 1974 to take account of the importance of the significant port city. In return, Draguignan became the center for artillery development and testing. The town flourished in the nineteenth-century due to its flower-growing trade, a reminder of which is the unfinished neo-gothic church of St-Michel by Henri Revoil, built in 1869. The Clock Tower (see left) is at the highest point in the town. It has stood on the site of a previous tower since 1663. South of the town lies the charming little town of Trans, in which two old stone bridges built of stones taken from the river bed cross the little river Nartuby. A small town hall (1799) occupies the site of a former château.

Landscape near Le Muy
(above)

Draguignan
Tour de l'Horloge (left)

OPPOSITE:
Gorges du Pennafort
View of the little known Ravine east of Draguignan

Magnificent Nature

The Valley of the Durance and the Gorges du Verdon

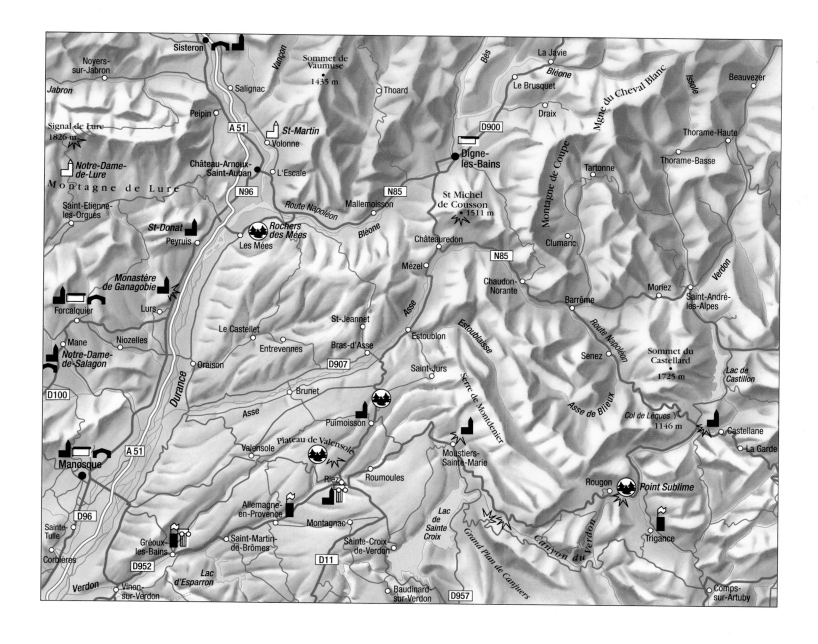

Noyers-sur-Jabron

Sisteron

Vançon

Sommet de Vaumuse
1435 m

Bès

La Javie

Bléone

Beauvezer

Jabron

Salignac

Thoard

Le Brusquet

Peipin

Draix

Signal de Lure
1826 m

A 51

St-Martin

Volonne

Digne-les-Bains

Thorame-Haute

Thorame-Basse

Notre-Dame-de-Lure

Château-Arnoux-Saint-Auban

L'Escale

N85

St Michel de Cousson
1511 m

Tartonne

M o n t a g n e   d e   L u r e

N96

Route Napoléon

Mallemoisson

Bléone

Saint-Etienne-les-Orgues

St-Donat

Rochers des Mées

Châteauredon

Clumanc

Verdon

Peyruis

Les Mées

Mézel

N85

Monastère de Ganagobie

Chaudon-Norante

Moriez

Saint-André-les-Alpes

Forcalquier

Lurs

Barrême

St-Jeannet

Asse

Estoublaisse

Senez

Sommet du Castellard
1725 m

Lac de Castillon

Mane

Niozelles

Le Castellet

Entrevennes

Bras-d'Asse

Estoublon

Notre-Dame-de-Salagon

D907

Saint-Jurs

Serre de Mondenier

Asse de Blieux

Col de Lèques
1146 m

Castellane

D100

Oraison

Brunet

Asse

La Garde

A 51

Puimoisson

Moustiers-Sainte-Marie

Rougon

Point Sublime

Manosque

Valensole

Plateau de Valensole

D96

Riez

Roumoules

Lac de Sainte Croix

Sainte-Tulle

Allemagne-en-Provence

Montagnac

Trigance

Gréoux-les-Bains

Saint-Martin-de-Brômes

Sainte-Croix-de-Verdon

Canyon du Verdon

Corbières

D11

Grand Plan de Canjuers

D952

Lac d'Esparron

Comps-sur-Artuby

Verdon

Vinon-sur-Verdon

Baudinard-sur-Verdon

D957

Durance

Flood plain of the Durance
near Manosque

The Mistral, an icy wind, used to be counted as one of the plagues of the Provence, along with the Parlement of Aix and the flooding of the Durance. The wind's name derives appropriately from *maestre*, or "master." The most beautiful sunshine loses its appeal when the bitter wind tears relentlessly at trees, houses, and clothing. The wind whistling down from the north-north-west is channeled through the bottleneck of the Rhône valley, increasing its intensity. In winter and spring, wind speeds can measure 94 m.p.h. (150 km/h)! The Mistral is created by high pressure in the Atlantic meeting low pressure over the Gulf of Genoa, producing cold air in the western Mediterranean.

The Durance Valley

"The Mistral, the Parlement, and the Durance, those are the plagues of Provence," is an old Provençal saying. Today, only one of these hardships is left. The Parlement d'Aix has been dissolved since the Revolution and the Durance has been tamed. The river, one of the most important waterways of the southern Alps and the second-mightiest branch of the Rhône, after the Saône, was once feared for the sudden rises of the water-level which caused terrible floods. The phenomenon is the result of the Provençal climate, where it only rains twice a year, in spring and fall. When the rain finally falls, it comes in such torrential downpours that all the streams are turned into raging torrents in a matter of a few hours. These flow into the Durance, over half of whose water consists of melting snow, and its tributary, the Verdon, contributes its own additional waters. The combination of these factors in the spring created a true natural disaster, in which the dikes were breached and houses, animals, and people, washed away. For this reason, the river frequently altered course.

Attempts to dam the floodwaters were made as early as the thirteenth century. Since

that time basins and side-canals have been built in an effort to bring the river somewhat under control, as well as to irrigate the lands of the Comtat Venaisson and the area around Aix. Decisive steps were taken in the nineteenth century by two competing canal works. When Marseilles was expanding rapidly and on the way to becoming a trading metropolis, a 52 mile (84 km) long side-canal was connected to the Durance between 1834 and 1851. Its capacity was calculated far enough into the future to be able to manage an additional population boom. Soon afterwards, between 1857 and 1875, a canal was built from the estuary of the Verdon to supply Aix with water. Finally, beginning in 1948, the technically difficult task of damming up water flowing from the mountains was undertaken in the hopes of controlling the river. The waters of the Durance were dammed south of Embrun in the Lac de Serre-Ponçon. The waters of the Verdon are collected west of the Gorges du Verdon in the artificial lake of Lac de Ste-Croix. Although the creation of such reservoirs destroys large swathes of the natural environment, the associated benefits for this otherwise economically disadvantaged region of the Pré-Alpes cannot be overlooked.

Better irrigation makes it possible to plant orchards and grow fruit, while these huge manmade lakes are also extremely valuable for fighting forest fires. Above all, the artificial lakes have created a new interest for those tourists who are alienated by the overcrowded beaches of the coast. Furthermore, the hilltop villages are able to benefit from the advantages of having a nearby lake.

Manosque

Today, Manosque is an important administrative center of the southern Alps and since the 1950s it has had a nearby nuclear research facility. The narrow lanes of the old city still exudes the atmosphere so aptly described in the books of Jean Giono—remote, somewhat eccentric, and earthy. Originally the city was a manor of the Counts of Forqualquier which was later handed over to the order of the Knights of St. John of Jerusalem. For protection against plundering bands of soldiers, a circular wall was built to enclose the city in the fourteenth century. The medieval structure of the old city is easy to follow today and is grouped around the two main churches, St-Sauveur and Notre-Dame-du-Romigier. Notre-Dame contains an

Manosque
Notre-Dame-du-Romigier
Detail of the early Christian altar, depicting Adam and Eve.
Early 5th century.

early-Christian altar (illus. above), that shows the apostles honoring the Cross. The shorter sides depict Adam and Eve and the three youths in the fiery furnace, which are considered to be Old Testament allusions to the Resurrection.

Manosque
Clock tower (above) and
view of the old town (below)

Jean Giono
Jean Giono, one of France's great modern writers and poets, was born in Manosque. He was underestimated in the past for as being merely a recorder of folkways. In his numerous novels ("The Hill" 1929; "The Hussar on the Roof" 1934; "Stay, my Joy" 1935), the people and the landscape of the Provençal Pré-Alpes indeed take center stage. His home town, Manosque, where he was born in 1895 and died in 1970, often features as the setting. However these portrayals of the earthy, simple folk with their curious natures, should not be understood as being mere caricatures. Introduced in clear, polished language these characters embody archetypes that experience passion, love, contempt, and pain as a natural part of life. Not for nothing do allusions to antique mythology appear time and again, since these myths never seem to have died in the Provence. This fact is used by Giono as a critique of modern civilization. Despite his closeness to Communist circles in the 1920s, Giono quickly became a sharp critic of all forms of political totalitarianism and modern mass society. In this regard, Giono is important as a native intellectual, by correcting the misinterpretation of Provence as the picturesque backdrop to folkore, and local customs and traditions, produced by many of his Parisian colleagues. Giono's wonderful descriptions of the landscape are symbolic of the original lifestyle of the inhabitants.

On the Boulevard E. Bourges a convent church was built in neo-classical style in 1840. In 1992, it was reopened as the *Fondation Jean Carzou*. Carzou was an Armenian painter, born in 1907, who painted the entire church into a fantastic-surrealist idiom. Themes from the Apocalypse are given special emphasis. In the direct vicinity, at the medieval Porte Saunerie, the city has devoted a museum to its most famous son, the poet and author Jean Giono.

Forcalquier

Forcalquier was the main seat of one of Provence's three noble families in the eleventh and twelfth centuries who through marriage ruled the county of Provence from 1209. The city suffered badly from the attentions of the Grandes Compagnies in the fourteenth and the Wars of Religion in the sixteenth century and only first began to recover in the second half of the nineteenth century. The Théâtre de l'Athénée and the curved road and rail viaduct are manifestations of the redevelopment. From 1486 until the French Revolution, Notre-Dame-du-Bourguet and the cathedral of Sisteron, were the city's main churches. The present structure is a conglomeration of different periods. The Gothic transept and a polygonal choir were added to the twelfth century nave, which had originally had only one aisle in the Provençal tradition. These additions were, however, some of the earliest examples of Gothic elements in Provence. Finally, side-aisles were added to the nave in the seventeenth century. The city has two bell-towers, one medieval the other baroque. The former Franciscan monastery

(Cordeliers) around which the city grew up, was founded in 1236, and also contains some of the earliest Gothic elements in Provence. The remodeled medieval sections (the main church and cloister) date from the thirteenth and fourteenth centuries. To the north lies the city graveyard, laid out in the form of a beautiful formal garden in the French style, with a box-hedge maze.

South of Mane stands another magnificent example of Provençal Romanesque architecture, the former priory church of Notre-Dame-de-Salagon (see opposite). This sheltered priory was under the aegis of St-André in Villeneuve-lès-Avignon and was one of the richest in the region during the Middle Ages. The cloister was built over the ruins of a Gallo-Roman villa. In the sixteenth century, the monastery buildings were refurbished. After the Revolution, however, the buildings fell into disrepair and were used as a farmhouse before being restored relatively recently. The entrance is on three inset levels and is accompanied by lavishly fluted columns in the west wall. The late twelfth-century church has a very unique foundation. The three-bayed nave is connected to the north by a single, somewhat narrower side-aisle. The capitals are Corinthian and and on one of the free-standing pilasters on the side-aisle there is a carved scene of a type that is rarely found in Provence. At different places on the stonework, there are small carvings by craftsmen in stone panels representing hunting scenes, angels, and other religious motifs. About 120 ft (400 m) to the west of the cloister, there is an old stone bridge over the Laye which was built at the same time as the church.

Forcalquier
View of the town with the pilgrim church of Notre-Dame-de-Provence at the top.

OPPOSITE:
The former priory church of Notre-Dame-de-Salagon (late 12th century) (above and below left) Medieval stone bridge over the Laye near the Priory church (below right)

Ganagobie

The Benedictine priory of Ganagobie dominates the Durance Valley in complete isolation. It was founded by Bishop Jean III of Sisteron and handed over to the powerful Abbey of Cluny. Thanks to the contributions of the Counts of Forcalquier the priory flourished from the twelfth through the fourteenth century. It was later abandoned and fell into ruin, despite being temporarily occupied in the seventeenth century, until the Benedictines returned in the late nineteenth century. A major renovation was begun in 1957.

In prehistoric times, a Celtic settlement stood here, as is proven by the numerous fragments found on the site. A small town also existed to the northeast of the monastery during the Middle Ages, of which some ruins are left. The western porch of the priory church (see opposite) is surprising with its unusual wavy profile of the walls and archivolts. The style is certainly not original, but was part of a restoration that occurred at an unspecified time in which the stones, that originally served as pillar profiles, were turned in a 90-degree right angle and layered on top of one another. The tympanum relief shows Christ in an almond-shaped aureola with a victoriously raised right hand, surrounded by the winged symbols of the Evangelists. The twelve apostles are depicted on the lintel. The representational scheme is the same as in Arles or St-Gilles, although in an abbreviated form. The sculpture is not an example of great craftsmanship, but it is lively and expressive. The ground-plan of the church—a one-aisled nave, transept, and three apses—is typical of Provence, although unusually the transept has two aisles. The eastern parts of the church were demolished during the Revolution and first rebuilt in 1975. The most important part of the interior is the floor mosaics in the apses, first discovered and documented in 1893-98 and finally excavated in 1975. The transept contains

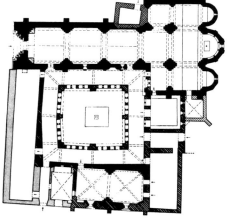
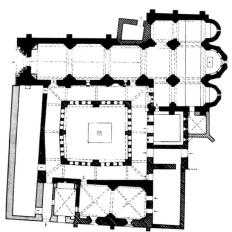

OPPOSITE:
Ganagobie
The 12th-century Benedictine priory of Notre-Dame-du-Puy, west portal of the priory church.
Ground plan of the priory buildings (right)

representations of numerous mythological beasts, including griffins, a centaur, and an elephant with a tower on its back. The battle between Good and Evil is represented pictorially. In the right apse a knight in armor appears to be attacking a winged dragon. Around the choir circle there is an inscription requesting that the donor of the mosaics and the "head of the workshop" Prior Bertrand and Petrus Trutbert, be remembered. The single stones consist of rather large pieces of brick, white marble, and a darker basalt.

The cloister is similar in design to the cloisters in Arles and Montmajour. Ganagobie also has an unidentified, clothed figure on one of the corner pilasters (to southwest). The capitals of the columns mostly show sculpted ornamentation such as is found in Vaison-la-Romaine; however it should be borne in mind that large parts of the cloister were completely rebuilt during the restoration work.

Walking on this narrow ridge, one's gaze is invited in all directions: toward the Durance Valley as well as to Forcalquier in the west.

Ganagobie
Priory garden
In 1992, the priory was once more inhabited by Benedictine monks

The Valley of the Durance and the Gorges of the Verdon

LEFT AND OPPOSITE:
Ganagobie
Mosaics on the floor of the priory church, 1122. The Ganagobie mosaics cover an area of about 233 sq. ft (70 sq. m) and are thus the largest preserved Romanesque floor mosaics in France.

Further to the north along the valley, there is another interesting example of Provençal Romanesque. The small church of *St-Donat-le-Bas* (or Eglise majeure) is one of the few examples of the early Romanesque in Provence. In the fifth century, Donatus the hermit is said to have settled here and is alleged to be buried here. Count Guillaume II of Provence handed over the monastic community to St-André in Villeneuve-lès-Avignon. St-Donat actually consists of four churches (the Eglise majeure and Eglise mineure de St-Donat-le-Bas, St-Donat-le-Haut, and a oratory). Apparently a church was built on the site of the saint's first place of residence (St-Donat-le-Haut) as well as over his grave (St-Donau-le-Bass, Eglise mineure). The complex was finally completed with the building of the large Eglise majeure (see right), which was large enough to accommodate the pilgrims. It is the largest and the only completely preserved church in the complex. It has a three-aisled basilica with a transept to which three apses are attached. The whole design is compressed and compact. The nave is only 13 ft (4 m) long, the side-aisles only 5 ft (1.5 m) long. The church is built from small pieces of stone, reinforced with larger stones at the edges. The slender round pilasters have rounded bases but there are no capitals. The nave ceiling is barrel-vaulted. and the transept has ogival vaulting. The building was most probably erected in the mid-eleventh century. It is now a prime example of how the church-building tradition was created which the masters of the twelfth century considerably improved upon by returning to antiquity for their inspiration.

The church of St-Donat-le-Haut was built on the other side of a mountain stream, inside a collapsed cave. The present church dates from the twelfth century. For reasons of space, the three apses extend from the nave.

On the opposite side of the Durance, massive triangular outcrops of rock known as Les Mées, cover an a stretch of almost 1 mile (2 km) and rise to a height of 3,303 ft (100 m) (see opposite). They are formed from scree boulders that hardened into a cement-like masses in some places and was less effected by erosion than the rest of the river valley. Ghastly legends surround the Mées; they are supposed to be repentant pilgrims or monks turned to stone for daring to give an indecent glance from under their cowls.

The village of Volonne stands at the foot of a cliff ridge which was once dominated by a château. To the north is the church of St-Martin which was part of another priory belonging to St-Victor in Marseilles in the eleventh century, later becoming the parish church of the village. The extremely simple five-bayed church, built in the late eleventh century is another example of early Romanesque building art in Provence (see right). The three aisles of today's ruined church each end in a apse. It has slender round pilasters and wide arcades.

OPPOSITE:
Les Mées
Bizarre rock formation near Les Ortes

RIGHT:
St-Donat
Church of St-Donat-le-Bas (Eglise majeure), first half of the eleventh century, north-western aspect (above)

Volonne
Ruins of St-Martin (late 11th century) (below)

Sisteron

At the confluence of the Buëch and the Durance a stopper-like boulder once blocked the further flow of the river to the south. In time, the water created an opening that has become a narrows, with steep cliffs on both sides of the river bed. The Rocher de la Baume on the left bank, which is 233 ft (70 m) wide, has been worn into deep grooves or clefts over time. A landing-place was settled on the west bank next to the Via Domitia which the Romans expanded and named Segustero. The Counts of Forcalquier once had a residence here. In the sixteenth century, the ancient fortifications of the city were redeveloped. In 1944, the Allies wishing to speed the retreat of German forces, destroyed much of Sisteron's old city in a bombing raid in which 300 citizens lost their lives. Much of the old city has been rebuilt, however.

Just outside the old city stands the Cathedral of Notre-Dame (see below). This twelfth-century building was once part of a complex with two additional churches, St-Thyrse and St-Jean, as well as a cloister. Notre-Dame is an important example of a style based on the architecture of Lombardy with its three-aisled basilica, three apses on the east end, and no transept. The striped, two-colored masonry in the east and west is clearly Italianate. The west portal has a unique blind arcade whose side-arches seem to be intersected by the buttresses. A similar portal can be found at the cathedral of Embrun. Finally, the tower in the center of the cross is in Lombard style. It is octagonal in shape and has a miniature balcony. The interior of the cathedral offers a simple and unadorned space. As in St-Donat, the nave is not set higher as in a basilica, but rather forms a hall in which all the vaulting is set at the same height.

Sisteron
View of the old town with the late-16th-century citadel at the top.

West face of the late 12th-century cathedral (extension)

Mountain landscape near Sisteron.
View to the north toward the Montagne de Gache

OPPOSITE:
Sisteron with Rocher de la Baume
The massive rock overlooking the Durance (in the east)

The citadel above the city (illus. 374-75) was altered by one of Henry IV's military engineers, Jean Erard, in the late sixteenth century. Sections of the old castle dating from the thirteenth and fifteenth century still remain intact. The fortifications were reinforced again in 1842-52, when a 365-step flight of steps was cut into the cliffs, leading down to the Durance. On the plateau of the fortress there is a open-air theater in which "Les Nuits de la citadel" are staged every summer. The impressive natural theater of the surrounding landscape, especially the rock formations "nightmare become stone" (see opposite) on the other side of the river, is available for free at any time of year.

Sisteron is a useful base for many excursions into the mountains on the left bank of the Durance. There are small river valleys dotted with unspoiled villages. Clamensane and Bayons lie in the valley of Sasse. Valernes and Sigoyer (on the D 304) also offer beautiful views. There is a curious Latin inscription cut into the mountain on the left-hand side of the road at the Défilé de Pierre-Écrite where the D 3 begins to climb sharply.

The Roman Praetor, Claudius Postumus Dardanus, reports how he, his family, and his followers retreated into the wilderness in the year 415 after converting to Christianity in order to found a community with the name of Theopolis ("God's city"). The problem here is that no archeological evidence has been found up to this point that could be associated with such a community. After St-Geniez, the road turns to the right to a small Romanesque chapel, Notre-Dame du Dromon, which has a tiny crypt (a short walk away along a footpath).

The ravines of the Méouge that flows into the Buëch northwest of Sisteron are also worthy of a visit. And finally, the Montagne de Lure rises to the southwest of Sisteron, a continuation of the Mont Ventoux mountain chain. A narrow mountain road lead up to a height of 6,086 ft (1,826 m), almost as high as Mont Ventoux. However, the important difference is that this mountain is not packed with tourists at all times of the year. On the gentler, south-facing slope—a paradise of rare wild plants—stands the Chalaisan monastery of Notre-Dame-du-Lure (see pp.378-79).

ABOVE:
**Chalaisan monastery of
Notre-Dame-de-Lure,**
founded in 1165, and
its surroundings

RIGHT:
Montagne de Lure
Near the summit of the
Signal de Lure 6,086 ft
(1,826 m)

The Valley of the Durance and the Gorges of the Verdon

Allemagne-de-Provence
Château, dating from the late
15th and early 16th century in
Renaissance style.

Along the Verdon Valley

The hot springs of Gréoux-les-Bains were known to the Romans. In the Middle Ages, the spa belonged to the Abbey of St-Victor and later to the Order of the Knights Templar, builders of a mighty fortress here whose ruins still dominate the town. The modern baths were installed at the beginning of the nineteenth century.

Allemagne-en-Provence was the property of de Castellane who built a château here in the late fifteenth and early sixteenth the century on a square plot of land (see above).

The small city of Riez was one of the earliest in Gaul with a bishopric. One of the first cathedrals was probably built in the fifth century on the site of today's baptistery. In the early Middle Ages, the city moved to the defensive heights of St-Maxime to the northeast. A new episcopal church, Notre-Dame-de-la-Sed was built. It is mentioned as a parish church as early as the thirteenth century, because the population had settled below the heights and begun to build and fortify a new city. A third episcopal church was built, while the city on the heights was abandoned and fell into ruins. Today's city still has the remains of the fortifications, and the parish church shows traces of construction done in the sixteenth century, particularly the bell tower.

In a pleasant park-like complex Roman and early-Christian monuments can be viewed. Four columns with entablature trace back to a Roman podium temple whose front faced towards the south (see opposite). The ca. 30 ft (6 m) high columns are made of a gray granite taken from the area around Esterel. The elaborate details of the capitals can still be seen despite weathering.

Not far away rises the *Baptisterium,* looking rather like an shapeless stone block. The entire building, originally surrounded by a columned portico, is somewhat disfigured by security and restoration measures. Over a quadrilateral foundation the central building rises around the baptismal font while a circle of eight columns sets off the gallery. The capitals, spoils from a Roman construction, carry a high climbing tambour that is closed by a small cupola. The edging seen today stems from Romanesque times. The cathedral church, whose foundation remains across the street, was set in the axis and width of the baptisterium to the east. It was a three-aisled, slender building with a choir apse surrounded by sitting steps. The cathedral group was obviously laid over a large Roman public building at the end of the fifth century and whose arrangement reminds one of the church complex in Fréjus.

Riez
Ground plan of the
5th-century baptistery

OPPOSITE:
Riez
Four columns of a 1st-century
ruined Roman podium temple

The village of Puimoisson on the Plateau de Valensole, above Reiz, is surrounded by almond trees and fields of poppies that bloom in spring and summer, later giving way to the purple of the fields of lavender, a plant abundantly cultivated in this area (illus. opposite).

Moustiers-Ste-Marie

The small city of Moustiers-Ste-Marie is in a lovely natural setting nestling at the foot of high, bare rocks (see pp.384-85). The site was first settled by St. Maximin, first a hermit in Lérins and later a bishop in Riez, who brought some monks here in 435 to live in caves in the mountains. They also built a small chapel dedicated to the Virgin. Fearing attacks from robbers, the monks abandoned their settlement, before returning from Lérins in the eleventh century to found a priory. Moustiers was an important administrative center for the Counts of Provence. The city was heavily fortified and like the larger cities of the region, had its own local government.

Moustiers flourished in the seventeenth-century as a center for paper-making and its worldwide famous faïence (earthenware) pottery. The ceramics industry prospered until the mid-nineteenth century, but then had to wait some long 100 years before the rediscovery of the art caused the local kilns to be fired up again. The requirements for ceramic production were sources of water from the mountains, namely the streams known as the Rioul and Maïre which run through the city, dividing it into several neighborhoods. These areas' steep gradients mean they have to be connected by numerous bridges.

The parish church has an auditorium-like nave with a wealth of Provençal Romanesque carvings. The choir was built in the fourteenth century and has a flat, rather than polygonal design. A faïence museum of pottery explains the technique of making the local pottery and its history in Moustiers.

A small path leads up to a flight of steps to the ravine of the pilgrim's chapel of Notre-Dame-de-Beauvoir (ilus. above). The symbol of the city, a star called the *Cadeno*, hangs at a height of 666 ft (200 m) between two cliff summits. This is apparently the work of a Knight of St. John of Jerusalem named Blacas who hung it here in the thirteenth century in gratitude for his miraculous release from captivity. The pilgrim's church stands on the site of the Marian shrine built by the monks in the fifth century. The nave stems from the twelfth and the choir from the fifteenth century.

OPPOSITE:
Landscape of the Plateau de Valensole near Puimoisson

Moustiers-Ste-Marie
Pilgrim chapel of Notre-Dame-de-Beauvoir (12th and 15th century) in the ravine behind the city.

PP. 384-85:
Moustiers-Ste-Marie
General view with the rocky outcrop.

Ste-Croix-de-Verdon
Village by the lake (above)

Lac-de-Ste-Croix
The artificial lake created from
the floodwaters of the Verdon
(right)

Gorges du Verdon

The Lac de Ste-Croix (1975), a large lake
surrounded by mountains, was the last of the
reservoirs to be built in the 1960s and 1970s.
The village of Salles-sur-Verdon was submerged
and rebuilt on the eastern shore. A large Roman
bridge was not saved, however, and now lies
at a depth of 166 ft (50 m) on the bottom of
the lake. The small, village of Ste-Croix (see
above), after which the lake is named, once
stood high in the mountains but now has well-
maintained beach.

Just east of the Lac de Ste-Croix begins the
Gorges du Verdon, whose deep rocky gorges
are one of Europe's most important natural
formations. The Verdon starts at an altitude of
8,333 ft (2,500 m) on the Col d'Allos, turning
west near Castellane before winding through
16 miles (25 km) of narrow gorges, whose
maximum depth is 2,333 ft (700 m). The Lac de
Ste-Croix is the first of the river dams, followed
by further dams before it flows into the
Durance. The reason why the river gouged a
course through this giant limestone massif,
rather than taking an alternative route, is
because the plateau was once much lower.
The Verdon dug out a natural bed, while the
limestone massif was forced higher and higher
during the Tertiary Period due to pressure
applied laterally by the neighboring strata of
rock. The river being more powerful than it
is today and the current much stronger, then
gradually hollowed out the existing valley.

The Grand Canyon du Verdon (illus. pp. 388-
90) can be seen from the corniche road running
above it along the limestone plateau. There is
a northern and a southern route, both offering
dizzying perspectives of the majestic, rocky landscape through which the Verdon winds like
a thin ribbon below. From La Palud-sur-Verdon
on the north side there is a scenic route known
as the Route des Crêtes, a hair's breadth
from the cliff edge. Everywhere cliff walls,
some higher than 333 ft (100 m), offer chal-
lenges for rock-climbers. Near the lookout of

The Valley of the Durance and the Gorges of the Verdon

RIGHT AND OPPOSITE:
Gorges du Verdon

OPPOSITE:
Gorges du Verdon

Point Sublime, by the Tunnel de Tusset, a cul-de-sac leads down almost to the valley bottom at Couloir Samson. For a hiker equipped with provisions, good shoes, and a flashlight it is possible to follow the river down in the gorge on the Sentier Martel. The path leads through several tunnels and, by using ladders, it is possible to get to the Baume-aux-Pigeons, a giant cave 100 ft (30 m) high. At a bend in the river, one of the Verdon's tributaries, the Artuby joins it at a deep gorge formation.

Castellane

Castellane lies at the other end of the Verdon gorges. Originally, it was a settlement on one of the cliffs around the current location of the town, which was inhabited by the Celtic-Ligurian tribe of the Suetrii. The settlement was named Salinae by the Romans because of the salty springs in the area. During the Teutonic invasions, the inhabitants took to the steep cliffs above the town; the name of Petra Castellana dates back to this time. As early as the fifth century, a bishop resided in Castellane, but a century later the episcopal see was moved to Senez. In the early twelfth century, the city became the family seat of one of France's most noble families, the de Castellanes.

The former parish church of St-Victor was expanded northward in the fifteenth and seventeenth century, with the addition of side-aisles. The main section, which dates from the thirteenth century, has thick banded rib-vaulting similar to that found in the cathedrals of Grasse and Fréjus. The climb up to the rocky outcrop at an altitude of 600 ft (180 m) occupied by the chapel of Notre-Dame-de-Roc is worth the effort. At the foot of the cliffs, a medieval bridge leads over the Verdon. Every year, the city celebrates the *Féte du Pétardier* (Festival of the Gunner) on January 31 in honor of Judith Andrau whose heroic maneuvers repelled an artillery attack by the Huguenots in 1586.

Castellane
Town and chapel of Notre-Dame-du-Roc on the heights

P. 392:
Gorse
In the spring and early summer the gorse flowers make for a bright yellow spread that is typical of Provence at this season.

Short biographies

Augustus, originally Gaius Octavius, Octavian after his adoption, first Roman emperor (63 BC– 14 AD). As the adoptive son of Cesar, who was murdered in 44 BC, he was initially made Consul. The victory over his fellow Consul, Anthony, in the naval battle of Actium made Octavian sole ruler with the cognomen Augustus in 30 BC. As emperor, Augustus succeeded in fully reorganizing the Roman Empire through the newly centralized powers of government. He also initiated an extensive cultural rebirth. In Provence, too, the consequences of his rule can still be seen in numerous Roman monuments.

Benedict XII, originally Jacques Fournier (ca. 1285-1342), Pope. This Cistercian friar became a cardinal in 1327, succeeding Pope Peter in 1334. Under his rule, the alliance with the French monarchy and the opposition to the German Emperor Ludwig the Bavarian were strengthened. This also found expression in the fact that Benedict began construction of the Papal residence in Avignon.

Benedict XIII, Pedro de Luna (ca. 1342-1423), antipope pretender from 1395-1423. During the Great Schism, he was elected by the French cardinals who remained in Avignon. Despite initial successes, he was unable to gain acceptance as Pope. He was declared deposed on numerous occasions and was besieged in Avignon.

Bonaparte, Napoleon (See p. 356)

Boniface VIII, originally Benedetto Gaetani (around 1235-1303), Pope. After the dramatic abdication of Celestine V, he succeeded to the Papal throne in 1294. He pursued an aggressive campaign to ensure the supremacy of the papacy over the secular powers, which led to the bitter opposition of the French kings and a large section of the French episcopate. The resulting polarization led indirectly to a weakening of the Papacy after Boniface's death and the move of the papal residence to Avignon.

Bréa, Louis (around 1450-1523), Provençal painter. Eminent member of the Nice school of painting in the transition from late gothic to the Renaissance.

Caesar, Gaius Julius (100-44 BC), Roman general and statesman. He was one of the Triumvirate, with Licinius Crassus and Pompey, the three men who became the center of political power in Rome, having been in constant dispute with the Roman oligarchy. Caesar succeeded in extending and

consolidating the Roman Empire through numerous victorious campaigns. His conquest of the tribes between the Pyrenees and the Rhine (58-52 BC), including the Gallic population of Provence, did much to enhance his prestige. Colonies of war veterans were founded in the provinces to secure Roman rule. The removal of his fellow rulers led to extensive domestic opposition, of which Caesar became a victim when he himself was murdered by Brutus in 44 BC.

Camus, Albert (See p. 182)

Canavésio, Jean (Giovanni) active in the second half of the 15th century Provençal-Ligurian painter. He has been identified as the artist of several reredos and cycles of frescos, such as the Passion and Last Judgement (1482) in Pigna, Liguria, and a polytych of the Madonna and saints (Turin, Gal. Sabaudia), among others. The French chapels decorated by him include Notre-Dame-des-Fontaines (illus. p. 341) and St-Etienne in St-Etienne-de-Tinée. The dramatic, strongly narrative paintings draw on Provençal, northern Italian, and Dutch painting traditions.

Charles I of Anjou (1226-85), King of Sicily and Count of Provence. The Duke of Anjou and brother of the French King Louis IX obtained Provence through marriage in 1246. After victory over the last Hohenstaufens, Manfred and Conrad, Charles was rewarded with the Kingdom of Sicily in 1265 by Pope Clement IV. Charles set up his principal residence in Naples, while in Provence, Aix was enlarged as a second seat. Following the French example, Charles set up a central administration which greatly reduced the traditional independence of many Provençal cities.

Charles II of Anjou (1254-1309), King of Sicily and Count of Provence. As the son of Charles I, he continued in the political tradition of his father, in particular in the plan to establish a spiritual center for Provence in St.-Maximim-la-Ste-Baume (illus. p. 284 ff.). Support for the cult of St. Mary Magdalene, said to be buried there, was one of the most important measures adopted to achieve this.

Cézanne, Paul (See p. 206)

Chéret, Jules (1836-1932), French painter and graphic artist. He was one of the first to use color lithography to produce posters. His often unusual use of color in his breezy, neo-Rococo paintings is characteristic of the decorative arts of the Belle Epoque period on the Côte d' Azur, especially in Nice.

Clement IV, originally Guy Foulquy (d. 1268), Pope. He was born in the Provençal town of St-Gilles and was first active as an advisor to King Louis IX. He became Bishop of Le Puy in 1257, Archbishop of Narbonne in 1259, Cardinal in 1261, and finally Pope in 1265. As Pope he granted Charles I, Count of Provence, the Royal

Kingdom of Sicily. He thus played a major role in supporting French supremacy in the western Mediterranean.

Clement V, originally Bertrand de Got (d. 1314), Pope. Bishop of St-Bertrand-de-Cominges from 1295, then Pope from 1305. Under the political influence of King Philippe IV, Clement reversed the autocratic papal politics of his predecessor Boniface VIII, who believed that the spiritual leader should also be the secular ruler. In agreement with the King, Clement disbanded the Order of the Templars, the assets of which devolved to Philippe. Clement was also the first Pope to take up residence in Avignon.

Clement VI, originally Pierre Roger (1292-1352), Pope. This Benedictine monk was initially Archbishop of Sens and of Rouens, and also chancellor to King Philippe VI. In 1338, he became a cardinal. After being elected Pope in 1342, he purchased the Comtat Venaissin and doubled the size of the Papal palace. This seemed to secure Avignon's status as the definitive Papal residence, although some, including Petrarch, continued to advocate Rome. Clement also played a significant role in ensuring that the king of Bohemia could succeed to the Imperial throne as Charles IV.

Clement VII, originally Robert de Genève (1342-1394), antipope pretender. Earlier Bishop of Thérouame and Cambrai, he became a cardinal in 1371. After the election of Urban VI was declared invalid, the French cardinals agreed on Robert de Genève as the new Pope. As antipope pretender, he further enhanced the status of Avignon as a Papal residence.

Cocteau, Jean (1889-1963), French author, playwright, director, graphic artist, and costume designer. Although influenced by Dadaism and Surrealism, Cocteau always returned to the classical themes of ancient mythology, for instance in *Orphée* and *Antigone*, two of his plays. Cocteau's works can be seen in various places in Provence, such as the Cocteau Museum in Menton, where he occasionally lived, the church in Villefranche-sur-Mer (illus. p. 320) and in the museum in the city hall (hôtel de ville) of St-Jean-Cap-Ferrat.

D'Eyck, Barthélemy (active mid-15th century), illustrator and painter. He was painter at the court of René I of Anjou, Count of Provence, and may have been related to the Dutch painter Jan van Eyck. Some of the most important works of art of the time have been ascribed to him, above all the illustrations for the allegorical tale of knights written by King René himself, *Le Livre du Cuer d'amours espris*, along with the *Annunciation* in Aix (See p. 197).

Daudet, Alphonse (1840-1897), French writer. He traces the life stories of various characters from different social backgrounds. His humorous descriptions of life in Provence are contained in *Letters from*

My Mill and *The Amazing adventures of the Noble Tatarin of Tarascon*.

Fabre, Jean-Henri (See p. 28)

François I (1494-1547), King of France (from 1515). After victory over the Swiss at Marignano this king's main political aim was to fight the supremacy of the House of Hapsburg under Emperor Charles V, whose soldiers attempted a landing on the Provençal coast, a course doomed to failure given the reinforced defenses ordered by François. The King can be termed the first French Renaissance prince. His extensive patronage of the arts can also be seen in the fact that famous Italian artists such as Cellini, Leonardo, and Primaticcio were summoned to France.

Franque, François (1710-1793), French architect. Son of Jean-Baptiste Franque. He became a member of the Royal Academy in Paris in 1730 and a celebrated architect who worked throughout France.

Franque, Jean-Baptiste (1683-1758), French architect. After his apprenticeship at the Royal Academy in Paris he was the architect of numerous buildings in and around Avignon and Aix, including the Musée Calvet (illus. p. 62).

Froment, Nicolas (c. 1430-1483-86), French painter. Along with Bartélemy D'Eyck, Froment was an important painter at the court of René I of Anjou. Among other paintings he was responsible for a triptych ordered by René I, with a representation of the Burning Bush (1475-1476; illus. p. 196), in the cathedral of Aix-en-Provence.

Garnier, Charles (1825-1898), French architect. After traveling through Italy and Greece to study classical architecture, he won a competition for the rebuilding of the Paris opera house (1861-1875), becoming one of the most important proponents of an extravagant but subtle architectural eclecticism. This predestined him for the sophisticated society of the Côte d'Azur, where his designs included the Casino in Monte Carlo (illus. p.332) and the Planetarium in Nice.

Gaugin, Paul (1848-1903), French painter. He began his career as a self-taught painter in the style of the Impressionists, but his understanding of his art was soon transformed into a radical artistic form of expression with a spiritual dimension. His resulting contempt for civilization led him to move first to Brittany and in the year 1888, following Van Gogh, to Provence. Both regions were considered at that time the most rural and unspoiled in France. Soon, however, Gaugin was drawn to even more exotic locations. He lived and worked in the South Sea Islands, where he eventually died.

Giono, Jean (See p. 366)

Gogh, Vincent Van (1853-1890), Dutch painter. The self-taught painter was initially influenced by the dark colors and tones of the paintings of Frans Hals and Rembrand. In 1886, in Paris he began to incorporate elements of the Post-impressionists and the so-called Japanese style. The style of painting he developed, comprising many small brushstrokes, came to fruition above all during his stay in Arles in 1888-1889, resulting in powerful colorful compositions (illus. pp. 50-51). His attempt to set up an artists' colony there with Gaugin failed. After mutilating himself by cutting off an ear, he stayed for a while at a sanatorium in St-Rémy (illus. p. 113), where he mostly painted landscapes. In 1890, Van Gogh returned to Auvers-sur-Oise near Paris. He committed suicide in July of that year.

Grimaldi, Albert (1848-1923), Prince of Monaco. The Grimaldis, who originally came from Genoa, are an old established aristocratic family with origins in the 12th century. Since the late 13th century, their territories have covered that section of the French Riviera which includes Monaco. They initiated the princely title in 1612. From 1860, the principality became their only remaining territory, after referendums in the other regions brought them under French rule. Prince Albert I, who ruled from 1889, made Monaco a center for opera, ballet, and marine biology. He also initiated the famous Grand Prix in this tiny state.

John XXII, originally Jacques Duèze (1245-1334), Pope. Onetime Bishop of Frèjus (from 1300), he became Bishop of Avignon from 1310 and Cardinal in 1312. He was finally elected Pope in 1316 in Lyon. John was the first Pope to rule definitively from Avignon. The alliance with the French monarchy led him into opposition to the German Emperor Ludwig the Bavarian, whom John finally excommunicated and declared deposed. In addition, this Pope played a significant role in the persecution of the religious movements which attempted to reform the Church in line with their strict ideals of poverty.

Laurana, Francesco (around 1425-1502), Italian-Dalmatian sculptor. His career began with work on the triumphal arch at Castel Nuovo in Naples. From the 1560s, he increasingly worked at the Provençal court of René I, where he completed the Lazarus altar in the Marseille cathedral and a crucifixion group for the Celestine church in Avignon (illus. p. 64). He introduced new elements into Provençal sculpture with his realistic and elegant concept of figures and the illusionary backgrounds to his reliefs. In later years, the sculptor was active in the south of France as well as Naples and Sicily.

Le Courbusier originally Charles-Edouard Jeanneret (1887-1965), Swiss-French architect, town planner, painter, and sculptor. The architect began his career before World War I in his native La-Chaux-de-Fonds. Following his move to Paris in 1917, he devised an architectural theory based on purely geometrical forms and determined by its function. The architect had early contacts with Provence through personal acquaintances which also led to contracts for country homes such as the Villa la Pradet near Hyères for Hélène de Mandrot in 1930. The most important contract was for the Unité d'Habitation in Marseilles (illus. p. 240-241). In 1956, Le Corbusier built himself a vacation home, Le Cabanon, at Roquebrune-Cap-Martin. (See p. 332).

Louis IX (Saint Louis) (1214-70), French king. Under his rule from 1226, initially under the guardianship of his mother, France reached its zenith in the Middle Ages. A strict administrative system was set up in the recently acquired regions of Normandy, Languedoc, and Provence, and treaties were signed with foreign enemies. Louis was a strong believer in the divine right of the French kings. As well as founding numerous churches, he also undertook two Crusades, both of which failed. He died of the Plague during the second of these and was beatified in 1297. The port of Aigue-Mortes was established by him as an important embarkation point for journeys to the Holy Land (see p. 130).

Louis XI (1423-83), French king. His reign from 1461 marked a watershed in French history, as he greatly reduced the power of the feudal lords such as Burgundy, Berry, and Anjou. Under Louis, the foundations of the modern monarchy were created with the introduction of a modern administration, absolute power of the monarch, and a rejection of the obsolete forms of chivalry in court life. It is symptomatic that Provence, on the death of René I and his childless successor, was also incorporated into France in 1481.

Matisse, Henri (1869-1954), French painter and sculptor. After Impressionist beginnings, this student of Gustave Moreau from 1904 onward developed a style of painting based on strong colors and an almost complete rejection of the third dimension. From 1917, he mostly lived in Nice. After World War I the flat color compositions become almost abstract patterns which, however, retained some elements of realism. In the 1940s, this led to silhouette-like color collages, while his drawings became abstractions of lines and curves. This was also the form used by the artist for the decoration of the chapel of Rosaire in Vence 1948-51 (illus. p. 351).

Mistral, Frédéric (See p. 114)

Nostradamus (See p. 214)

Pagnol, Marcel (See p. 226)

Petrarch, Francesco (See p. 45)

Picasso, Pablo (1881-1973), French-Spanish painter, graphic artist, and sculptor. After studying in Barcelona and Madrid, he developed new artistic forms in Paris from 1900 onward. He was an early exponent of Cubism, developed in 1907, which was to be of great significance in European art. After World War I, Picasso made a partial return to classical forms. A cross-fertilization of different forms was taking place in his work at this time. After World War II, the artist mainly lived on the Côte d'Azur – in Antibes, Vallauras, Golfe-Juan, at the Villa Californie near Cannes, and in Mougins – and in Provence, where he acquired the château at Vauvenarges (illus. p. 211) in 1955. He was also buried here in Mougins.

Quarton, Enguerrand (around 1420-around 1466), one of the most important painters of the French Late Gothic. He was born in Picardy in northern France and from 1447 through 1466 worked in Avignon, where he was one of the leading masters of the school of painting. See *The Coronation of the Virgin* (145-54; illus. p. 67)

Raymond IV (ca. 1041-1105), Count of Toulouse and Vicomte de Provence. He was one of the principal figures of the first crusade, founder of Tripoli, and discoverer of the Holy Lance.

Raymond VI (1156-1222), Count of Toulouse. His policy of antagonism towards France contributed to the French King's crusade against the south of France, using the heretic movement of the Albigensians as a pretext. In this conflict, the Count, on the whole, emerged victorious.

Raymond VII (d. 1249), Count of Toulouse. The son of Raymond VI, he continued his father's policy of retaining sovereignty over his territories. The military success of the French in the Albigensian Wars, however, persuaded him of the need for negotiation. This led to the marriage of his daughter to Alphonse de Poitiers, the brother of the French King, Louis IX. As in the case of the Count of Barcelona, Raymond Bérenger V, the Provençal territories fell to another branch of the House of Capet.

Raymond Bérenger IV (ca. 1159-1181), Count of Provence. Sharing the extensive territories in Northern Spain and Southern France with his brother, King Alphonso II of Aragon, Raymond Bérenger ruled Aragon from 1168, even after the Emperor, Barbarossa, had himself crowned King of Provence in Arles in 1178.

Raymond Bérenger V (1205-1245), Count of Provence. This last of the pre-Capetian rulers of Provence attempted to stem the power of the cities and actively opposed the claims of the German Empire. After his death, Provence fell to his daughter, Béatrice. Through her marriage to Charles I of Anjou, Provence was incorporated into the Capetian territories.

René I (See p. 100)

René II, (1451-1508), Duke of Lorraine and Bar. He inherited the Duchy of Bar from his grandfather, King René I of Anjou. The rest of his territories were inherited from his parents. He repelled attacks on his sovereignty and established a magnificent court in Nancy.

Renoir, Auguste (1841-1919), French painter and sculptor. Originally a porcelain painter, he joined the Parisian Ecole des Beaux-Arts, where he was initially influenced by Courbet. He began using a paler color scheme in the 1860s, and soon produced scenes of Parisian life in shimmering color. Renoir was among the most influential Impressionists of the 1860s. In the following decades, his numerous portraits and nudes were increasingly influenced by Ingres' classicism. His later work is also characterized by elegant and sensual paintings of luminous color, which he created despite suffering from increasing arthritis in his hands. In 1907, Renoir retired to Cagnes-sur-Mer, where he also produced sculptures, such as the Venus Victrix (illus. p. 346).

Sade, Donatien Alphonse François Marquis de (1740-1814), French author and playwright. Born to an established aristocratic Provençal family, the Marquis de Sade grew up in Paris and Avignon. In 1763, he was already imprisoned for the first time. Altogether, he spent a total of 27 years in prison and little time at his family seat at Lacoste (illus. p. 180). This was due mainly to his scandalous lifestyle, but above all to his even more scandalous writings, which were only rediscovered in the twentieth century. The indescribable cruelties and sexual torture which are described there contrast with the often overly optimistic ideas of emancipation of the Enlightenment and show how emancipation can also lead to the expression of the darker side of the soul. He has given his name to the word "sadism."

Sévigné, Madame de (See p. 22)

Index of persons

Index of Place Names

Glossary

Acanthus variety of thistle, whose leaves are carved on Corinthian captals.

Aedicule wall niche framed by pilasters, rectangular columns, pediments, etc.)

Alcove hollow or recess in the wall in the form of a concave depression

Ambulatory vault Vault of a (choir) surround

Apse semicircular or polygonal extension, usually in churches, where it is attached to the eastern end of the choir

Arcade wall arches and concentric frames in relief on a wall

Arcading Series of arches, usually small, a frequent decorative element

Arch frieze A frieze which is crated from a series of small arches

Architrave horizontal vault across columns, decorated with classical friezes with cornices.

Archivolt Arches and concentric frames set off from a wall.

Atrium An open court, often surrounded by columns in front of early Christian and medieval churches.

Attic base A column base characterized by a cleft profile created by the separation of two circular rings.

Band ribs the ribs of a cross-ribbed vault with a square cross-section

Baptistery area where the font stands, sometimes in its own chapel, usually in the center of the building

Barrel-arch arch with semi-circular cross-section

Barrel-vault curved arch in the shape of a barrel or tunnel generally strengthened with transverse arches or squinches.

Base profile Cross-section of a column base

Basilica originally a Roman market hall or courthouse, but in Christian architecture it is a church with several aisles, lit by high windows

Bay vaulted section

Blind arcades, arches, triforium carving in relief of columns and colonnades on flat surfaces such as walls.

Boss generally molded in stone at the base of an arch or vault.

Bossed vault stone vault with visible services which are deliberately roughly hewn.

Buttress support for the relief of transmitted pressure.

Cannelation vertical grooves or fluting in the shaft of a column or pilaster

Capital the molded top of a support, introduced between the support and the load.

Cardo a Roman road, at right angles to the grid system between the Decumanus and the main street

Cartouche decorative element of the baroque period in the form of a shield or other panel with surface bearing inscriptions or heraldic devices.

Caryatid architectural support in the form of a female figure

Cavea Rows of seating arranged in a semicircle in Roman theaters and amphitheaters.

Cella open central area of a Greek temple.

Chapterhouse the meeting-room of a cathedral or monastery, usually in the eastern part of the cloister.

Choir in Christian liturgy, these are the prayers of the clergy who are usually grouped around the altar. In church architecture it is the area between the transpect and the apse.

Choir bay one or two more bays in the choir area before the choir apse was introduced.

Choir-stalls stepped rows of seats on two sdes of the choir area, used by the clergy.

Choir surround the passages around the inner choir, similar to the side-aisles and often branching radially from a chapel

Church hall single-aisled undivided internal space of a religious building.

Cippus platform from an Etruscan tomb.

Civitas since the days of the Emperors, the description given to all lands outside Rome which were divided into cities and colonies.

Civitas confœderata lands which were subservient to Ancient Rome though they had a measure of self-government

Cloister the open square of a monastery or convent around which the other buildings are set.

Clustered pier a medieval way of grouping small and larger three-quarter columns around a single core pillar.

Colonia new or conquered Ancient Roman settlements whose inhabitants enjoyed full Roman citizenship.

Colonnade series of columns with architrave.

Colossal order order of columns or pilars which enclose several floors.

Column, column order a round supporting pillar consisting of a base, a shaft, and a capital of about one-and-a-half-times human height. There are three classical orders, depending on the shape of the capital. The Doric, the simplest with a plain round cushion at the top, the Ionic with two curled scrolls like ram's horns, and the Corinithian with two rows of carved acanthus leaves and corner volutes.

Column supporting element with a circular cross-section, consisting of a base, a shaft, decoration, and a capital.

Composite pillar gothic pillar shape, consisting ofstepped pillar core and a number of circular supports.

Compound arch An arch construction incorporting several smaller arches and other architectural elements.

Console a supporting bracket

Conversion building in Cistercian abbeys in which the lay monks sleep.

Corbel construction which protrudes markedly from the surface of a building, on which a bay window, balcony or similar structure can be supported.

Corbel stone stone protruding from a wall on which a statue, vault, scaffolding or other item can be placed.

Corner volute scroll which is introduced into the angle of a capital or similar device.

Cornice horizontal molding to disguise or cover the join of the roof or ceiling and the wall.

Cross-edged vault vault created from two intersecting barrel-vaults.

Cross-ribbed vault vault created from two intersecting barrel-vaults, whose edges are outlined with ribs.

Crown found between the arches and rib-vaults at the top joint.

Crown cornice the main cornice on the façade under the roof.

Crypt space beneath the church, used for burials and other purposes.

Crypt ambulatory semicircular passageway around the crypt

Cupola round, square, or polygonal dome or boss.

Cupola funnel the transition from a square underpinning to an eight-sided or round cupola base.

Decumanus see Cardo

Diagonal ribs these appear on vaults which lead diagonally from ground-floor windows.

Dividing arch arch between the individual aisles of a multi-aisle building.

Dormitory the dormitory used as sleeping quarters by monks in a monastery. Individual cells were introduced later, but the term is also used for the floor on which the cells are located

Double-columns/pillars Pairs of two columns or two pilasters

Drollery an amusing motif by a medieval painter or sculptor (gargoyle, etc.).

Dungeon or castle keep central defensive tower in French châteaux or towns

Erotism the representation in ancient art of the message of love in the form of small, naked, winged children, called cherubs in later art.

Finial stylized, leaf in the form of a cross to top pediments, pinnacles, and towers.

Forum the central square in Ancient Roman times, usually at the intersection of the Cardo and the Decumanus and surrounded by public buildings and temples

Free pillars the opposite of standing supports which are attached to the walls of a building.

Fresco wall painting applied using pigments dissolved in lime water and applied to plaster that is still damp and fresh, so that the colors remain locked into the wall.

Frieze molded or carved horizontal band of decoration

Funnel, funnel vault funnel-shaped vault with a hollow half-ball opening at the bottom.

Guide scaffold scaffold erected externally to support the vaults and arch constructions during the application and binding of mortar

Hall church a church building with aisles of equal height, particularly in the late gothic period.

Hall-column column introduced into the wall so that only half of its molded diameter projects.

Hanging arch a late gothic form of decoration. Rows of small arches which appear to hang from the main structure.

High relief deeply carved, heavily molded relief (generally on flat sur (opposite of bas-relief)

Iconography study of the subject-matter of images

Insula city block in the Roman grid system of town-planning, consisting of a group of houses surrounded by roads. Also represents a Roman house rented to several tenants.

Keel arch generally in late goathic architecture, arches which appear to curve inward on the shafts of the columns but are narrowly ogival in shape.

Lancet arch, pointed barrel barrel-vault with pointed arch cross-section. Lancet in gothic architecture, a high, narrow pointed arch framing a wall or window.

Leaf Capital A capital decorated with carved or applied leaves.

Lesene vertical strip of decoration, otherwise a pilaster without a base or capital

Loggia arched entrance to room or hall at ground level or on an upper story.

Machicolation projecting wall on battlement, from below which shafts opened so that missiles or boiling oil could be thrown over attackers attempting to scale the walls.

Main aisle central aisle or nave or the upper parts thereof.

Mandorla almond-shaped stylized radiating crown used only for the enthroned Christ or the Mother of God.

Molded wallwork Roman wall technique in which concrete is introduced into a mold within a brickwork shell.

Municipium cities of the ancient world which volunteered to accept Roman rule, thus acquiring a measure of autonomy for themselves.

Nave main part of the church from the front to the transept.

Overstory the upper walls of the central aisle of a basilica with windows to the outside.

Oculus round window

Oppidum refuge and settlements of the Celto-Ligurian population of southern Gaul.

Opus mixtum Roman wall-building technique alternating between brickwork and natural layers of stone.

Orchestra the semi-circular area in a Roman theater, as well as the surface used for plays that lay between the stage and the seating.

Order see Column orders

Palestra, Palaestra in ancient Greece, the competition surface of the gymnasium. In Roman times, the free area within the baths for physical exercise and meetings.

Palmette an ancient decorative pattern based on palm-leaves

Parlatorium part of the cloisters which were provided for conversations.

Pediment beam or rafter in gothic architecture, often covered in engravings and moldings.

Peristyle rows of columns surrounding a building or inner courtyard.

Pillar arcade arcade supported by pillars and columns.

Pre-church specially dedicated room which in the Romanesque period was used for special services and rites.

Pedestal base supporting a column

Pilaster architectural decoration in the form of a column projecting from the wall.

Pinnacle gothic ornamentation in the form of a narrow pyramid with a shaft.

Podium temple Roman temple on a high base with a flight of steps leading up to the entrance on a narrow side of the rectangle.

Portico arched entrance hall

Postament plinthlike base for statues, memorials, etc.

Pre-bay bay before the apse

Predella base for shrines and altars

Profile stone a carved stone with a prfile on one side which enables the assembly in cross-section of curved ribs, bases, and cornices.

Radial chapels chapels radiating from a semi-circular or polygonal choir

Recliner Roman furniture in the shape of a couch or sofa, on which Romans slept and took their meals.

Refectory dining-room of a monastery or convent.

Reredos or retable decorative screen, usually heavily carved and generally monumental.

Rib frame over which part of a gothic vault is constructed. Ribs were decorated in the late gothic period.

Rib-start the first stone of the ribs of a rib-vault.

Ribbed vault see cross-ribbed vault

Risalit accentuation of the features projecting from a wall surface

Romano-Byzantine style French variant of the 19th-century "round arch style" which combined Romanesque and Byzantine elements.

Rose, rose window round window filled with pieces of stained glass.

Rosette floral decoration and structural element in the form of a flower.

Round support a vertical support element in medieval architecture, used to create elongated posts.

Round barrel barrel-vault whose cross-section forms a semi-circle.

Rustic work rusticated walling with masonry incorporated into the brickwork. It has been used since the Renaissance.

Semicircular projection used in Romanesque and gothic architecture for the semicircular cross-section projection

Shaft ring ring-shaped annulet, strengthening the column shaft and often attached to the wall.

Side-aisle aisle parallel to the central aisle of nave of a long building, such as a church.

Serlina Series of supports topped alternately with a beam and an arch.

Sinopia natural ocher the color of cinnabar often used for preparatory sketches for frescoes and wall-paintings.

Scriptorium originally writing equiment but later used to describe the writing-room of a medieval monastery.

Spoil reused architectural or decorative element from an older building

Stereotomy part of the sterometry of the surface cross-section of bodies, used for alignment of stones in complex vault formations.

Squinch self-supporting semicircular arch.

Support profile The typical cross-section of the supports (rounded, pointed, bundled, etc.)

Tambour, drum cylindrical or polygonal underpinning of cupola.

Tempera painting Technique used mainly in the middle ages in which egg yolk or resin was used to dilute the colors.

Thermae Large public baths in Greece and Rome.

Torus Ring as profile element on cornices, bases, and ribs. Torus Ring as profile element on cornices, bases, and ribs.

Triple apse in Romanesque architecture, the eastern extension of three apses in a church of which the central one supports the arcades.

Three-shell/cross extension church building with three semi-circular or polygonal apses, which are arranged in a cross.

Three-way vault ribbed vault on a triangular base, leading from the three corners of the common boss stone.

Three-quarter column a column in front of and partly attached to a wall.

Triforium originally a "three-arch opening" to the central aisle of a church building, the open passage between arcades, galleries, or an upper story.

Triptych Altarpiece or reredos in three pieces.

Triumphal arch ancient monumental arch in honor of the Emperor or a battle. In the Christian church, an arch between the nave or the choir and the transept.

Tracery geometric patterns used as decoration in the gothic and late gothic periods, below windows, on railings and on ceilings.

Transept aisle which crosses at right-angles to the nave in a building with one or more aisles or naves, to form the traditional cross shape of the ground plan. The transept is shorter than the nave but in some churches it is extended.

Tropaion ancient victory memorial

Tympanum in antiquity, the pediment of a temple, most decorated with carvings and moldings. In medieval churches it was the area over a door within the arch area and was usually heavily decorated.

Transept cross-shaped section of the church where the nave intersects with the transverse aisle, dividing the building into a cross-shape.

Transept tower tower built over the transept cross.

Under church in churches divided into two areas of worship, this is the part of the church below the transept.

Upper church the remaining area of the church beyond the various branching structures.

Votive offering tangible expressions of thanks for answered prayers in Christian churches, in the form of medallions and small gifts.

399

Picture credits

The majority of the photographs are the work of Achim Bednorz, and have been specially commissioned for this book.
The publishers and author would like to thank the museums, archives, and photographers for their generous assistance and for the photographs they supplied as well as the reproductions they permitted. Specific acknowledgements to institutions and other photographers are as follows:

AKB, Berlin: p. 182 above left

Beer, Günter: p. 222, 233 above, 233 below left 233 below right

Bildarchiv Foto Marburg: S. 66 below right

Dominé, André: S. 119 above , 119 below

Guerrand, A.: S. 59 below

Giraudon, Foto: Lauros: S. 196, 197

Meauxoone: S. 137 above

Photo Daspet: S. 67 above

Photo Office Municipal de Tourisme d'Arles: S. 77 below

Roger-Viollet: S. 34 below right

Sander, Wolfgang: p. 195 below right, 213 right, 233 below right, 233 below left, 265 above left, 287 left, 287 below right

Wood, Graydon: p. 209 above